FIELD GUIDE TO RIVERS OF THE ROCKY MOUNTAINS

Field Guide to Rivers of the Rocky Mountains is an encyclopedia of essentials for paddling and streamside hiking, but far more than that with rich back-stories, natural history, and stunning photos. It inspires my next round of adventures here in Montana and throughout the Rockies."

—Al Kesselheim, author of *The Wilderness Paddler's Handbook* and *Let Them Paddle*

"Whether you're a seasoned river rat or new to the culture, this book is a must-have companion for your glove box and dry box as you explore the incomparable rivers of the Rocky Mountain West."

—Mike Fiebig, American Rivers' director of river protection in Colorado, raft guide, and kayaker

Lower Falls,
Yellowstone River,
Wyoming

FIELD GUIDE TO RIVERS OF THE ROCKY MOUNTAINS

Tim Palmer

FALCONGUIDES

GUILFORD, CONNECTICUT

Disclaimer

Please note: This book describes the nature of Rocky Mountain rivers, and Part 2 focuses on tips for boating, hiking, and other activities. These sports can be hazardous to one degree or another. River users need to know about their own limitations as well as conditions at the time of their outing. This book assumes that each person is responsible for his or her own safety, and each accepts all risks. The author and publisher assume no responsibility or liability with respect to personal injury, property damage, loss of time or money, or other loss or damage caused directly or indirectly by activities in or near the rivers covered here. With recognition of a wide range of readers and respective abilities, information here cannot be construed to be a recommendation for any particular individual to visit the rivers covered, and this book makes no representations that any activity mentioned here is safe particularly for you or your party. In other words, information here is no substitute for experience, training, skill, prudence, common sense, adequate equipment, safe levels of flow, and competent personal assessment of dangers. See "To the Water" for more on safety. With all that in mind, let's go out and enjoy all that these waters have to offer!

FALCONGUIDES®

An imprint of Globe Pequot, the trade division of
The Rowman & Littlefield Publishing Group, Inc.
4501 Forbes Blvd., Ste. 200
Lanham, MD 20706
www.rowman.com

Falcon and FalconGuides are registered trademarks and Make Adventure Your Story is a trademark of The Rowman & Littlefield Publishing Group, Inc.

Distributed by NATIONAL BOOK NETWORK

Copyright © 2021 Tim Palmer

Photos by Tim Palmer
Maps by Steven Gordon of Cartagram

British Library Cataloguing-in-Publication Information available

Library of Congress Cataloging-in-Publication Data available

ISBN 978-1-4930-5239-4 (paper : alk. paper)
ISBN 978-1-4930-5240-0 (electronic)

∞™ The paper used in this publication meets the minimum requirements of American National Standard for Information Sciences—Permanence of Paper for Printed Library Materials, ANSI/NISO Z39.48-1992.

CONTENTS

The Yellowstone River drifts
from its Rocky Mountain origins
to the Great Plains in Montana.

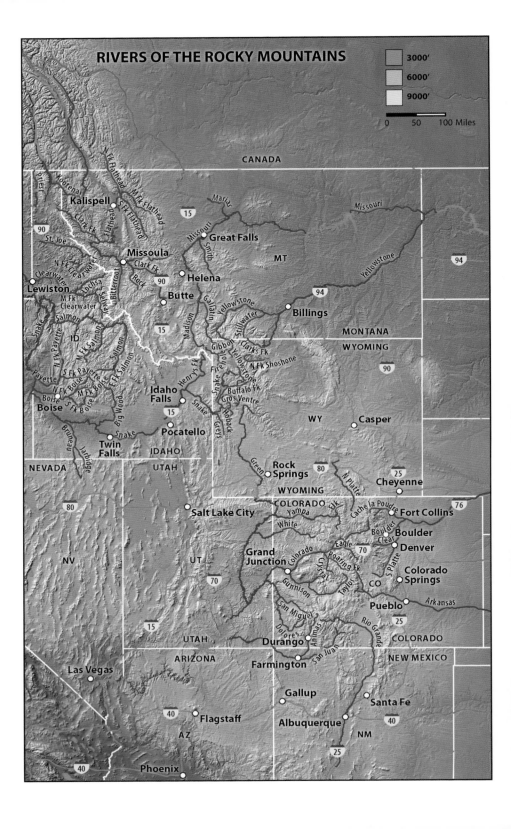

RIVERS OF THE ROCKY MOUNTAINS

ACKNOWLEDGMENTS

Let me offer deep appreciation here to the Western Rivers Conservancy for the use of information I gleaned while preparing their Great Rivers of the West Report. Thanks to WRC even more for the fine work it does in protecting streams throughout eleven western states.

For reviews of state chapters, thanks to the following experts. Many others reviewed specific river segments.

Colorado: Mike Fiebig and Matt Rice of American Rivers' Colorado office

Idaho: Bill Sedivy, former director of Idaho Rivers United; Russ Thurow, fisheries biologist, US Forest Service

Montana: Scott Bosse of American Rivers' Montana office; Kit Fischer, author of *Paddling Montana*

Wyoming: David Cernicek of the US Forest Service; Roger Smith, river enthusiast and director of the Teton Raptor Center

Matt Mayfield calculated data at the openings of each river description using Geographic Information System technology.

Steve Gordon of Cartagram prepared the maps with his special technical and artistic skill.

For review of specific river descriptions, thanks to Kirk Blaine of the Eagle River and now the Native Fish Society; Sam Carter of Dolores River Boating Advocates on the Dolores and San Miguel; Kent Ford on the Animas River; Gary Gadwa from the upper Salmon River; Bill Hoblitzell of the Eagle River; Hilary Hutcheson, rafting/fishing guide and owner of Lary's Fly and Supply at the Flathead River; Patrick Kennedy, eastern Idaho regional fisheries biologist, Idaho Department of Fish and Game; Torsten Krell in Denver; Holly Loff of the Eagle River Watershed Council; Colter Pence of Flathead National Forest; Chuck Pezeshki of the North Fork Clearwater; Lisa Ronald at the Clark Fork; George Sibley, author and historian from the Gunnison River; and Kent Vertrees, Friends of the Yampa.

For logistical help, information, and other aid, thanks to Bob Banks at the Yellowstone River; Len Carlman in Jackson; Curtis Chang of OARS in Lewiston; Bill, Jackie, and Matt Dvorjak of Dvorjak Expeditions on the Arkansas River; Matias Floras of Dvorjak Expeditions; Verne Huser of the Snake River and many river writings; Al Kesselheim, river-running sage of Montana; Caroline and Mike Kurz of the Clark Fork River in Missoula; Doug Proctor of Selway River Adventures; Leo Rosenthal of Montana Fish, Wildlife and Parks at the Flathead; and Ron Watters and Katherine Daly, coauthors of *Guide to Idaho Paddling*.

My wife, Ann Vileisis, was a source of inspiration and help of every kind imaginable, and her companionship on many of these rivers was the finest part of the journey.

PART I
RIVERS OF THE ROCKIES

The Kootenai River foams through its multi-pitch falls in northern Montana.

In the wake of a summer thunderstorm, an evening rainbow arcs over the Salmon River upstream from Stanley, Idaho.

Mountains and Rivers

"Rivers of the Rockies" conjures up some of the finest, wildest, and most mythic free-flowing waters in America. Bubbling from our largest mountain range, these streams provide for practical and recreational needs, but more fundamentally they serve an entire web of life in the waters, near them, and even far beyond the shores. In the pages that follow, let me help you to see and experience these extraordinary places.

Traveling on and hiking along these rivers makes it possible—if not irresistible—to learn about and enjoy a remarkable network of watery lifelines and all that they touch. This book is written in the spirit of adventure and discovery so that everyone who is open to the beauty, excitement, and solace of these streams might come to know and appreciate them better for the natural values they offer to all.

My first experience with rivers of the Rockies came as a teenager. From home in Pennsylvania I hitchhiked to the Front Range of Colorado, where I savored a suite of remarkable streams as they rushed from their mountain strongholds with power, mystique, and allure. My hiking path up and over the Continental Divide took me past one captivating waterfall after another. Ill prepared, I awoke with ice on the poncho thrown over my sleeping bag, and I used spare socks for gloves, but the high-country wilds and waters filled me with awe and a fresh view of the world, opening whole volumes of curiosity and desire.

The next summer, 1969, I scored a job as a landscape architect at Sawtooth National Forest in Idaho where, on one of my first weekends, I sought out the source of the Salmon River. Below there I saw, with unrestrained amazement, swarms of chinook salmon that still finned their way 900 miles on spawning journeys from the Pacific. I had no idea that, because of dams recently built downstream, those fish would soon become endangered, or that my life would someday become entangled in their fate and committed to their survival.

With a borrowed raft, I set off in the opposite direction—*down* the Salmon River—if only for a day, because on Monday I had to return to work, and I needed to return the raft to our backcountry trails foreman. But that day showed me a new universe and opened my eyes to what was possible in the realm of river travel.

The shorelines passed effortlessly by like the wildest fantasy of mountain scenery, the flow of water enchanted me, and the simple idea of living with the river filled an awaiting space in my heart. That night I envisioned rowing a raft the whole way down the Salmon River to the end, wherever that was, far off in the great unknown, and I thought that someday—maybe some lucky day, or week, or month—I could live out that dream.

Soon I took up a passion for canoeing and rafting on every free-flowing waterway I could reach. Over the years I launched illuminating expeditions down all the Rocky Mountains' great rivers and many of the smaller ones as well. I especially sought out extended trips that take us away for days and weeks into lotic worlds of wonder—voyages of 530 miles on the Yellowstone, 377 on the Green, 109 on the Flathead, and more—and I lived out my dream of rafting all the way down the Salmon River, 420 miles—not once but twice over the years—with plans now to launch that epic trip of my adolescent fantasy one more time.

By these and other channels I became professionally engaged in a lifetime of river conservation in dozens of campaigns nationwide. Stitching much of this experience together, ten years ago I was fortunate to research and write a report for the Western Rivers Conservancy, whose lofty goal is to protect the best natural rivers of the West, and whose need at that time was to determine which rivers those were. Immersing myself on their behalf, I investigated the work of dozens of scientists and managers who have spent decades on the rivers of eleven western states. I read their work described in stacks of reports, interviewed them, and synthesized their findings with descriptions, analyses, narratives, and reflections from my own personal exposure, which was accumulating faster than I could take notes and file my photos.

In this book I'd like to share some of what I learned from all those explorations and sources, and from more that just keep coming, recent months of exciting travels included.

The Rocky Mountain region has some fabulously long reaches of free-flowing water. Hundreds of other streams flow with grace, life, and importance to us all. These might include the creek outside your back door or at the edge of town.

Owing to the Rocky Mountains' span of 1,000 miles north-to-south and up to 450 miles in width, a number of rare and unique species of fish populate rivers here, their endemism separated by seismic upheavals, isolation of sub-ranges, and variability of climate and gradient. A careful exam shows other biological aspects of the rivers as well: outstanding riparian corridors of cottonwoods, refuges for once phenomenal runs of salmon, and key locations for restoration of healthy waters having importance throughout the region and far downstream—even to the oceans.

If we're to share the wonders of our rivers with future generations, the Rocky Mountains' freshwater estate of today must be safeguarded, and the qualities of its past need to be reclaimed where possible. Seeing, knowing, and realizing these values is the first step.

So let's go explore!

A BOOK OF RIVERS

This field guide provides information, travel tips, and perhaps a bit of inspiration so that we might know our network of rivers better and thereby enrich our lives by experiencing and taking better care of these streams.

Over the years I've found other excellent guidebooks specifically aimed at boating, hiking, and fishing, but none offered a fuller view of the rivers, and none featured the streams themselves, with attention to their geography, ecology, fish, and other intrinsic qualities. So I went to work on this book.

The Rocky Mountains extend from Canada southward nearly to Mexico, and from the Front Range of Colorado or the Rocky Mountain Front of Montana westward to the Great Basin desert, Colorado Plateau, or Columbia Plateau. I've organized chapters by four states: Colorado, Idaho, Montana, and Wyoming. I've included waters that flow explicitly in the Rocky

Rafts are capable and forgiving craft for big whitewater, for carrying gear on extended trips, and for groups of people. Here veteran guide and river conservationist Mike Fiebig is ready to launch on the Middle Fork Flathead River in Montana.

Kayaks are the choice for many paddlers, especially for whitewater here on "The Numbers" of the Arkansas River, Colorado.

Mountain domain, and to a lesser degree downstream extensions of those rivers eastward onto the Great Plains and westward into drylands beyond the mountains. While Utah and New Mexico include smaller portions of the Rockies, those states are principally in southwestern geographic regions, best covered in another book.

In the interest of full disclosure here, let me say that I would like to have included narratives about many more rivers, but the allotted space required me to trim. So, if you feel that not all worthy streams are included between these two covers, I'm with you. The sixty-five rivers highlighted here might best be regarded as a starting point.

The focus here is on nature and tips for paddling, rowing, and hiking along Rocky Mountain streams, large and small. For each river I include notes about fish, which might be of value to anglers, though my attention is more on fish as essential players in these ecosystems than on fishing. This book is principally a guide to nature—not to culture—and so my photos show less-altered riverscapes rather than human-made ones, even though evidence of our presence appears everywhere.

Some people might think that river travel is exclusively the province of skilled whitewater paddlers. Well, it's not. This four-state region's collection of waterways offers appeal not just to the seasoned aficionado, but to everybody who paddles through easy or difficult rapids, and to anyone who walks along, wades in, sits beside, or is quietly grateful for water that flows. The paddling information here is meant to help kayakers, canoeists, rafters, and stand-up paddleboarders. Rivers can be a pastime and passion for all of us.

I admit that I'm unabashedly fond of long river journeys. So, you'll see here rivers that are not only great for day trips, weekend outings, and whitewater workouts, but also for river traveling—launching a raft or canoe and going downstream for a weekend, a week, or a month. Extended trips take us across whole landscapes, watersheds, and states, and

Canoes are traditional craft for river running, typically in moderate whitewater and gentler flows but also in challenging rapids by expert paddlers. Unlike kayaks, they can easily be loaded with gear for overnight and extended trips lasting weeks and more. Here Ann Vileisis surfs a small wave on the upper Snake River, Wyoming.

in this way we can fully engage in the escape that comes with an intimate connection to the natural world by way of the waters that run through it.

Along this line, I don't want to dampen the sense of discovery that each of us can feel when we head out into the unknown and immerse ourselves in the natural world. Adventure is good! But much can be gained by learning about a river, and a little help along the way can save a lot of gasoline and time while avoiding unwelcome danger that might go beyond any reasonable spirit of adventure.

In short, I'd be honored to help you figure out where to go, yet I make no pretense about running your trip. A river journey should be an exploration. My personal preference is to know enough about the river so that I don't get in over my head, so to speak, but not so much that I dampen an awaiting sense of discovery. I want to know the class of whitewater I'll be encountering so that I can safely choose my trips accordingly. But except in a few consequential cases, I don't want others telling

Rivers of all sizes call on us to jump in and cool off on hot summer days. This bubbling pool refreshes in Hells Canyon of the Snake River.

Trails follow the shorelines of many streams, such as here in the depths of Hells Canyon of the Snake River, Idaho, and hiking is a great way to see many of the Rocky Mountain rivers.

me how to run the rapids or, for that matter, what's around the next bend of the river or the trail. That's for each of us to determine and discover. Go find it!

Just so you know, I've paddled my canoe or rowed my raft on virtually all the boatable rivers covered in this book, and on most of the individual outings. For some reaches, however, I rely on other guidebooks prepared by a cadre of esteemed boaters referenced in the sources section at the end of this book. I recommend those sources for paddlers seeking the most difficult whitewater and also for additional streams to see.

Writing a guidebook presents a dilemma: Some favorite places that I've had to myself might become more visited. Yet each of us deserves our share of nature, and the old axiom is true: We only protect the places we love, and we only love the places we know. So think of your guardianship as the cost of admittance here, and join in efforts to safeguard these special places that lack voice if we—as boaters, hikers, and anglers—don't come to know and adopt each river as our own, and to care for each stream with the same type of love and reverence that we have for other places and other lives dear to us.

For each highlighted stream I present a summary of the waterway and its character, with notes about its nature, fish, ongoing threats, and protection efforts. Then—getting to the core of guidebook functions—I point to routes for driving there, to hiking trails along the shores, and to bikeways, and then with more emphasis I detail reaches for canoeing, kayaking, rafting, and even paddleboarding. I flag many potential dangers—especially those that might not be expected—but certainly not all.

RIVER RUNNING IN THE AGE OF THE CLIMATE CRISIS

The day has come for us to consider the climate crisis in everything we do, including river time. Most of us burn fossil fuels when we head out for an expedition or simply a day on or near the water, so it's difficult to enjoy our rivers without incurring some cost in global warming.

Yet without nourishing our ties to nature, people tend to lack the incentive and the passion to take care of the earth and our waters. Losing that motivation and failing to instill it in the next generation are the worst things that can happen regarding the fate of the earth. I believe that river connections are one of the finest ways to sustain and increase our attachments to nature. Can we benefit from river time yet minimize the costs to global warming? Here's how I've adjusted my own habits and love of rivers.

See, learn about, and experience streams near home, which requires less gas. This may sound insignificant, but think about the opposite: global travel. There's no need to fly halfway around the globe, or even to Canada or Alaska, to engage in a fabulous river adventure or eye-opening experience. My selection of rivers for this book includes not only classic wild rivers, but also Rocky Mountain streams near cities where the most people live, plus other waters that are easily reached.

Get the most out of your approach to the water. If you're driving to Idaho, do a long trip instead of a short one. Maximize time on the river, letting the current do the work rather than driving around all the time. Less driving is one reason I love long river trips, and why I often launch above the usual put-in and float beyond the usual takeout. When possible, aim for efficiency by going out for larger blocks of time and linking trips back-to-back.

Biking shuttles can save gas and are feasible for many short trips and for outings alone or with just my wife (and we do a lot of those!). Along this line, professional shuttle services can obviate the need to drive two cars from home, and shuttlers can caravan more than one vehicle at a time to the takeout and efficiently return multiple shuttle drivers together. Similarly, commercial river trips can save highway mileage by serving a whole group at once. By the way, an entirely new market may evolve with outfitters facilitating private boaters who are willing to ride in a van to avoid the usual shuttle requirements. I've rowed my own boat on a number of commercial trips where the outfitter was amenable, and I've always had a terrific time.

Get a fuel-efficient vehicle the next time you trade up. Drive slower to use less gas. Reuse old equipment instead of consuming more. My boats were born in—well, I'm a bit embarrassed to say how old they are, but they remain great boats. Pool rides and resources with friends.

There are few entirely guilt-free ways to visit, enjoy, and explore rivers, but an uninterrupted week or two on the water is better than a vacation where we drive and drive every day.

The waters await. But first let me offer some background about the natural systems that govern this remarkable suite of Rocky Mountain rivers.

The Nature of Rocky Mountain Rivers

THE WEST'S NETWORK OF RIVERS AND STREAMS

From the top of the continent, ten arterial rivers and thousands of tributaries flow in a loosely radial pattern outward from the Rocky Mountains to low country beyond.

Starting in the north, the Missouri River begins with its triad of headwater sources—the Jefferson, Madison, and Gallatin Rivers—and drains eastward across the Great Plains. Clockwise from those, the Yellowstone begins in the Teton Wilderness of Wyoming, flows through our first national park and much of Montana's length, and meets the Missouri just a few miles into North Dakota.

Further clockwise around these heights of the continent, we see the North and South Platte flowing from Wyoming and Colorado before joining in Nebraska and winding onward to the lower Missouri. South of them, the Arkansas River gathers headwaters from peaks in central Colorado and flows south and then east to Kansas and ultimately the lower Mississippi River. The Rio Grande sources in the San Juan Mountains of southern Colorado and exits southward through New Mexico before defining the international border between Texas and Mexico.

West of the Continental Divide, the Colorado River flows from Rocky Mountain National Park and crosses into Utah, Arizona, and California on its way to the Gulf of California and the Pacific. North of it, the Green River forms in the Wind River Range of southern Wyoming and becomes the southbound artery of Utah before joining the

From peaks called the Maroon Bells, Maroon Creek flows to the Roaring Fork and then the Colorado River.

The Snake River curves beneath the seismic rise and glacially carved face of the Teton Range, Wyoming.

Colorado. Northward, the Snake River flows from Yellowstone National Park, crosses the Snake River Plain of southern Idaho, then defines the border of Idaho and Oregon as it grows northward to become the second-largest river in the West.

Completing our rotation, the Pend Oreille and Kootenai Rivers of northern Montana and Idaho flow to the Columbia—the largest river of the entire West. Not included here, the Columbia's upper reach through the Rockies lies entirely in Canada, where it grows to become the United States' sixth-largest river at the point where it enters the country in Washington (it later grows to become the nation's fourth-largest river).

A multitude of dams and diversions impound and deplete the Rocky Mountain rivers throughout their canyons and pastured valleys, but this network of streams still claims more undeveloped riverfront than any other region in the United States except Alaska. The Salmon is the longest undammed river in forty-nine states with its 420-mile length. The Yellowstone has six diversion structures but—properly approached—only one requires the portage of a canoe.

The nature of these rivers—the way they look and function—depends on five factors.

First, geologic events created the mountain ranges, topography, and bedrock through which rivers flow—the big backdrop. Second, climate prescribes the amount and timing of the crucial rain and snow. Third, the forces of geology and climate together determine hydrology—characteristics of flow, including rapids, pools, and cycles of flood and drought. Fourth, the combined effects of geology, climate, and hydrology govern what plants live in and along a river. Finally, all these factors influence what fish and other wildlife will thrive, and ultimately how we can use the streams, whether by boating, hiking, or otherwise appreciating their life force. The diversity of Rocky Mountain rivers owes to the ways that these five factors vary across the region.

GEOLOGY

The paths of rivers we know today are determined by seismic activity and volcanism of the earth around them, and also by subsequent geologic forces of erosion—mostly by water but also by glaciers—that sculpt the valleys and canyons.

The entire Rocky Mountain region has long been subject to buckling and folding of geologic strata as the North American plate floats on top of an underlying semi-molten layer of the earth and migrates slowly westward by continental drift. This 200-million-year phenomenon includes what geologists call the Laramide Revolution of seismic uplifts occurring over the past 40 million years, forming the peaks, plateaus, and foothills with intervening valleys of the Rocky Mountain region. The highest summits rise in the south; Colorado has fifty-eight over 14,000 feet. The greatest continuous mass of mountains lies in central and northern Idaho.

The simplest configuration of Rocky Mountain rivers shows streams that take form at high elevations of mountain uplifts where precipitation is greatest, and then flow somewhat directly down the slope to flattening terrain below. Rivers at the east-facing Rocky Mountain Front of Montana are one example of this; the Front Range of Colorado is another with gems such as the Cache la Poudre pounding down from its abrupt fault-block rise with steep rapids.

Other rivers have been deflected by uplifts of sub-ranges, forcing them into routes of greater complexity. The west side of the Colorado Rockies is inclined more gradually than the east side, and so rivers there take longer paths down the Continental Divide's

Durable volcanic rock has resisted erosion and created this falls on the Firehole River in Yellowstone National Park, dusted here by an autumn snow shower.

west slope. Even more geologically elaborate on the west slope, the Salmon River, sourced in the Sawtooth Mountains of Idaho, flows 100 miles *toward* the Continental Divide and is then deflected away from it by the Bitterroot Range at the Idaho-Montana border. Westbound, the river penetrates one of America's wildest mountain strongholds before exiting the Rockies in the second-deepest canyon on the continent.

Scenery is everything we see from the river, and prominent here are mountains that geologically rise up into views that would otherwise be inconsequentially flat with only the next bend of the river in sight. The Tetons are among our most abrupt mountain masses, veering 7,000 feet above the Snake River while the valley seismically sinks to lower levels, together creating extreme relief that many consider the most captivating scenic backdrop of any river in America.

Geology determines not only the overarching trajectories of our rivers along with the landscapes we see from the water, but also important details including location and steepness of rapids. The largest drops indicate resistance points where the toughest bedrock—often granite but also gneiss, schist, and igneous basalt—is exposed to the water's flow.

The region's many waterfalls are the best examples of these bedrock bastions of resistance; see the cataracts at Kootenai Falls in Montana, the Yellowstone's Lower Falls, and Lower Mesa Falls on the Henry's Fork of the Snake in Idaho. In Colorado, a "basement complex" of underlying hardrock strata—exposed only after layers of softer overlying sedimentary and volcanic rocks have eroded away—account for the state's steepest and most intense whitewater gorges: Gore Canyon of the Colorado, Black Canyon of the Gunnison, Royal Gorge of the Arkansas, and the Animas River Canyon.

Layers of sedimentary rock have been metamorphosed into brilliant colors and shaped by the river's currents into cobbles and gravel in the bed of the South Fork Flathead, seen here through an underwater camera.

Rapids are also caused by land-slides that terminate in streams and congest the current; for example, the 1925 slide on the Gros Ventre River east of Grand Teton National Park. A 225-foot-high plume of rock and soil debris blocked the river temporarily, then burst with a flooding maelstrom. A still-formi-dable rapid remains today. On the Yampa River of Colorado, a land-slide in 1965 created a turbulent new rapid called Warm Springs—an unfortunate surprise to rafters the next day.

Other rapids are formed when steep tributaries reach their con-fluences with receiving rivers and enter the larger flow, which slows the incoming water's speed and allows heavy rocks carried by the steeper side streams to settle in the river's channel and force the water around them.

Salient features including the colors of riverbeds in the Rockies are tied to geology. The Northern Rockies at the Montana-Canada border are metamorphosed, or altered by pressure and heat, into mineralized cake-layers of maroon, gray, white, and black rock, and as those rocks crumble and wash downstream they become cobbles and gravel of dazzling colors, like mosaics of stained glass paving the bottom of the Flathead and its three forks. The chemistry of the mountains' rock strata gives these streams the most brilliant riverbeds in America.

At a subtler level, the geologically related chemistry of the rivers governs much about the life that will thrive there. A key component of biological productivity is limestone, formed from compacted layers of shells and organic matter that accumulated in ancient seas. This is especially conducive to invertebrate life needing dissolved elements from the whitish sedimentary rock for construction of shells, carapaces, and body structures. Flowing through limestone, the Blackfoot River of Idaho, for example, is exceptionally productive. Its conductivity, or measure of nutrients, reaches 700 parts per million. The granite-based Salmon River, in comparison, rates 40 to 70. Trout in the Blackfoot grow at twice the rate found in many other good trout streams.

Glaciers have also played a geologic role in the paths of rivers. In a cooler climate than that of today, localized mountain glaciers formed on the north and northeast sides of many peaks and grew to become linked along the Continental Divide and high sub-ranges. The grinding creep of ice transported and pulverized underlying rock to cre-ate the boulders, stones, and gravels that constitute the beds of many rivers today—key sources of spawning gravels and rapids-forming boulders spread for many miles in rivers below historic and surviving (but not for long) glaciers.

Plate tectonics, volcanism, and erosion created the landscape across which all rivers flow, but without rain and snow, the rivers would not exist.

CLIMATE

Patterns of precipitation shape rivers from beginning to end, and the temperature of the air affects the water and all its life.

As the prevailing eastbound winds of North America's mid-latitudes push storms up and over the Rockies, the air cools. Temperatures typically drop 3 degrees for each 1,000-foot rise. Cold air holds less water vapor, so it sheds moisture as it rises, giving higher elevations more precipitation. Because of complex solar and jet-stream effects and low-pressure phenomena that deliver most major storms in winter, Rocky Mountain precipitation comes principally as snow, which piles up and melts slowly relative to rainfall's rapid runoff. Snowmelt crests at its highest levels in late spring, but continuing melt nourishes waterways well into summer if not autumn.

Once the moisture-laden, prevailing westerly winds top the summits, the air descends the east side, rewarms, and regains capacity to hold water vapor. The clouds have also spent much of their content by dumping snow on their approach from the west, and the combined effect reduces precipitation markedly on the downwind, east-facing slope—a "rain shadow."

Also reflecting the interplay between geology and climate, the north sides of mountains and the north-facing slopes of canyons tend to be shaded from sun and therefore cooler,

Much of the Rocky Mountains' precipitation comes as snowfall, with melting that spreads runoff over a period of months or even years. The Rockies' reservoirs of frozen water and all that depend on them are imperiled by the warming climate. Boulder Creek, in Colorado, flows beneath the ice of December.

with longer-lasting snowpacks at their sources, and so temperatures in those streams are chilled. High-elevation and north-side streams are vital to coldwater species such as trout, salmon, and whitefish, and will be increasingly important as the climate warms further, causing profound effects on rivers.

HYDROLOGY

Geology and climate together determine characteristics of flow, including volume, direction, and gradient of streams.

Rivers of the Rockies typically run low during winter's freeze, rise with snowmelt, peak in late May or so, then recede. The floods of snowmelt are essential to everything from cottonwood groves to endangered fish. Responding to climatic imperatives, nine of the region's ten largest rivers lie in the north.

Largest in volume and length, the Snake River, with its tributary Henry's Fork, leaves the Rocky Mountains with 8,779 cubic feet per second (cfs) and enters the Snake River Plain, where the main stem later receives more tributaries from the Rockies and grows to 56,900 cfs by the time it joins the Columbia in the Pacific Northwest.

Second in volume in the Rocky Mountain region of the United States is the Pend Oreille (pond-er-RAY) of Idaho and northern Washington, though dams block its length

Lower Yellowstone Falls foams downward in the upper reaches of a river that will flow nearly 700 miles before joining the Missouri River on the Great Plains.

in the United States. The Clark Fork of Montana is really the same river, being the 20,010-cfs inlet to Pend Oreille Lake but going by a different name.

Third in volume, the Clearwater carries 15,500 cfs to the lower Snake.

The Yellowstone grows to 12,523 cfs above its confluence with the Missouri on the Great Plains—fourth in size among Rocky Mountain rivers in the United States.

The Kootenai of Montana and Idaho carries 11,740 cfs where it leaves the US Rockies and returns to Canada, though it grows significantly to 27,600 cfs north of the border before it joins the Columbia River there. The Flathead of Montana flows with 11,638 cfs as the principal tributary to the Clark Fork and is actually larger at the confluence. The Salmon of Idaho averages 11,420 cfs. The Missouri flows with 11,000 cfs where it meets the shorter but larger Yellowstone in North Dakota.

As the ninth-ranking river flowing within the Rocky Mountain region but the largest in the southern two-thirds of the range, the Colorado carries 6,559 cfs where it enters the Colorado Plateau province of southwestern deserts. The Colorado historically carried 17,850 cfs in the desert farther downstream at Lees Ferry—just above the Grand Canyon—though flows plagued by drought are now diminishing. Ultimately diversions from the Colorado deplete it to nothing at its Gulf of California terminus in Mexico— the most extreme exhaustion of a river on the continent.

With 775 miles, the Green River of Wyoming is longer than the Colorado's 439 where the two join but carries only 5,302 cfs compared to the Colorado's 7,600 at the confluence of the two arteries in Utah's canyonlands of the Colorado Plateau province.

Rivers' hydrologic phenomena include cycles of high and low runoff. Floods cause losses and suffering where people have built in harm's way, but periodic high water is essential to the health of streams. Floods scour out pools where fast water picks up silt, gravel, and cobbles and jettisons them downstream. The resulting deep pools keep water cold in summer and provide shelter for fish and other life. Alternately, floods deposit their heaviest and densest cargo—large cobbles—at riffle and rapid sites where the imported rocks further congest runoff, aerate water, and increase its oxygen supply while also providing anchoring structures for invertebrates at the base of the food chain. The pool-and-riffle sequence—maintained by floods—is essential to a healthy river.

Seasonal flow variation is also crucial to shorelines and riparian corridors—the most valuable of all habitats biologically. By centrifugal force, water dislodges silt, sand, and gravel from channels and banks on the outsides of bends, carries that bedload downstream, and deposits it on the insides of bends where the current slows. These hydrologic processes constantly renew the shape and condition of the shores. The biological health of floodplains and riparian forests depends on this periodic flooding and cyclical erosion and deposition—a "disturbance ecosystem."

Keystone species such as cottonwoods require these disturbances for germination and growth. Fish also benefit from floods. Aside from their dependence on the flood-sculpted pool-and-riffle sequence, many fish need seasonal high water that makes available the rich food sources of river-edge wetlands and floodplains—also important refuges for small fish evading predators, including alien species such as bass, lurking in the main channels.

Floods and other natural processes result in channel complexity—the mix of pools, riffles, scoured depths, gravel bars, riverfront wetlands, flooded forests, and sloughs—all crucial for wildlife.

Where floods have been stopped by dams or where the channels have been homogenized by levees, pools fill in with sediment and riffles subside by erosion—the dual effect serving to even out the gradient and create a constant glide with less biological productivity than in the alternating pool-and-riffle sequence. Heavily dammed and diverted rivers, such as the Gunnison and South Platte, are primed for this problem. The Yampa and Yellowstone, in contrast, retain the dynamics of natural flood-flows, and with them the complexity of back channels, hydrologic features, and a distinct pool-and-riffle sequence.

For another connection between hydrology, plants, and wildlife, consider trees that fall into streams during floods. Driftwood is not just floating debris that clogs the channel and requires boaters to portage; rather, logs in rivers are vital contributors to the ecosystem. Fallen and flood-borne trees become grounded in shallows or on bends and then partially block the flow and redirect the current, creating hydrologic and biological complexity. One stranded log entraps another, making a logjam. These form pools where water backs up, and rapids where water is forced around.

Wood in streams provides anchorage and habitat to invertebrates that fish need for food, and it offers underwater cover from predators. Fish hide from dive-bombing ospreys, for example, under the shelter of logs suspended at the water's surface. The wood's rot nourishes microbes, insects, and invertebrates important in rivers, estuaries, and even the sea. In the past, massive logjams in many rivers backed up water enough to spill over the banks, cover low flats alongside, and trigger deposition of suspended gravels needed for fishes' spawning beds, or "redds." Birds, mammals, and riparian plants thrive in the resulting forested wetlands, and the log-induced overflows recharge groundwater tables, enabling them to store water and discharge it back into streams as levels wane, to the benefit of many players.

Fallen trees and logjams in the Swan River, Montana, pose challenges for boaters while providing needed habitat for fish and creating healthy complexity in the shape and morphology of the riverbed, enriching to all the life that depends on it.

Biologists agree that large woody debris must be reinstated into waterways to restore streams and the life that depends on them. A key difficulty is that most of the old-growth trees—capable of lodging themselves in the streams after they've fallen—have been logged and taken away. The benefit of logjams is one among many compelling reasons to protect and reinstate mature riparian forests.

Hydrology and the rhythms of runoff affect everything from rapids to flooding to logjams, and also to riparian plants, which are vital to other life and to recreational use of the rivers.

PLANT LIFE

From the microscopic to some of the largest organisms on earth, plant life determines the character of rivers, their health, and their suitability to all creatures.

At the base of this chain of dependencies, algae appear as small and inconspicuous diatom and desmid species—waterborne or slimy on rocks, slippery to the step but nutrient rich. Other forms of algae grow as filamentous green fibers that cling to the bottom with holdfasts—the waving micro-forests of "seaweed" in quiet warm shallows of rivers. Algae are eaten by larvae of stoneflies, mayflies, caddisflies, and dragonflies, and on up the food chain these insects and other invertebrates become prime food for fish. These primitive plants can grow profusely and benefit the entire ecosystem, but with pollution or siltation algae can multiply to stifling mats that ultimately die and rot, consuming oxygen in the process and further degrading water quality.

As keystone species in the riparian community, cottonwood trees serve many birds, mammals, and fish with food and habitat. These Fremont cottonwoods line the banks of the Colorado River downstream from Grand Junction.

Algae are fundamental to the life of rivers, but when most of us think of plant life along waterways, we think of trees. The Rocky Mountains have two timberlines: one low, where aridity prevents tree growth from that elevation down, and one high, where snow, cold, wind, or rock limit growth from there up. While many streams begin with rivulets of snowmelt at high elevations above timberline, most mileage is through the mountains' mid-levels of spruces and lodgepole pines, followed by ponderosa pines and then junipers.

Below the juniper belt, the low-elevation timberline follows, and it would render deep valleys of the Rockies plus long reaches across the plains and plateaus treeless except for the extraordinary gift of rivers. In these dry areas, water delivered by the streams soaks into the ground near the shores and nourishes riparian or stream-dependent vegetation, including the *only* trees through much of the arid country that dominates the majority of the West's acreage. In those drylands as well as many riverfronts in mountain terrain, rich green ribbons of cottonwoods, willows, box elders, and red osier dogwoods are vital to the life around them.

In natural river systems at all elevations, trees and shrubs shade the waters, keep them cool, and protect banks from erosion. Fallen trees provide food, spawning habitat, and protection. Riverfront vegetation delivers essential nutrients to the water as fallen leaves and insects that drop from overhanging branches and thereby feed fish.

The health of riparian plant life is a key indicator of the health of the streams themselves and one of the easiest of those indicators to identify. Owing to the availability of water, the depth of soil delivered as water-transported alluvium, and the moisture-rich deterrence of fire, floodplains along rivers often support the largest trees, healthiest forests, and most important food sources for wildlife. Western redcedars elegantly thrive as arboreal champions of size and age along floodplains, adding beauty and serving life along the Selway, Clearwater, and other rivers of the Northern Rockies.

Black, narrowleaf, and Fremont cottonwoods reign as the Rockies' largest riparian trees. They cast shade and produce the greatest quantities of nutrient-bearing leaves. Their foliage, twigs, bark, and sprouts are food for beavers, deer, and elk, and their crowns form nesting habitat for songbirds. Dead or broken snags provide nesting platforms for ospreys, eagles, and herons. Cavities become homes for woodpeckers, wood ducks, mergansers, and raccoons. All this describes cottonwoods as keystone species—life forms that many others depend upon.

The river-and-cottonwood relationship works both ways: The health of the rivers needs the trees, but the life of the trees also depends on the rivers. Cottonwoods might be considered the ultimate riparian tree not just because they serve other life so well, but also because they require flooding rivers to reproduce. The trees' seeds are genetically coded to ripen just after high waters of springtime recede, and those seeds generally need a freshly scoured floodplain or new silt deposit on which to germinate—in other words, a flood. An entire class of young trees will arise in the wake of a specific high-water event. When mature, the trees' roots grip soil and protect stream banks from excess erosion, and those trees later fall into the water and enrich the entire aquatic ecosystem. Where floods are controlled by dams, cottonwood forests lack the fresh silt or scoured sand, and they eventually die and disappear without replacement.

Some of the country's longest and nearly continuous cottonwood corridors lie in the Rockies along the Snake River in Wyoming and eastern Idaho, the upper Salmon in Idaho, the Yellowstone in Montana, the Yampa in Colorado, and the North Platte in

Wyoming. These and all the plant life in and along rivers make possible the greater community of life in the water.

FISH AND WILDLIFE

Fish

Fish are not as easily seen as trees, but they indicate river health even more explicitly. Their nourishment depends on an elaborate food chain beginning—as we've seen—with algae, and their lives depend on all the factors that create essential habitat.

For both food and places to spawn, rear, feed, and hide from predators, fish need varieties of habitats that come with channel complexity. Less-healthy streams have been simplified into a single channel with relatively uniform banks and beds, which sustain fewer and smaller fish. In contrast, healthy streams support a full complement of fish that are native to the Rocky Mountain waters.

Emblematic here, cutthroat trout evolved even as the mountains were formed, and populations diversified into subspecies secluded by geographic barriers. Westslope cutthroat occupy streams on the Pacific side of the Rockies in Montana and Idaho. Yellowstone cutthroat live in the upper Yellowstone basin of Wyoming and Montana.

Fishing and rafting guide Hilary Hutcheson carefully returns a westslope cutthroat to the Middle Fork Flathead.

Bonneville cutthroat became distinctive in the sprawling meltwater basin of Bonneville Lake during the ice ages when that lake's aquatic reach effectively linked all the rivers and streams flowing into it from southern Wyoming and Idaho through much of Utah. As the post-ice-age lake receded to become the comparatively miniaturized Great Salt Lake of today, its tributaries became isolated from each other, permanently segregating each stream's population of cutthroat.

Also west of the Continental Divide but east of the Bonneville cutthroat zone, Colorado River cutthroat make their home in the upper Green and Colorado River basins of Wyoming and Colorado. On the eastern side of the Continental Divide, greenback cutthroat are native to the upper Arkansas and South Platte in Colorado. Separated by high mountains, Rio Grande cutthroat survive in tributaries of the upper Rio Grande in southern Colorado.

All cutthroat species are imperiled or endangered owing to habitat damage and, more universally, to the introduction and domination of nonnative gamefish including brown and rainbow trout.

Bull trout (sometimes called Dolly Varden, which is a separate species) migrate great distances in rivers and require especially cold water. These large fish once thrived throughout much of the northwestern Rocky Mountains, but their numbers have been sharply reduced. Their range today in Idaho and western Montana is an indicator of quality waters and can be regarded as a proxy for the best natural streams remaining.

Other native resident fish—each important in its way—include whitefish, squawfish, chiselmouth, shiners, chubs, dace, suckers, and paddlefish. Native arctic grayling, once ranging broadly across the upper Missouri basin, are found only in the Beaverhead and Ruby Rivers of the Missouri headwaters today, though they've been reintroduced to some other streams.

Unlike resident fish that stay in their rivers all their lives, anadromous species spawn and hatch in rivers but bide much of their lives at sea, where they grow larger in a greater nutrient pool. These fish are among our most valued, iconic, and ecologically important species, more prevalent in the Pacific Northwest than in the Rocky Mountains owing to their dependence on an undammed continuity of flow between headwater spawning areas and the ocean. But in the Rockies of Idaho, anadromous species include steelhead trout and chinook, sockeye, and coho salmon.

Anadromous fish historically occupied many other rivers in the northern reaches of the Rockies, but dams, such as those on the Snake River, have blocked their passage. According to the *Atlas of Pacific Salmon*, 231 distinct stocks of salmon have been extirpated in the United States—most in the heavily dammed Columbia basin. Mind-boggling numbers of salmon once spawned there, and intensive efforts seek to sustain these fish and restore populations to healthy levels.

Steelhead are anadromous rainbow trout that grow larger than their freshwater counterparts by migrating to the ocean's greater food source for most of their lives. Like salmon, different and genetically distinctive "runs" return to their natal rivers at different times. They rear one or more years before migrating to sea, and thus can be threatened in basins with heavy logging, grazing, and farming. Healthy populations of these muscular fish, adapted to the long spawning journey upstream, thrived in the Salmon and Snake River basins and could do so once again if the critical dams blocking their migration are removed.

White sturgeon—historically anadromous but capable of breeding without migrating to the ocean—survive in a few large rivers of Idaho and Montana but are imperiled because they need long reaches unbroken by dams in order for their eggs and fry to be viable.

Native fishes have evolved in their home basins for millennia and are uniquely suited to natural conditions, while alien species from other parts of the country or globe pose fatal problems to native fish by preying on them, competing for food, preempting habitat, and introducing exotic diseases for which native fish have no resistance, including whirling disease affecting cherished trout waters. In addition to brown and rainbow trout, which are popular among sport anglers but nonetheless exotic and threatening to native fish, alien fishes include bass, bluegill, walleye, crappie, brown bullhead, carp, catfish, and pike. These perversely tend to thrive in manipulated environments created by dams, diversions, and warm water. Nonnative gamefishes in the Rockies include shad, bass, bluegill, brown trout, and brook trout. While recognizing the appeal that these fish have to many anglers, this field guide gives emphasis to native fish and the need for their protection.

While many people enjoy fish by catching them, fish watching is an important reward of spending time on rivers. To see fish better, use a mask and snorkel, which can open a whole new world to river travelers' eyes. From the front of a raft, fish can often be seen while the boat drifts downriver.

The health of fish populations governs the lives of other wildlife, and the river conditions determining the status of fish also affect birds, mammals, reptiles, amphibians, and invertebrates.

Wildlife

Near the base of the food chain, aquatic insects fill vital needs in the lives of fish and larger wildlife. Crawfish, mussels, and other invertebrates likewise play pivotal roles in river ecosystems.

Among river-dependent wildlife, waterfowl and other birds are the most easily seen. Mergansers dive underwater and subsist largely on fish. Mallards, wood ducks, and pintails feed at the surface.

Wading birds that spear minnows, crayfish, and other small animals include great blue herons, snowy egrets, and green herons. Kingfishers spear fish, sound their rattling call while flying over the waters, and nest in riverbanks.

As the most common duck on rivers of the Rockies, mergansers subsist mostly on fish and serve as an indicator of healthy waters.

White pelicans thrive on some large rivers of the interior West. Their brilliant white plumage brightens gravel bars on the Yellowstone River below Livingston, Montana.

Water ouzels, or "dippers," catch larvae and insects along swift coldwater streams and live in nests at the edge of rapids and waterfalls. Swallows and flycatchers dart above the water to snatch insects. Spotted sandpipers peck for insects on shore.

Ospreys dive from great heights for fish that unwittingly appear near the surface. Spectacular white pelicans, with striking black wingtips, dive for fish and lounge on gravel bars of the Yellowstone and other large rivers flowing to the plains or some western lowlands.

As the quintessential river mammals, fur-bearers are capable of staying warm in cold water. Beavers are a keystone species, building dams of sticks and mud, which raise the level of water and arrest erosive down-cutting of streambeds. The edges of beaver ponds become wetlands benefitting many creatures. Stream systems across the West still suffer from the near-extinction of beavers 200 years ago, when the fur trade formed the basis of the first exploitive industry in the Rockies. Another fur-bearer, the otter, lives on fish, crayfish, and frogs. Minks scurry at water's edge seeking similar prey.

The water ouzel, or "dipper," feeds on aquatic insects of coldwater streams, often diving underwater and into the spray of waterfalls. This plainly gray but beautifully singing bird chatters, dips, and snatches larvae along the North Fork Flathead, Montana.

Terrestrial mammals such as deer, elk, squirrels, foxes, bears, and coyotes all come to drink at streams, or for cover in the riparian zones, which are often the only natural habitat remaining in farmed or developed areas. Riverfronts are corridors that link otherwise fragmented natural landscapes.

All aspects of nature along the waters of the Rockies make these rivers what they are, and the life systems throughout are affected by overuse and abuse in the past and by increasing threats today. Many people and organizations have launched efforts to protect what remains of natural rivers and to restore intrinsic qualities where possible. These are the subjects of the next chapter.

The quintessential ungulate of the riparian zone, moose depend on it for 80 percent of their food. This mother and calf linger in their salad bar of willows along Lake Fork of Rock Creek, Montana.

Beavers have backed up Lee Creek at the headwaters of the North Fork Gunnison in Colorado. Their dams of sticks and mud create wetlands, recharge groundwater, sequester silt and carbon, store floodwater, and prevent damaging down-cutting of stream channels.

Threats, Protection, and Restoration

DIMINISHED RIVERS AND ONGOING THREATS

The clarity, wildness, and beauty of Rocky Mountain rivers attract and impress us, yet it's also important to recognize what has been lost and to encourage protection aimed to sustain and restore the best of this remarkable network of streams.

The entire range might once have been considered "Rocky Mountain National Park." But only a small portion of that estate remains in excellent condition.

The organization Pacific Rivers surveyed the waters of the Northern Rockies and reported, "While many think of the northern Rockies as 'the last best place,' growing scientific evidence shows that stream ecosystem degradation is severe and is continuing almost unabated throughout the region." Many of the most valuable stream miles for native fish and wildlife lie in lower elevation and lower gradient rivers, and these are the streams that have been altered the most by mining, diversions, logging, dams, and development.

The mining industry is responsible for the worst stream pollution in the West. The Environmental Protection Agency (EPA) in 2018 reported that just 88 mining facilities caused 47 percent of all toxic pollution in the nation, and identified 161,000 abandoned hardrock mines—mostly in the Rockies and desert ranges. Expected cleanup cost in 2015 topped $50 billion, probably a low estimate and, in any event, unlikely to be spent.

The Lewis River cascades toward its confluence with the Snake River in Yellowstone National Park—America's first large protected landscape.

Mining has resulted in the worst toxic water pollution in the West, according to the Environmental Protection Agency. This abandoned mine encroached on Howard Fork of the South Fork San Miguel, Colorado—a site that has been partially restored.

Consider the Summitville Mine in the Alamosa and Rio Grande basins of Colorado. Gold mining began in 1873, and after a century of degradation, a Canadian corporation in 1984 was permitted to start new operations with an open pit. The company filed for bankruptcy eight years later, and toxic leakage with disastrous potential led the EPA to spend $155 million in public funds on cleanup.

The reason for this problem is the Mining Law of 1872, which prioritized mining over all other uses. It enables mining interests—once sourdoughs working from a mule with a pick and shovel but now faceless multinational corporations with draglines six stories tall—to claim mineral rights across public land of the West. The law lacks adequate provisions for pollution control, wildlife protection, fish kills, restoration, fees for public costs, and bonds to cover failures. Miners acquired tens of thousands of acres of public land in the West for a token $3.50 per acre—much of it later sold at windfall profits for resorts, second homes, and more mining. Reform efforts—like that of Oregon Representative Peter DeFazio in 2014—have failed to crack the mining lobbyists' blockades, and the 1872 law remains in place, much like a communications law would be if passed before the invention of the telephone.

Logging likewise denuded entire watersheds on private and public land. Most Forest Service timber sales in the Rockies have lost money for the government with the cost of roads, planning, and administration vastly exceeding fees collected, according to Mark C. Phares in *Public Land and Resources Law Review*. Meanwhile the costs of watershed restoration go unaddressed, or are borne by taxpayers after the loggers have departed.

In 2001, after overwhelmingly positive comment, Forest Service Chief Mike Dombeck instituted a Roadless Rule that administratively protected virtually all the remaining unroaded national forest land in the West from new road construction—land also protected, by association, from most logging. Included were 58 million of the Forest Service's 190-million-acre estate. The rule withstood a decade of attack from timber and mining interests that wanted to open the wildlands to clear-cuts and roads, but political pressure to overturn the rule in Alaska and elsewhere was rekindled by the Trump administration in 2020.

Dams block the flow of rivers in many of the finest valleys and are found on nearly all major rivers of the Rockies. The Salmon River in Idaho and the Yellowstone in Montana are the only two large waterways without storage reservoirs, though the waters of each encounter multiple dams below. Dams have permanently flooded irreplaceable canyons, depleted flows downstream, transformed water temperatures in the rivers, altered the water's silt content in ways that disrupt whole ecosystems, and blocked migration of salmon, bull trout, pikeminnows, sturgeon, and other fishes that need free-flowing mileage.

Owing to economic forces, the lack of feasible dam sites remaining, and conservation activism, the construction of large dams in the United States has been halted, at least for now. However, smaller sites for hydropower, water supply, and other uses as odd as

Thousands of dams have blocked at least one section of nearly all major rivers in the Rockies, in the process flooding canyons and valleys, halting migration of fish, diverting water out of the channels, altering temperatures, and transforming flows and movement of silt downstream. One of the largest dams, in Hells Canyon of the Snake River in Idaho, has blocked salmon from hundreds of miles of spawning grounds.

Even as a large river in southern Idaho, the Snake is drained virtually dry for irrigation storage and canals through much of the year. From the identical vantage point (but different times of day), these photos picture Shoshone Falls during springtime runoff and later during irrigation season.

preventing ice from washing up in the town of Rangely along the White River in Colorado continue to be proposed.

Worse, irrigation withdrawals desiccate hundreds of streams in valleys from the Bitterroot to the Rio Grande. Ever since the first white settlement, state laws have recognized irrigation diversions as the best use of western waterways, and consequently limits on withdrawals to protect streams are rare. In Idaho, for example, instream flows can be reserved by the state Department of Water Resources but only after an almost insurmountable process within a hostile political arena. Even then protections provide for "minimum" flows to sustain stream life—not optimum or even adequate flows—and reservations apply only after diversions are taken for "senior" water rights, which include the claims of virtually every farmer, rancher, or city wanting to divert water since settlement began.

In Montana, 3,600 miles of streams are dewatered each year. Efforts to reform western water law that lopsidedly favors agriculture have been stonewalled in spite of changing times and dramatically altered demography with people moving to the West for its "quality of life" values. As western analyst and *High Country News* publisher Ed Marston wrote, "One rancher still carries the political weight of a hundred other people."

Meanwhile, the accidental or deliberate introduction of exotic species has driven native fish toward scarcity or extinction. Problems include not only the opprobrious tamarisk along rivers in the Southern Rockies and star thistle in the north, but also popular gamefish including pike and brown, lake, and rainbow trout.

Along this line, fish hatcheries intended to increase the sport and commercial catch diminish native fish in egregious ways. They introduce great numbers of hatchlings to rivers where native species are already struggling. The stocked fish compete for food and habitat, introduce diseases that thrive in the feedlot tanks of the hatcheries, stray into wild habitat, and compromise the genetic makeup of wild fish by interbreeding. Stocking large numbers of fish masks the decline of native fish and obscures the need to protect them. Though popular among many anglers, the hatcheries diminish wild stocks and may ultimately fail as hatchery difficulties such as epidemic diseases increase, costs rise, and availability of wild fish with their superior genetic makeup needed for essential brood stock become scarce.

Consider, instead, Montana's experience with hatcheries. Facing decline and imperilment of its cherished native trout, the state recognized the hazards of hatcheries and closed all those affecting native fish in 1972. An immediate rebound of native populations has persisted and angling became an enduring mainstay of Montana's economy with the best trout fishing in America.

Also affecting Rocky Mountain streams, people flock here as a new and promised homeland. In 2019 Idaho and Colorado ranked among the top eight states nationwide in population growth rates (though not in absolute numbers of people). While newcomers consume more land, pollute the air in valley towns during winter inversions, and displace wildlife with roads, homes, horses, cats, and dogs, many also bring a desire to preserve what's left and to reform dependence on subsidized commodities. Resort communities that feature rivers include some of the fastest growing and most popular real estate in the West, but many of those arriving people become committed to saving as much of what remains as possible.

Affecting rivers everywhere, a hotter climate will mean that water temperatures rise, threatening if not killing coldwater fish including trout and salmon. Warmer water causes explosive growth of algae, and as it dies and decomposes it depresses the supply of oxygen needed by fish and other life. Climate change also means that floods will be more severe and droughts more intense. Stream flow in the Rockies has declined by 20 percent, and another reduction of 60 percent is expected within thirty years, according to the Lawrence Livermore National Laboratory in an April 18, 2017, report. Flows diminished by diversions already limit aquatic health and food chains in virtually all our rivers.

With climate change, mountain streams delivering cold water from the snowfields and glaciers of Rocky Mountain high country will become ever more important to ecosystems and communities below. Everywhere along our rivers, protection of riparian forests for shade, improved flows during low runoff, reinstated infiltration of groundwater, and reservation of floodplains as open space will all have to be done more, faster, and better as the stress of a warming climate increases in years and decades to come.

SAFEGUARDS AND RESTORATION

Well protected, some streams rise in our largest wilderness areas and national parks. The Yellowstone, Madison, and Gallatin Rivers flow from Yellowstone National Park, and the Snake from Grand Teton National Park. The Flathead forks lie at the borders of Glacier National Park, and the headwaters of Saint Vrain Creek and the Colorado River begin in Rocky Mountain National Park.

Only sixteen areas in the country outside Alaska are wild enough for a person to retreat 10 miles or more from a road, and half of those are in the Rockies: five in the Yellowstone/Beartooth/Wind River region, two in central Idaho, and one in Montana's Bob Marshall Wilderness. Large parts of these areas are designated in the National Wilderness Preservation System—the gold standard for safeguarding wild land and, indirectly, rivers.

National Wild and Scenic Rivers are—or should be—the exemplar of river protection. Congressional designation puts these rivers off-limits to further damming or damage by federal actions, and the law mandates protection of "outstandingly remarkable" values. Original Rocky Mountain members of this elite group include the Middle Fork Salmon, Selway, Lochsa, and Middle Fork Clearwater, all in Idaho. Additions have been the Snake and St. Joe in Idaho; the Flathead forks, East Rosebud Creek, and Missouri in Montana;

Cascading from Colorado's Front Range, Glacier Creek is protected within Rocky Mountain National Park.

the Clark's Fork, upper Snake, and fifteen tributaries of the Snake in Wyoming; and the Cache la Poudre with its South Fork in Colorado.

Wild and Scenic status barred dams once proposed on the Snake in Hells Canyon, the Selway at Penny Cliffs, the Clark's Fork at Box Canyon, the Middle Fork Flathead at Spruce Park, and East Rosebud Creek as it enters ranchland. Wild and Scenic designations have encouraged and required improved management of floating and recreation.

However, the prescribed directives of the Wild and Scenic Act are not always followed when other uses and outlooks interfere, and the Rockies have more rivers deserving protection in the Wild and Scenic system. West Coast states have had far more rivers included in the program; the Rocky Mountains' low number does not owe to a dearth of eligible streams but rather a lack of political support.

The issue of water rights is a principal reason for conflict regarding Wild and Scenic status because designation includes provision for a federal water right as an instream flow. When enacted by a state's water agency, that right can reserve a minimum flow below which further diversions are not allowed. As a practical matter, most eligible Wild and Scenic reaches are high in their basins—above points of existing or potential withdrawals—and so instream reservations should not be a concern. Furthermore, designation comes with the expectation of customized language about water rights. This allows for negotiation and final action by the states. Even so, fear of federal involvement or the potential to usurp private water rights has thwarted efforts to designate more Wild and Scenic Rivers.

Nonetheless, a promising campaign is under way to add as many as 600 miles of Wild and Scenic Rivers in Montana, including pristine tributaries of the Flathead and public-land portions of the Gallatin, Smith, Dearborn, and Blackfoot. In Colorado the blockade

Montanans for Healthy Rivers has launched a campaign to protect 600 miles of waterways in the National Wild and Scenic Rivers system, including the Swan River here below Point Pleasant Campground.

to new Wild and Scenic designations may be opened with Deep Creek, a tributary to the Colorado.

While the issue of diversions persists as one of the most troublesome for the health of western rivers, nominal gains have been made. Several states have adopted procedures for recognizing instream needs, though the reservations typically address unlikely water left in rivers after 150 years of claims already granted by state agencies.

The Yellowstone is the only major river where significant flows have been reserved for instream uses, fish, and the natural maintenance of a healthy riverbed. This pioneering effort came in the wake of industrial proposals for dams and withdrawals that would have diminished the Yellowstone during the energy boom of the 1970s. Instead, much of the runoff was reserved for hydrologic maintenance of the river and its community of life and for protecting downstream ranch withdrawals.

On another front, river conservationists have succeeded in a few of the most intense mining controversies threatening cherished rivers. At the Clark's Fork of the Yellowstone, the Fisher Mine proposal was defeated in the 1990s and mineral rights bought by federal agencies. A nearby threat north of Yellowstone National Park was defeated with a ban on new mining claims in 2018. Plans to mine at Montana's headwaters of the Blackfoot and Smith are pending at this writing.

The work of land trusts and conservancies is yet another thrust of river conservation. Regional organizations such as the Western Rivers Conservancy and national ones including the Nature Conservancy have acquired dozens of waterfront parcels, while local land trusts operate along many of the region's rivers.

The Clark's Fork of the Yellowstone was rescued from an industrial mining proposal in the 1990s when contested mineral rights were acquired by the federal government, averting acid spills in this and other streams nearby.

GET INVOLVED

As part of your own exploration and enjoyment of Rocky Mountain rivers and streams, join an organization that works for their conservation. Idaho Rivers United has been a vibrant voice where environmental protection is constantly under fire, yet the group has gained new designations of Wild and Scenic Rivers in desert canyonlands and protected instream flows there. The national group American Rivers, with regional staff in Colorado and Montana, effectively covers those states and Wyoming. American Whitewater works throughout the Rockies, as does Trout Unlimited. Local organizations such as the Jackson Hole Conservation Alliance, Clark Fork Coalition, Blackfoot Challenge, Eagle River Watershed Council, and dozens of others have likewise been active in protecting and restoring their streams.

Inquire about what's being done to safeguard or improve your waters. County and local planning commissions welcome citizen involvement, or at least they should, and positions on these important councils are often available for the asking.

Anyone interested in the future of a favorite stream can learn about it through local groups or agencies, by searching on the Internet and at the library, and by simply going to the river and taking time to look. Use this knowledge to engage others. Teach children, and encourage schools to become involved with nearby streams. Become politically active by supporting better care for our streams and electing politicians who will do the job.

To the Water

SAFETY FIRST

Even among the most safety-conscious of us, boating on and hiking along rivers can include exposure to hazards, so be prepared. Being safe requires not only the ability to cope with dangers as they arise, but even more the ability to identify potential dangers before they occur. This requires experience, good judgment, and training. Get the necessary instruction for your activity; paddling clubs, kayak schools, and others offer training courses, and much can be learned from competent friends. See the American Whitewater Safety Code and follow it. See also the disclaimer at the opening of this book.

Always beware: Judgments of hazards—even in the international system for classifying whitewater difficulty—vary with the individual. Fluctuations in water level and weather can alter risks greatly from assessments covered here or elsewhere, and hazards such as landslides or tree-fall can happen at any time and change conditions in a river dramatically. Logs across streams can create problems and are common on smaller waterways. Though always vigilant, I find streams of 30-foot width or less especially prone to log blockages.

ACCESS

For driving routes to rivers highlighted in this book, see the Part 2 narratives for each river, which include icons for road access as well as for fish, hiking, and paddling.

I expect that most boaters reading here will be independent rafters, kayakers, and canoeists. Commercial river trips also serve people and fill an important recreational need. For guided trips, search the Internet by river name. Reputable outfitters are available for many of the runnable rivers in this book.

The North Fork Flathead is an outstanding river for canoeing and easy rafting.

Land along rivers is either public or private, and sometimes it's important to know which—see maps from the US Forest Service and Bureau of Land Management (BLM), or consult the agencies' recreation brochures for the most popular rivers.

Private owners reasonably restrict use of their property. For access to the water, public land is usually needed, which can include thin stream-front rights-of-way at bridges and next to roads.

Personally I've never had a problem with a landowner when floating on a river of any size. But it happens, so be low-key. I never camp within sight of a house, and rarely in sight of a road. I don't build fires, even on public land. I'm always quiet when on a river, as everyone should be when within earshot of other boaters or people on shore. When I've encountered landowners, most have not minded my stopping or even camping once they knew I was not going to create a problem.

In Idaho, state law allows boating on "navigable" waters, curiously defined as those that can float a 6-inch-diameter log, now interpreted to include streams boatable in kayaks or rafts. Walking, fishing, and camping are allowed below the "high-water mark"—use your best judgment for how high the water reaches on most years during peak flow. Portaging around dams, diversions, rapids, or other obstructions is allowed.

The Montana Stream Access Law permits boating on all streams regardless of "navigability" or ownership of property. Walking, fishing, and portage is allowed to the high-water mark.

In Wyoming, boating is legal on any stream, as are portages around obstructions.

In Colorado and Utah, boating is allowed, but contact with the shore or bottom can be barred at private land, even for wading. Assume that landowners control the beds of small streams. If safety requires getting out of the boat or walking, be quick!

On small ranchland streams—and some not so small—barbed wire might be strung across the water, creating a serious hazard. Carefully pass through or around those fences. Beware: Wire barriers are difficult to see when approaching in the current, doubly so in swift flow or with glare. I've been surprised and had to scramble on small and medium-size streams in ranching country, but I've negotiated dozens of wires over the years without causing or suffering damage.

FLOW LEVELS AND SEASONS

Boating conditions that I report are typically based on medium and lower (but doable) levels of flow, rarely on high flows. Owing to continuous fast current making recovery difficult, hypothermia induced by cold water, and increased turbulence and lack of time to respond, hazards generally increase as water level rises. At high flows paddling runs can escalate a full whitewater class of difficulty (1 through 5; see "Whitewater Difficulty" below) from ratings listed here. So work that into your expectations.

Each month has its specialties, but July is a great time to tour many of the Rocky Mountain rivers. Rivers in spring and early summer amaze me with the power of their high flows. Some boaters relish the excitement of high volume, but I usually pass on paddling and rowing then except for smaller streams that are runnable only near their peak. Midsummer through early fall are delightful for boating where flows are adequate, and, personally, I love lower levels when the water is clear with distinct rocky rapids, sandbar campsites, and time to appreciate everything. I often enjoy boating on volumes below what are listed in other guidebooks.

Late summer is also great for hiking along high-country streams. However, mid and late summer weather—once so perfect in the Rockies—is increasingly hot and smoky from fires. Yet in August and September most bugs are gone, the hottest weather is past, and a lot of streams still offer great paddling by canoe or kayak if not raft. Winter has its appeal in lower terrain. See my river-by-river descriptions for seasonal notes.

Simply choosing the proper season for boating on a particular river is often an adequate trip-planning strategy, but sometimes it's necessary to know the specific flow, especially in high-water season and after storms, which can spike radically. Beware of launching on any rising river or during times of peak snowmelt or predicted storms. In my descriptions, see the average (mean) volume in cubic feet per second. Flows encountered will rarely be average, but this statistic enables comparison, one river to another.

Examine cfs levels online at the US Geological Survey (search "USGS gauge" plus the river's name) or National Oceanic and Atmospheric Administration river sites, plus short-term forecasts from NOAA. Relevant gauges are listed by river in this book. Flow levels itemized at the start of each river description are mostly taken near the mouth; paddling reaches will typically be less than that and also different from the nearest gauge, depending on whether your run is above or below it.

Useful for long-range planning, the Natural Resources Conservation Service tracks snowpack; for snow level/water content, see "Snow Survey NRCS" online and search by state. In any particular summer, for example, flows might be low in the Southern Rockies and high in the north.

Generalizations are fraught, but I typically regard flows of 200 to 300 cfs as a low but doable minimum for canoeing or kayaking in a narrow riverbed without a lot of dragging, though I often squeak through on even less. Eight hundred to several thousand cfs often yield good flows that cover most mid-channel rocks. Higher volumes in that range can generate large holes, breaking waves, and continuous turbulence.

Levels beyond 2,000 cfs in many rivers can be considered high, with inherent challenges and hazards. Constrictions including canyons can pose formidable hazards when high volume creates continuous rapids. Some large rivers, however, have wide channels and gentle gradients with relatively easy water for experienced boaters even when volume is up. But above a few thousand cfs, even easy water introduces risks owing simply to speed of current, distance from shore, and unexpected turbulence.

The advent of self-bailing rafts has sharply reduced the problem of rafts taking on water and becoming unmanageable, and thereby expanded upward the flow levels for skilled boaters. Likewise, inflatable kayaks (I-Ks) have expanded downward the opportunities for low-water paddling. Dozens of rivers long regarded as too low in summer—down to 50 cfs or even less in some tight channels—are now runnable with small inflatables and frequent dragging. While low-water hazards (foot entrapment among rocks, falling injuries, and rocky swims) replace big-water hazards (log entrapment, flips, long swims, and hypothermia), the low-water experience usually makes more deliberation and carefulness possible.

Plan well, but for the ultimate test, eyeball your flow at the put-in. More than once I've arrived but cancelled trips because I've found levels too high for safe boating or too low. Never be too committed. "Come hell or high water" is not a good MO here. Have in mind a backup river or reach nearby that's larger or smaller, and safer.

WHITEWATER DIFFICULTY

Paddling or rowing is rated Class 1 through 5 on American Whitewater's International Scale of River Difficulty. Ratings cited in this book are largely taken from other guidebooks.

In the past few decades, some boaters have downgraded ratings owing to refined equipment, rising skill levels, and intimate knowledge of routing through rapids. I tend not to do that, and may report ratings slightly higher than what appear in other guides. I rate by the hardest rapid; the class of a run might be bumped down a level with one or a few portages. Even Class 1 boating can present challenges to beginning paddlers owing to log hazards and currents against banks or logs. So, even for easy whitewater, boaters should have proper training and experience. Never launch on waters beyond your ability.

Standards, abridged by the BLM, are as follows:

Class 1: Small waves, passages clear, no serious obstacles.

Class 2: Medium-size regular waves, passages clear, some maneuvering required.

Class 3: Numerous, high, and irregular waves, rocks, eddies, narrow passages, scouting usually required.

Class 4: Powerful irregular waves, boiling eddies, dangerous rocks, congested passages, precise maneuvering required, scouting mandatory.

Class 5: Exceedingly difficult, violent rapids often following each other without interruption, big drops, violent current, scouting mandatory but often difficult.

Class 1 water includes riffles and calm flows such as this stretch of the Middle Fork Clearwater in Idaho.

Class 2 may have rocks to evade, moderate turbulence, and specific routes to follow. This rapid on the Grey's River of Wyoming is a swift Class 2.

EXOTIC SPECIES

A curse of globalizing times is that precautions must be taken to not spread invasive animals and plants from one stream to another on boating and fishing gear. If there's any chance of encountering quagga mussels, New Zealand mud snails, or other alien species (often in low-elevation waters), wash your gear—especially waders and shoes—before entering another stream, and definitely if your turnaround is within two days. I wash mud from hiking shoes and dispose of weed seeds.

Some states require permits even for small boats. If you're carrying one, you'll be required to stop at checkpoints where agency personnel will inspect the boat on your roof.

MILEAGE AND DATA SOURCES

Reliable statistics for river length, volume, and watershed area—itemized at the beginning of each river description here—are elsewhere surprisingly difficult to find for many rivers. No official gazetteer exists. Other published data may vary widely, so don't be surprised if you've seen different numbers.

Basin-wide figures here were mostly calculated by professional Geographic Information System analyst Matthew Mayfield. Lengths were taken from the USGS National Hydrography Dataset (high resolution 1:24,000).

Some rivers' names begin with the confluence of two tributaries; when that happens I also note the mileage of the longest tributary upstream and total mileage (the tributary sometimes has a different name only by quirks of nomenclature). Including the full upriver extent of stream mileage makes for an apples-to-apples comparison with rivers bearing the same name the entire way through the largest source.

Boatable mileages are always less than the river's length and follow in my paddling narratives. For specific reaches covered in popular guidebooks, I mostly use their mileages to avoid confusion. I round numbers above ten. River mileage is generally longer than that of shuttle roads, but only slightly so where the road stays in the valley (in those cases I add 5 to 10 percent for river miles as a rule of thumb). My directions to put-ins and takeouts list mileages of road, not river.

The size of a river (e.g., "second-largest") refers to amount of flow—not length—and I use mean (average) cubic feet per second. Data were collected mainly from USGS gauges, which typically reflect "impaired" flows including diversions. Where gauges are not available, volumes here were derived from a Unit Runoff Method (MAFlowU as a component of NHDPlus), established for runoff modeling by the USGS. Watershed area in square miles was derived from a GIS program, CUMDRAINAG.

MAPS

My directions to river access points begin with places on state highway maps. I also regard statewide DeLorme atlases as requisite for my travels. National forest and BLM maps show more—especially trails—and USGS topographic maps are the gold standard, though recreation maps for many popular destinations have now been published; buy these online, at outdoor stores, or visitor centers. Digital versions may be available.

Class 4 whitewater requires scouting to determine the best route through complex passages such as this lower drop in the Middle Fork Flathead below Spruce Park. Risks are augmented here because there is no road or easy trail access in the event of an accident.

For selected popular trips, brochures by the administering federal or state agencies include excellent mapping and details about rapids and campsites, available online or in print from the agencies. Many of these are mentioned in my Part 2 narratives. Other online sources are also available.

PERMITS AND SHUTTLES

For many popular rivers through public land, permits are required by the administering federal agency—Forest Service, National Park Service, or Bureau of Land Management. These may be needed for day trips but more likely for overnights. Some permits are self-issued without limits at put-ins. Others are required in advance, and numbers may be limited; investigate with the agency or at www.recreation.gov and apply early. My write-ups often note where permits are required.

The permits are needed to maintain a quality experience for the boater, to protect the place, and to provide a justifiable and presumably equitable method of apportioning use between commercial and independent boaters, though there is sometimes disagreement regarding the rationale used.

Every river trip requires a shuttle of your vehicle. My first choice for shuttling is a bicycle, which I often use for day trips, especially when the route is not long and follows the river rather than crossing a high pass, and especially when paddling alone or with a one-car group, which my wife and I often are. To have my rig with its comforts awaiting me, I prefer to drop my gear, drive to the takeout, and bike back before the trip. Of course, with two vehicles you can spot one at the bottom.

Commercial shuttles are often the best option, especially for long trips. For a list of services, consult your river's administering agency or search online. Commercial shuttlers may be able to store your car safely during overnight trips and deliver it to the takeout when requested. Though reluctant to hand my keys to strangers or to leave them hidden outside my van awaiting pickup, I've never had a problem with a commercial shuttle.

ADDITIONAL INFORMATION

See the sources section at the end of the book for guidebooks covering difficult whitewater and additional rivers. American Whitewater maintains a website with detailed paddling information for many rivers, and for paddlers of difficult whitewater, that organization's information is well worth the cost of membership.

If you fish, angling restrictions are by necessity detailed, complex, and variable; see state agency websites for regulations by specific rivers and fish species. Fishing tips are available online and not covered here; search by river.

In the text that follows, BLM means Bureau of Land Management—a federal agency overseeing vast acreage in the West. FR means a road maintained by the Forest Service. CR means county road. "River right" means the right side of the river when facing downstream.

Onward to the rivers!

PART II
RIVER PORTRAITS

Known as the wildest river in Montana, the Middle Fork Flathead's crystal-clear water is difficult to reach but rewards boaters who pack their gear into backcountry sites and float out for three to seven days.

Rafters speed through swift waters at Five Points in Parkdale Canyon on the Arkansas River.

Rivers of Colorado

The Rocky Mountains rise as a north–south backbone through Colorado, and with their foothills they account for half the terrain of the West's sixth-largest state. The other half lies eastward in the Great Plains or west in red-rock canyons of the Colorado Plateau.

Colorado has exceptionally popular recreational rivers, including the Arkansas, with the most-floated whitewater in the West; the Yampa as a highlight of Steamboat Springs; the Animas at the heart of downtown Durango; and the South Platte, recreational centerpiece of Denver. Pristine and long wild rivers are not as plentiful here as in some other regions of the Rockies, but much intriguing appeal awaits, as do some fine but less celebrated multiday river trips.

This is one of America's key headwaters; runoff from Colorado's Rockies brushes up against nineteen states—narrowly outdone only by Wyoming. Towering mountains boast more peaks over 14,000 feet than any other state and 75 percent of the nation's land topping 10,000 feet.

All this high country is key to the state's hydrology. Three-quarters of Colorado's precipitation comes as snow, blanketing mountains with a deep pack that melts into rivers in late spring and early summer, then subsides. Wet storms also come from the south as summer monsoons, causing unexpected spikes in flows. Still, lying in an extended rain shadow, and positioned south of storm patterns that soak the West's upper latitudes, Colorado receives less precipitation than the Northern Rockies.

The mountains here give rise to four major river systems: the Platte in the northeast portion of Colorado's Rockies, the Arkansas in the southeast, the Rio Grande in the south, and the Colorado in the west. All these rivers include green corridors of cottonwoods, willows, box elders, and red osier dogwoods, providing habitat for birds, fish, and other wildlife often surrounded by semiarid terrain.

Endemic fish are rare but a biological highlight, including three imperiled subspecies of cutthroat trout. Greenback cutthroat were thought to be extinct but then found in the widely separated Como Creek of the South Arkansas River basin and South Fork Cache la Poudre. Reintroductions have increased the greenbacks' range to forty-two streams—still only 5 percent of historic territory scattered in stream segments along the Front Range from the Poudre in the north to Apache Creek in the south. Rio Grande cutthroat survive in a cluster of streams at headwaters of that river. Colorado River cutthroat once claimed 144 distinct populations, sharply reduced but now increased to 56 in short stream segments across Colorado's western Rockies, including upper tributaries of the Green, Yampa, Elk, and White. It's too late for yellowfin cutthroat, extinct by the early 1900s, underscoring the urgency of protecting aquatic habitat.

No less important, four species of warmwater fishes—the Colorado River pikeminnow, humpback chub, bonytail chub, and razorback sucker—survive in the Colorado River basin, but populations have been drastically reduced. In that watershed blanketing western expanses of the state, forty of forty-nine native fish species are endangered or imperiled. Over the millennia many of these had adapted to warm, turbid, fluctuating levels typical west of the Continental Divide but are now rare owing to changes in flow regimes that occurred figuratively overnight from dams and diversions, and also

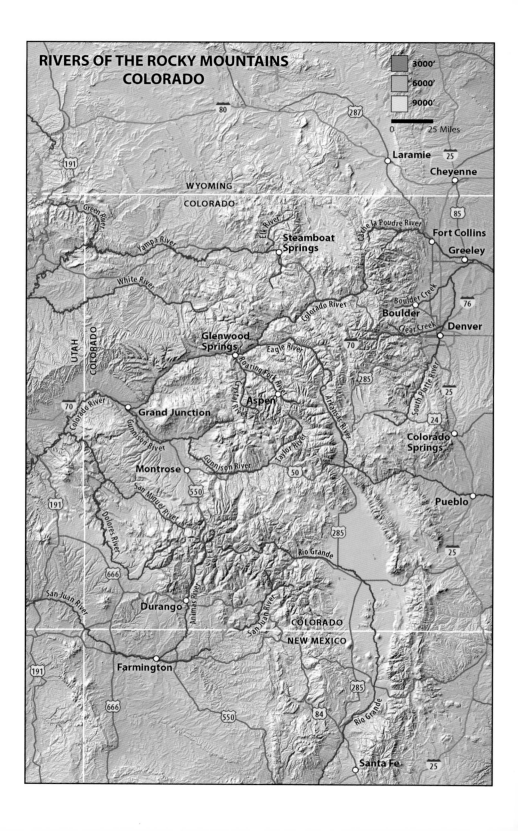

from predation by introduced species including vora-cious northern pike that were shortsightedly planted for anglers.

Strongholds of the ancient native warmwater fishes include the Yampa River below Craig, the Colorado below Rifle, the White below Rangely, the Gunnison below Delta, and the Green below the Yampa con-fluence. These are designated critical habitat for the pikeminnow, humpback, bonytail, and razorback, and represent 29, 28, 14, and 49 percent respectively of his-torical range, according to the Upper Colorado River Endangered Fish Recovery Program.

Among the state's 105,000 miles of streams, portions of only the Cache la Poudre and its South Fork have been designated as National Wild and Scenic Rivers. The Forest Service in the 1970s studied twelve rivers for designation and portions of eleven were recom-mended, but Congress acted only on the Poudre. In spite of ample evidence that water users would not be threatened—including negotiations that led to the Poudre's designation in 1986 and to its management ever since—the Colorado water industry thus far abides by fear that water rights will be eroded through Wild and Scenic status.

COLORADO RIVERS

Animas River
Arkansas River
Boulder Creek
Cache la Poudre
Clear Creek
Colorado River
Crystal River
Dolores River
Eagle River
Elk River
Green River
Gunnison River
Platte River, South
Rio Grande
Roaring Fork River
San Juan River
San Miguel River
Taylor River
White River
Yampa River

As with other western states, rivers in Colorado are degraded by dams, diversions, ranching, farming, logging, mining, urbanization, and global warming, and losses are severe owing to a dry climate and long history of intensive commodity use.

Early in the state's settlement, pioneering ranchers diverted all major streams and many minor ones where runoff flowed out of the mountains and entered tillable or grazed lowlands, creating a pattern of irrigation dominance and cultural hegemony that persists. Meanwhile, hard-rock mining (silver, copper, gold, lead, nickel, and molybdenum, as opposed to gravel, sand, coal, and limestone) has scarred more mountains and polluted more waterways here than elsewhere in the Rockies and left a grim legacy of neglect in thousands of abandoned sites that have killed fish, eliminated invertebrates, and threat-ened human health. The abandoned mines of Colorado contribute heavily to the fact that mining waste is the worst toxic pollution in the West, according to the Environmen-tal Protection Agency's annual Toxic Release Inventory.

More recently, energy development intensified in oil and gas fields on both the west slope and Great Plains. Problems include fracking of natural gas and the recurrent pos-sibility of water-intensive oil-shale extraction, though at this writing the more urgent threat is the abandonment without proper closure of gas wells that leak methane at fossil fuel facilities facing bankruptcy in the oil and gas industry bust of 2020.

Finally, increasing population with sprawl is rampant at the Front Range and at moun-tain ski towns, where water is drawn from streams and development crowds riverfronts.

Magnificent rivers remain in Colorado, but they need to be protected from energy devel-opment and gas-well abandonment, population growth, damming, and global warming.

Animas River

Length: 125 miles, including 30 in New Mexico
Average flow: 844 cfs
Watershed: 1,347 square miles
Location: North and south of Durango
Hiking: Backpacking in Animas Canyon, urban trails in Durango

Boating: Kayak, canoe, raft, day trips
Whitewater: Class 1-5 and unrunnable
Gauge: Silverton (upper), Durango (middle)
Highlights: Extraordinary canyon, urban whitewater

This largest tributary to the San Juan River flows through a 5,000-foot-deep canyon, nearly equal in depth to the Colorado River's Grand Canyon though in a region of peaks soaring to 14,000 feet, which makes the Animas one of the deepest high-elevation canyons on the continent.

The stream begins at 9,230 feet with its West and North Fork confluence and drains one of the Rockies' most intensively mined regions. Below Silverton it enters its canyon with frothing Class 5 rapids sluicing rugged terrain. No road penetrates, but a railroad remaining from the mining boom carries tourists between Durango and Silverton—fire danger permitting, which is becoming an ever larger concern.

Emerging from the canyon, the Animas glides across meadows and bubbles through Durango with whitewater, followed by a cottonwood corridor in the Southern Ute Indian Reservation. It then creates New Mexico's best riparian zone, ending at the San Juan confluence in Farmington.

The Animas is dammed only by a few diversion structures and a low hydropower dam in New Mexico, but has incurred significant damage otherwise. Major water exports came in 2015 with the hotly contested Animas–La Plata Project of the US Bureau of Reclamation—one of the last major water development schemes by the federal government and one of few in the post-1980s era when most of the potentially damaging water projects still proposed in the West were halted. Though damming of the Animas was averted, the Durango Pumping Plant diverts 57,000 acre-feet per year westward to the La Plata basin for irrigation of low-value crops, mostly hay and pasture.

The headwaters of the Animas were intensively mined before regulations existed, and rules have never been effective owing to the Mining Law of 1872. The miners' legacy brew of zinc, copper, lead, and mercury poisons invertebrate life and fish in upper reaches, especially via Mineral and Cement Creeks. Water quality recovers in the canyon, but spills include the Gold King Mine disaster of 2015 that released three million gallons of mine waste via Cement Creek and sterilized the Animas in shocking red toxic sediment through Durango and beyond.

The lower Animas in New Mexico is blocked by a private hydroelectric dam and pumping station that for decades halted upstream migration of native flannelmouth and bluehead suckers but has been upgraded by Farmington for better fish and boater passage. The lower river is also infested with thorny Russian olive trees in their distinctive gray-green foliage, displacing cottonwoods and willows that had provided vital food and cover for wildlife.

The river remains a regional boon for the wildness of its canyon, for its recreational reach through Durango, and for its cottonwood corridor below.

Boaters in kayaks, canoes, and inner tubes enjoy the Animas River through Durango, paddling down to a takeout above a Class 3-4 rapid at the lower end of town.

 FISH

In 2018 state biologists confirmed that a distinct lineage of Colorado River trout—San Juan cutthroat—survived in the basin of Hermosa Creek, a mostly wild Animas tributary north of Durango. The subspecies was thought to have been extinct for many years. With fires and silty runoff threatening, state biologists collected some of the rare fish for captive breeding.

The lower Animas Canyon is fished for brown and rainbow trout, which are also stocked below Durango in "gold medal" angling waters. Some native Colorado cutthroat and mottled sculpins survive, and the lower river supports native warmwater flannel-mouth and bluehead suckers.

 ACCESS

US 550 serves headwaters at Silverton, bypasses the Animas Canyon, then splits Durango and follows the lower valley to Farmington.

The Durango & Silverton Narrow Gauge Railroad runs daily in summer through the Animas Canyon and 45 miles altogether between Durango and Silverton; reserve seats for this popular tourist draw.

HIKING

The upper river, complete with ubiquitous mining remains, can be seen with urban walks in Silverton and an unimproved road upstream—a mountain biking hot spot.

To hike the lower canyon, drive north of Durango to Purgatory Creek Campground and trailhead, and trek southeast 3 miles to the Animas and up its canyon 7 miles to Needleton, with options to catch the train back to Durango or climb eastward to the Chicago Basin's 14,000-foot peaks—favorites of acclimatized backpackers.

Through Durango a bike and pedestrian trail follows the river in one of the Rockies' outstanding urban greenways.

PADDLING

The Animas Canyon's 28 miles of Class 4-5 whitewater are for expert kayakers only, best as a two-day for paddlers capable of carrying gear while negotiating extreme rapids. High water is especially dangerous. The put-in is at Silverton and takeout at Tacoma, where a train shuttle can be arranged for 2 miles south to a road at Rockwood. Below Tacoma the Rockwood Gorge of intense whitewater is followed by extreme gradient and a log-jam that's unrunnable at any level.

For the rest of us, paddling the Animas begins 21 miles north of Durango. The Upper Valley Class 1+ reach of 8 miles meanders open meadows. To put in, drive north from Durango on US 550 for 8 miles; at CR 250 turn right and go to the bridge. To take out, drive north of Durango on US 550 for 6 miles and turn east on Trimble Lane to the bridge. Avoid the privately owned shorelines.

Next, the Animas Valley reach winds 13 miles as Class 1+. Put in at Trimble Lane. To take out, from US 550 in north Durango drive east on 32nd Street, cross the river, turn left, and go 1 block.

The Durango Town Run has Class 2 whitewater with the option for a Class 3-4 finale. Put in off 32nd Street. Class 2 flows 4 miles, with takeout for most paddlers along the west bank just north of the US 160 bridge. The next mile includes Class 3-4 Smelter Rapid, made gnarly with a city diversion structure installed at the top of the drop in 2017. Scouting recommended! Even experienced boaters avoid this drop at high flows. Structural improvements to the diversion have improved navigability, but the rapid remains tough, especially at medium and high water levels. Avoiding Smelter, boaters launch in Santa Rita Park—immediately below the rapid off US 550 at the south end of town—and paddle Class 2 for 4 miles to Dallabetta Park, west of the US 160/550 intersection.

The lower Animas is Class 1-2 in foothills south of Durango crossing the Southern Ute Indian Reservation, where floating is allowed but roadside access is not. However, at 20 miles below Dallabetta, access is possible at RV parks just beyond the New Mexico line. Another 30 miles continue to the San Juan River in Farmington with several normally runnable diversion structures, a few BLM parcels, and commercial campground landings. Up from the mouth 5 miles, Penny Lane Dam was rebuilt in 2017 to include safe boater passage where hazards had been severe. Landings in Farmington include Whitewater Park with two Class 2 rapids and a riverfront trail between Animas and Berg Parks.

Below Durango the lower Animas riffles through its cottonwood corridor.

Arkansas River

Length: 1,460 miles plus 21 of the East Fork, total 1,481; 123 at Cañon City
Average flow: 40,000 cfs at the Mississippi River, 720 at Cañon City
Watershed: 170,000 square miles, 3,100 at Cañon City
Location: South of Leadville

Hiking: High-country day hikes and backpacking
Boating: Raft, kayak, canoe, day trips and overnights
Whitewater: Class 2-5
Gauge: Nathrop, Salida
Highlights: Popular whitewater, challenging rapids, mountain views

The upper end of this major Mississippi River tributary flows with only a few minor diversion dams through the Southern Rockies, dropping 4,600 feet in 123 miles before reaching the Great Plains. Here are some of the most popular rafting and kayaking waters in the West and some of the finest views of Rocky Mountain peaks seen from a major river.

The Arkansas makes for an excellent weeklong road-accessible river vacation with a different Class 2-5 stretch of rapids every day, plus headwater hiking, backpacking, fishing, and a full suite of whitewater amenities awaiting, including paddling schools, rentals, restaurants, lodging, commercial rafting, and campgrounds.

The river flows south along the base of Colorado's highest mountains rising westward in the Sawatch Range, including the state's top summit, 14,422-foot Mount Elbert—second-highest in the United States outside Alaska. Near Salida the Sangre de Cristo Mountains deflect the river eastward, where it cuts through one of the West's narrowest major chasms, 1,200-foot-deep Royal Gorge.

After emerging at Cañon City, the river is dammed and diverted as it staggers across the Great Plains of southern Colorado, Kansas, and Oklahoma. It ultimately gains water from humid Gulf of Mexico storms and becomes the sixth-longest river in the United States before it meets the Mississippi in Arkansas.

The upper corridor is mostly publicly owned and managed essentially as a river-oriented state park—one of the finest and busiest such examples in the West—but also includes private land and several towns.

The Arkansas is augmented by trans-basin diversions from the Fryingpan and Roaring Fork basins—water taken from the Rockies' west side, tunneled east, and run down the Arkansas for withdrawal by cities and farms. Delivery schedules cause the rapids of the upper river to drop too low for most commercial rafting by early August. Kayaking continues later.

Headwater reaches are polluted by Superfund waste sites at abandoned hard-rock mines leaking zinc, lead, and cadmium—still chemically detected at Salida, 70 miles downstream—yet the mine waste is not evident to paddlers or anglers in recreational reaches.

While several sections, including Brown's Canyon and Royal Gorge, are isolated from roads, much of the corridor is shared with highways and local byways, and an active railroad crowds the depths of Royal Gorge.

A commercial group of paddle-rafters negotiate "The Numbers" in the upper Arkansas River.

 FISH

Introduced rainbow and brown trout thrive, and Trout Unlimited lists the Arkansas from Buena Vista through Salida among the top 100 trout-fishing streams in America.

 ACCESS

US 24 tracks the upper Arkansas from Leadville down to Buena Vista, followed by US 285, then US 50 to Salida and through middle canyons. The road eastward climbs beyond the north rim of Royal Gorge, then reconnects via streets in Cañon City, where the Arkansas exits the Rocky Mountains for its sojourn across the plains.

 HIKING

Headwaters include hikes and backpacking in the Sawatch, Mosquito, and Sangre de Cristo Ranges. On urban river trails edging Buena Vista and in downtown Salida, thousands of people delight at the cool riverfront with its boating, swimming, and refreshing urban interface.

Royal Gorge can be seen from commercial tourist facilities at the north rim, including America's highest suspension bridge, for pedestrians, at 956 feet—acrophobics beware! Drive west on US 50 from Cañon City and turn south at the sign.

Brown's Canyon is a popular section of the Arkansas River, whose multiple reaches combine for the most-paddled whitewater in the West.

 PADDLING

The upper Arkansas is the most popular whitewater paddling river in the West, attracting 330,000 boaters in a typical year at six major reaches spanning 100 miles. The other two most popular rivers are the Snake near Jackson, Wyoming, and the South Fork American near Sacramento—each with boating concentrated in only two reaches. For detailed tips about whitewater, see *Arkansas River Guide* by Thomas Rampton. Boating can be subdivided any number of ways. Here's how I see it:

The Numbers and Fractions. The Numbers is a 6-mile Class 4+ challenge of technical whitewater named for seven rapids, continuously turbulent when high and intricately rocky when low. To put in, take US 24 north from Buena Vista 11 miles, turn right at milepost 200.3 (Scott's Bridge), cross the railroad tracks, turn upstream on the river's west side, and follow the dirt lane 1 mile. Take out at Railroad Bridge: From US 24 in Buena Vista, go east at the light, then north on Colorado Avenue/CR 371 for 6 miles. Just below The Numbers, the somewhat easier "Fractions"—another 7 miles of Class 3-4—continues to Buena Vista's riverfront directly east from town center. Altogether this is a challenging 13-mile run and an American classic.

Buena Vista to Brown's Canyon. Class 2-3+ for 8 miles offers both lively and quieter water. One mile below the put-in a diversion dam has a boat slot on the right, but a lot of rafters go left. In another mile US 24 bridges the river with a commercial access on the

From the Salida East ramp to Parkdale the Arkansas serves up a steady sequence of rapids.

left, and from there to Ruby Mountain ramp 5 miles of Class 2 suit experienced canoeists and beginning kayakers. To take out, drive US 285 south of Buena Vista 6 miles to milepost 144.8, turn east on CR 301, cross Fisherman's Bridge, go 0.5 mile, and turn east on CR 300 to the state park.

Brown's Canyon. This is one of the busiest paddling reaches in the West, a splendid Class 3-4 technical run of 7.6 miles to Hecla access or 9 miles to Stone Bridge including Seidel's Suckhole—an abrupt Class 4+ near the end. The water is buffered from roads, though not always from an abandoned railroad track, within a scenic, boulder-riddled canyon. Many boaters depart at Hecla; from US 285 north of Salida at mile 135.5, turn east on CR 194 and go 2 miles. For Stone Bridge, drive north from Salida on CO 291, and at mile 8.2 turn right on CR 191.

Next, 12 miles of Class 2+ is the finest reach for canoeists and beginning kayakers, though beware: 7 miles below Stone Bridge a constructed boat-flume bypasses a diversion dam. Go left at this serious safety hazard and into the flume, though canoeists will want to portage heavy turbulence with a path left of the bypass. Continue past downtown Salida to Salida East access; east of town on US 50 drive 3 miles to milepost 224 and turn north.

For 43 miles below Salida East the Arkansas is Class 3-4, mostly 3, with US 50 alongside, passing Cotopaxi village and continuing on through Parkdale Canyon. Multiple reaches are run as day trips with intermediate access, but the full length—plus 12 miles

Royal Gorge marks the grand finale of Arkansas whitewater with turbulent Class 4-5 rapids.

of Class 2 above—is delightful as the Arkansas's only extended multiday run with hundreds of rapids. I've found this to be a rollicking good three-day trip while tolerating the highway alongside and pretending it didn't exist. Most, but not all, of the Class 4 comes with 7.3 miles from Pinnacle Rock to Parkdale access. Disembark there at mile 266.2 on US 50—must-do takeout above Royal Gorge!

As the Arkansas's pounding Class 4-5 finale, 10 miles through Royal Gorge feature big drops while an active railroad crowds the north bank. Railroad infrastructure, occasional metal debris, and laboring trains are contrasted by the awesome power, turbulent drops, and sheer walls of this canyon. I chose to go in a paddle-and-oar raft with Dvorak Expeditions—running all sections of the Arkansas since the early 1980s. For independent boaters, take out at Cañon City's Centennial Park: From US 50 eastbound, turn right on Fourth Street, cross the river, and go right on Griffin.

For flatwater and a bit of Class 2, with diversion and weir complications, the Arkansas has several Great Plains reaches below Cañon City; see *Paddling Colorado*.

Boulder Creek

Length: 31 miles plus 12 of Middle Boulder Creek, total 43
Average flow: 298 cfs at Boulder
Watershed: 456 square miles
Location: City of Boulder
Hiking: Day hikes and biking

Boating: Tubes, kayak, day trips
Whitewater: Class 3-4
Gauge: Boulder
Highlights: Urban greenway, tubing, paved trails

After cutting one of the Front Range's most spectacular rock-walled canyons, this creek borders downtown Boulder with an excellent urban greenway featuring cottonwoods of impressive girth, walkways, rapids, and swimming holes for cool summer relief.

 FISH

Small brown trout are caught through Boulder. Urban anglers can avoid crowds of swimmers and tubers by fishing early in the morning.

 ACCESS

From northbound CO 93/Broadway on the east side of Boulder, turn west on Arapahoe Avenue and go to Eben Fine Park. Or from CO 93 follow Boulder Canyon Road/CO 119 west to the canyon mouth.

Boulder Creek foams through the city of Boulder with stair-step rapids and swimming holes serving the city and University of Colorado students nearby.

HIKING

A 6-mile paved trail extends from the canyon mouth down to diversions east of the city.

PADDLING

Boulder Creek is best known for tubing, with rentals available. Beware of high, frigid runoff into June, and wear a wetsuit whenever it's not superhot. Tubing is considered good at 100 to 200 cfs and closed at 700.

On 150 to 400 cfs, experienced kayakers paddle from Eben Fine Park through Class 3-4 rapids in a tight rocky channel with ledges and boulders placed for boaters. Avoid congestion at mid-afternoon tubing hours. Launch at the west end of Eben Fine Park for steep rapids, the east end for easier fun. Take out at Scott Carpenter Park; from CO 93 go east on Arapahoe Avenue to 30th Street, turn right, and right again into the park. *Paddling Colorado* notes that Class 2 rapids continue below to 55th Street.

Upstream along Boulder Canyon Road expert kayakers select from several Class 4-5+ reaches.

Cache la Poudre

Length: 126 miles, 72 at the canyon mouth before diversions
Average flow: 362 cfs at canyon mouth, diverted below
Watershed: 1,056 square miles at canyon mouth
Location: West of Fort Collins

Hiking: Headwaters day hikes and backpacking
Boating: Kayak, canoe, day trips
Whitewater: Class 2-5
Gauge: Fort Collins
Highlights: Scenic canyon with road access, whitewater, fishing

In a spectacular canyon where CO 14 winds upward, and undammed except for diversion structures and two small North Fork reservoirs, the Cache la Poudre is the Front Range's quintessential river flowing from mountains to plains.

The main-stem Poudre (POO-der) runs 21 roadless miles from trail-accessible headwaters in Rocky Mountain National Park and the Comanche Peak Wilderness. Then for 62 miles CO 14 parallels through a 1,000-foot-deep canyon. Trans-basin diversions from the Rockies' west slope add water—later extracted downstream where the lower river's heavily diverted, dammed, and developed mileage continues across the Great Plains to the South Platte. Wildlife in the canyon include elk, bighorn sheep, and mountain lions.

The Cache la Poudre is the finest semi-wild river bursting from the Front Range of Colorado.

The "Poudre" is the only Colorado stream designated in the National Wild and Scenic Rivers system, here flowing through its lower canyon.

The South Fork flows 32 mostly road-free miles in Rocky Mountain National Park, the Cache la Poudre Wilderness, and Roosevelt National Forest. The North Fork flows 70 miles, first with no roads, then with road access, two reservoirs, and diversions.

The Poudre and its South Fork are Colorado's only National Wild and Scenic Rivers.

 FISH

The South Fork is one of two streams where greenback cutthroat survived near-extinction. They've since been reintroduced into the main stem, North Fork, and other streams. Main-stem angling for brown trout is open all year.

 ACCESS

From Fort Collins drive west on CO 14 for most of the river's length, with twenty landings, campgrounds, and picnic sites. The lower South Fork is roadless, but FR 63E turns south from CO 14 and after 6 miles drops down to middle reaches of the South Fork and then ascends its canyon 9 miles.

The Cache la Poudre draws whitewater boaters to reaches of Class 2-5 boating separated by diversion structures and steeper cascades.

 HIKING

Trails reach main-stem and South Fork headwaters in Rocky Mountain National Park. Paths lead out from twelve national forest trailheads in the corridor, but no trails follow the river for long.

 PADDLING

The Poudre is one of Colorado's premier whitewater kayaking streams, with two little-used Class 2 sections, several Class 3 reaches, and harder rapids shaping the river's larger reputation. Runs are interspersed with weirs, diversion dams, and big drops, making a continuous journey impractical. High water in May and June can be hazardous. Flows drop in July, with good boating before levels recede later in summer. The paralleling road makes bike shuttles tempting but traffic is heavy.

Paddling Colorado lists a Class 2 reach for competent canoeists starting at Sleeping Elephant Campground along CO 14 and running 6.5 miles to a pullout below the fish hatchery—dangerous weir below!

Next downstream, the Upper Rustic section runs 7.8 miles with Class 3 from Idyllwild to Indian Meadows, below Elkhorn Creek at milepost 93.

Discontinuous with the run above, Lower Rustic is 3 miles of Class 2-3 from Mountain Park Campground to Narrows Campground—must-do takeout with severe rapids below.

Other sections include Class 4+ rapids. See *The Floater's Guide to Colorado*.

Clear Creek

Length: 66 miles, 49 at Golden
Average flow: 191 cfs at Golden, diversions below
Watershed: 1,465 square miles total
Location: West of Denver and Golden, east of Idaho Springs

Hiking: High-elevation headwaters, urban trails
Boating: Kayak, raft, day trips
Whitewater: Class 2-5
Gauge: Golden
Highlights: Steep whitewater near Denver, trout fishing, urban trail

At Denver's doorstep, Clear Creek is a developed and thoroughly mined stream, partially reclaimed even in its hectic highway corridor and now offering good whitewater boating and fishing. This and the South Platte are the most accessible streams to the Rocky Mountains' most concentrated urban population. Clear Creek also has some of the craggiest outcrops among streams plunging into the heavily populated Front Range–Great Plains interface.

With headwaters at the 14,000-foot peaks of Loveland Pass, the creek descends alongside I-70 and—channelized—passes through downtown Idaho Springs. Eastbound, I-70

West of Denver, US 6 and I-70 crowd Clear Creek but it still draws anglers and kayakers to its appealing waters at the edge of the city. Even under ice during December's deep freeze, a few trout were biting.

The austere beauty of Clear Creek Canyon can be found just off US 6—the stream looking all the wilder here in a chilled whitening of fresh snow.

then veers southward, but US 6 continues to crowd the shores and passes through five tunnels that leave the creek in briefly quiet respites. The lower creek bisects Golden and enters the north Denver area.

 ## FISH

Brown and rainbow trout make good fishing in pocket water for urban anglers—open season all winter for those who brave the ice and chill.

 ## ACCESS

The key recreation reach of Clear Creek lies from Idaho Springs downstream along US 6 to the canyon mouth at Golden. For the lower end of this, take I-70 west of Denver, exit on US 6, continue west, turn right on 19th Street, left (north) on Washington Avenue, then left on 10th Street to Whitewater Park. Throughout the canyon upstream, take care with traffic barreling up and down US 6.

 ## HIKING

A magnificent semi-urban trail and bike path has been built along most of the creek from Idaho Springs down and from below Golden upstream, with ambition to connect through impeding bedrock and complete a 65-mile-long "Peaks to Plains Trail," making possible a downhill spin of 7,000 vertical feet from Loveland Pass to Denver, mostly on bike trail after the upper elevation free fall.

Stream frontage makes for popular walking within Golden—the Denver area's premier riverfront community. Rock climbers scale the craggiest faces of the canyon between Tunnels 1 and 2, where the Little Eiger veers up south of the highway.

 ## PADDLING

Big on whitewater excitement and social boating but crowded by I-70 and US 6, Clear Creek is the closest good paddling for an after-work river fix in the Rocky Mountains' largest metropolis. Below Idaho Springs Class 3-4 drops are demanding through July, with commercial raft trips available.

Above Golden a 2-mile Class 2-3 run starts below Tunnel 1; take US 6 west from town and before the canyon entry look for an undeveloped pullout on the road's south side just below the first tunnel/diversion dam. Take out in Whitewater Park—a 300-yard-long constructed chain of Class 2 rapids with slalom gates, popular among kayakers and tubers and good April through July at 300 to 1,000 cfs.

Colorado River

Length: 1,450 miles; 103 at State Bridge, 168 at Glenwood Springs, 305 at the Colorado-Utah line, 439 at Green River confluence
Average flow: Heavily impaired (zero) at the mouth in Mexico, 1,745 cfs at State Bridge, 3,351 at Glenwood Springs, 6,066 at Colorado-Utah line, 7,600 at Green River confluence
Watershed: 246,000 square miles total, 17,822 at Colorado-Utah line
Location: Western Colorado
Hiking: Day hikes and headwaters backpacking
Boating: Canoe, raft, kayak, day trips and overnights
Whitewater: Class 1-4
Gauge: Dotsero, Glenwood, Utah line
Highlights: Long river, extended boating trip, whitewater

As the myth-making, life-giving, rock-carving centerpiece to the entire Southwest, this river flows through northern Colorado and onward through Utah, Arizona, Nevada, and California to Mexico in a series of spectacular sandstone canyons with oasis-like riparian corridors and habitat for endangered desert fish. Carrying more water than any other stream in the Southern Rockies and Southwest, this is the seventh-longest river in the United States.

The upper Colorado starts its 1,450-mile passage by tumbling from Rocky Mountain National Park and winding through the State Bridge reach—popular for easy rafting and trout fishing.

The Colorado picks up speed and gradient through Glenwood Canyon while the double-decker curves of I-70 recede in the background.

Along with sections of the Green River in its twin-like path southward through the Colorado Plateau of eastern Utah, the Colorado just west of the Rockies offers the nation's best and longest opportunities for river travel in deep desert canyonlands with monumental geologic features and a mix of flatwater and powerful rapids. Most of those legendary canyons—including the Grand Canyon—lie in Utah and Arizona, but the upper river is also extraordinary, and the river's second-longest free-flowing and boating reach, 209 miles, starts in Rocky Mountain foothills at Palisade and runs through the Colorado Plateau to the uppermost backwaters of Powell Reservoir, the "lake" where the river is impounded by Glen Canyon Dam in Arizona.

First of all, sources from the Continental Divide in Rocky Mountain National Park flow south and exit the park at Lake Granby behind the basin's uppermost dam. The Colorado then runs southwestward with riffles, rapids, cottonwoods, and several low dams as diversion structures. Roads follow some of the way to Dotsero, then I-70 shoulders alongside, including a 13-mile reach through the remarkable 1,300-foot-deep Glenwood Canyon.

Downstream from Grand Junction, sandstone walls at Colorado National Monument rise above the southern shore and the river leaves its Rocky Mountain foothills, enters the linked Horsethief and Ruby Canyons, crosses the Utah state line, and drops further into desert realms of the Colorado Plateau with the towering red-wall portal to 17-mile-long Westwater Canyon. Below, the Colorado shares its valley with UT 128, passing spectacular sandstone mesas and vertical walls to the recreational hot spot of Moab.

While stunning sections remain, the Colorado is the most stressed and exhausted river in America by the time it ends in Mexico; dams and diversions deplete flows and ecological functions through many miles. Pollution from mines affects stream life, highways and railroads intrude, and exotic species take a toll.

Adding to difficulties, global warming brings intensified droughts that will only worsen. In 2018 the mature river above Grand Junction receded to ankle depth. Climate scientist Brad Udall of Colorado State University calculated that flows will be reduced another 20 to 30 percent below the already unexpectedly low levels by 2050. Growth limits and efficiency improvements are needed, especially in irrigation, which accounts for 80 percent of withdrawals. Without effective reforms, recreation, fish, river health, and water-supply security will be further sacrificed.

 ## FISH

The basin's endemic Colorado cutthroat trout are the native coldwater species here, surviving in select remote tributaries totaling only 16 percent of historic range. The upper Colorado's introduced brown and rainbow trout make for popular fishing through the Hot Sulphur Springs area, which sees a lot of anglers at public ramps and in guided drift-boat trips.

Endangered warmwater fish survive in the river's lower Rocky Mountain passage and westward. Ruby-Horsethief Canyons have one of the healthiest populations of Colorado pikeminnows and, below, the river is important to humpback chubs, razorback suckers, bonytail chubs, bluehead suckers, flannelmouth suckers, and roundtail chubs.

 ## ACCESS

Roads provide easy access to much of the Colorado through the Rocky Mountain region, while lower mileage across the Colorado Plateau tends to be more remote. US 34 runs through the upper valley edging Rocky Mountain National Park. US 40 follows for another 23 miles, from Granby to Kremmling, then road-free Gore Canyon plunges downward. Access resumes above State Bridge and continues to Dotsero. From there I-70 follows the Colorado's path to Utah.

If one sets the disruption aside, the routing of I-70 through Glenwood Canyon can be seen as an engineering marvel of the American highway network, with double-decker lanes, curves cantilevered over riverbanks, and speedy transit through the most remarkable canyon of the entire Interstate Highway System.

 ## HIKING

Headwaters are reached by the Colorado River and La Poudre Pass Trail at the western limits of Rocky Mountain National Park via US 34, while other trails reach wetland-laced meanders southward to Grand Lake.

The Gore Canyon Trail offers a peek into the lower mile of the upper river's notorious Class 5 canyon; hike upstream from the BLM's Pumphouse Recreation Site, encroaching brush permitting (see below).

In the tourist hot spot of Glenwood Springs, a pedestrian/bike trail follows the river and its tributary, the Roaring Fork. From Two Rivers Park, on the north bank of the Colorado, the riverfront trail runs upstream along I-70 for 26 miles to Dotsero, with plans

The Colorado River leaves its Rocky Mountain foothills and enters the Colorado Plateau in Ruby-Horsethief Canyons with a relaxed current and gravel bar campsites.

to go farther up the Eagle River. Downstream 87 miles from Glenwood, Grand Junction likewise has a paved Colorado Riverfront Trail, 22 miles from Palisade to Loma.

 ## PADDLING

Several low dams cross the upper Colorado downstream from Granby, but then a scenic Class 1 paddle of 9 miles runs summerlong through Middle Park, west of Hot Sulphur Springs. Put in 9 miles east of Kremmling at Sunset landing off US 40. The must-do takeout lies south of Kremmling at the Blue River confluence ramp, 2 miles below the CO 9 bridge—don't miss!

Gore Canyon follows with an 11-mile blizzard of inaccessible whitewater and crazy-steep gradient. This is only for hazard-conscious expert kayakers prepped for multiple portages, though many of the best paddlers take a pass on this run, with its artificially sharp undercut rocks as artifacts of railroad blasting. Gore Canyon exemplifies the granite basement rock complex of the Southern Rockies, where entrained flows cut into resistant rock and create intense whitewater in constricted gorges.

Next, Pumphouse–State Bridge is a popular 14-mile Class 2 run with one Class 3 wave train at high flows, commercially rafted as a carefree day trip all summer. From I-70's Wolcott exit, go north on CO 131, cross the Colorado, at State Bridge turn east on CR 1, drive upstream past CR 11, and continue on CR 1 to the Pumphouse ramp. Take out at State Bridge/CO 131.

Leaving crowds of day-trippers behind, 44 miles from State Bridge to the Dotsero ramp above I-70 are mostly Class 2, runnable all summer, with two Class 3 drops when

The "Black Rocks" outcrops of Vishnu schist are among the oldest exposed rocks on earth at 1.7 billion years—a highlight of the canoe and raft run through Ruby-Horsethief Canyons.

high. Be alert to bridge abutments, and camp on BLM land. Intermediate takeouts include the Catamount access, 15 miles below State Bridge (4 miles above Burns). For this and other upstream runs, Kremmling to Glenwood, see the BLM brochure *Upper Colorado River Guide*.

Below Dotsero, flatwater is followed by a diversion dam, a nearly dry riverbed, and a hydropower plant precluding boating until water is returned in Shoshone Canyon—a busy commercial rafting run for 8 miles of big Class 3 turbulence above Glenwood Springs. Put in at I-70 exit 123. Take out in Glenwood Springs, I-70 exit 116. To drive there from the put-in, take US 6 downstream to Glenwood Springs and Two Rivers Park.

Next, South Canyon is a Class 2+ run of 11 miles from Two Rivers Park to I-70 exit 105 east of New Castle. For the takeout, from exit 105 cross to the south side of the river and turn upstream on the frontage road to a pullout.

The next 64 miles along I-70 to Palisade include several diversion dams, which I avoid.

From Palisade down to Powell Reservoir, the river flows dam-free, runnable all summer in one of the great but little-known extended trips at the Rocky Mountain–Colorado Plateau interface. Put in at Palisade's Riverbend Park; from I-70 exit 42 go south on 37.3 Road or, 10 miles downstream in Grand Junction, use Robb State Park below the CO 141 bridge.

From Grand Junction the river drifts 20 gentle miles and then enters what's called Ruby-Horsethief Canyons, though Horsethief Canyon comes first. A permit from the BLM, in advance, is required for overnight use but not for day trips. Sandstone cliffs continue into

Utah for 27 miles of easy Class 1–2 canoeing with a railroad but no road alongside. Put in at the BLM's Loma ramp, I-70 exit 15 west of Fruita. Below Loma 4 miles, hike up the south-side tributary Rattlesnake Canyon and climb to its east-side rim and arches as notable as some in Arches National Park. Mee Canyon, 14 miles below Loma, also has good hiking. The Black Rocks complex of elephantine shoreline bedrock appears with campsites at mile 16. Paddle on to the Westwater Canyon ramp—mandatory takeout for most boaters because of big rapids and a permit requirement below. Take I-70 west to exit 225 in Utah and drive south to the BLM campground and landing.

Westwater Canyon follows—17 miles of vertical walls, Class 3–4 high-volume white-water, and no road or trail. The BLM rations permits, reserved in advance. The intense turbulence of early summer eases after July with still-thrilling steep drops. Above the crux, Skull Rapid, scout left and enter center-left pulling left to avoid a flipping hole and the aptly named Room of Doom—an eddy where rafts or swimmers can get seriously stuck in one of the most unforgiving circular eddies anywhere.

Below Westwater the Colorado drifts gently through tablelands for 12 miles of road-less riverfront and cottonwoods—a rarely boated interlude with nice camping. Then 35 miles of swift river with UT 128 nearby pass the Fisher Tower obelisks, followed by a monument valley of free-standing mesas and onward through a sheer-wall red-rock canyon to Moab.

Below there, a less-visited Colorado continues 64 miles in deeply entrenched can-yonland meanders with quiet water to the Green River confluence. Most floaters catch a motorboat shuttle back up the Colorado—arrange in Moab—but the journey can continue through Cataract Canyon, which requires a National Park Service reservation for 15 miles of pushy foaming flows sometimes rivaling those of the Grand Canyon. The current ends in Lake Powell, with 32 miles of mud-ringed reservoir to road access at Hite Marina. For this reach I've resorted to tying up during windy afternoons and rowing through two nights in the awesome silent beauty of starlight overhead.

Colorado River day trips or overnights are popular in Ruby-Horsethief, Westwater, and the Fisher Tower reach above Moab. Though rarely run as such, the entire 130 miles from Palisade to Moab, scheduled around the single permit at Westwater, and even beyond for 241 miles, including 32 miles of reservoir to Hite Marina, make an outstand-ing dam-free journey—longest on the Colorado outside the Grand Canyon.

Crystal River

Length: 36 miles
Average flow: 488 cfs
Watershed: 939 square miles
Location: South of Glenwood Springs
Hiking: Headwaters and Avalanche Creek

Boating: Kayak, canoe, day trips
Whitewater: Class 2-5
Gauge: Above Avalanche Creek, Carbondale
Highlights: Mountain views, Avalanche Creek hike, whitewater

With headwaters in the Maroon Bells–Snowmass Wilderness, this Roaring Fork tributary tumbles northward as the fourth-longest undammed stream in the state.

FISH

Cool flows support rainbow trout, brown trout, and native mountain whitefish. Spared the crowds, the Crystal is not among the high-profile angling waters of Colorado.

ACCESS

CO 133 runs through most of the valley. For headwaters, take FR 314, which fades to four-wheel-drive routes for walking, mountain biking, or skiing.

The Crystal River swells with springtime snowmelt from the Elk Mountains of central Colorado.

Avalanche Creek rushes down to the Crystal River as one of the best backpacking streams in Colorado.

 HIKING

A bike trail runs from the lower river at Carbondale up to the BRB Campground (KOA) below Avalanche Creek, and is planned for extension up to aspen-clad McClure Pass, perched east of the upper river.

Hiking trails in this mountain-corrugated basin run up virtually all major tributaries. My favorite, Avalanche Creek, lies halfway between McClure Pass and Carbondale on the east side of the watershed. A 2-mile access road from the mouth ends at Avalanche Campground, followed by an 8-mile trail climbing through aspens, cottonwoods, spruces, and meadows to high country of the Maroon Bells–Snowmass Wilderness.

 PADDLING

The upper Crystal is Class 4+ whitewater including culvert portages and a carry for many boaters at the "Meatgrinder," Class 4-5 below the Redstone Campground bridge.

Below Redstone, Class 3 boaters enjoy a 5-mile section from milepost 57 on CO 133 at the Crystal River bridge just below the mouth of Avalanche Creek, ending with takeout just south of the BRB Campground (CO 133 milepost 62) below Nettle Creek.

Finally, 5 miles of Class 2 at lower flows through early July tour open country with awesome views of monumental Mount Sopris. Put in south of BRB Campground and go to an access at the first bridge of River Valley Ranch, a golf course community off CO 133 on River Valley Ranch Road 2 miles up from the Crystal River mouth.

Or, continue 12 miles down the Roaring Fork's big-volume Class 2, ending in Glenwood Springs. While you're at it, consider another 11 miles with much larger Class 2 down the Colorado through South Canyon, altogether a 29-mile reach virtually unrun as a piece but beautifully telescoping riverine Colorado from snowcaps to western foothills as no other river does.

Dolores River

Length: 252 miles, including 28 in Utah
Average flow: 570 cfs
Watershed: 4,632 square miles
Location: Northwest of Cortez
Hiking: Day hikes from river camps

Boating: Raft, kayak, canoe, overnights
Whitewater: Class 2-4
Gauge: Rico (upper river), Slick Rock, Bedrock, Gateway
Highlights: Multiday river trip, red-rock canyon

The mountain-centric Dolores headwaters begin at Bolam Pass in the San Juan Range south of Telluride and flow 6 miles with trail access, then with CO 145 westward 38 miles to the West Fork—itself a fine stream of 32 miles.

After 15 miles the main stem hits the 10-mile backwater of McPhee Reservoir. Built in 1984 after a decade of controversy—and as one of the last major dams built in the United States—this is the Dolores's only impoundment but one that struck to the heart of the river's life. With economics that never penciled out, stored water is diverted southward out of the basin for low-value crops, acutely diminishing flows and leaving little in the river even during normal high runoff.

From McPhee Dam to the mouth, 185 miles flow free though suffer from the diversion. Directly below the dam the river runs 12 miles with gravel FR 504 alongside, then drops into its great wild canyons with stately ponderosa pines and whitewater.

For 50 miles from Slick Rock to Bedrock, the Dolores winds through its most impressive canyon of vertical walls, cantilevered cliffs, and ancient junipers, regarded by many as one of America's most beautiful desert rivers—if only some semblance of its natural flows could be restored.

Below Bedrock the Dolores picks up the San Miguel River, running stronger than the impaired Dolores, which continues through both ranchland and wild country to Gateway, then in 8 more miles enters Utah for another 24 miles to the Colorado River.

 ## FISH

Below McPhee Dam the Dolores is important for bluehead suckers, flannelmouth suckers, and roundtail chubs—all warmwater fish of special concern owing to altered flows.

 ## ACCESS

Headwaters are reached from CO 145 south of Lizard Head Pass, and the West Fork from FR 535. Below McPhee Dam, FR 504 tracks the river 12 miles, followed by a long reach with only four-wheel-drive or no vehicle access.

Starting at US 491 at Dove Creek, CO 141 runs north to Slick Rock at the upstream end of the Dolores's signature red-rock canyon, which continues roadless to Bedrock, where the river cuts directly across the aptly named Paradox Valley, reached via CO 90 west of Naturita. Downstream another 10 miles, CO 141 follows the Dolores northwest to Gateway, where the river enters its last roadless reach, ending at the Colorado River and UT 128 north of Moab.

HIKING

Short walks can be taken along the West Fork at San Juan National Forest campgrounds. In the Dolores's famed Slick Rock–Bedrock reach, open sandstone terrain invites fascinating explorations from riverfront campsites.

PADDLING

The upper Dolores speeds past cottonwoods with Class 2 whitewater plus some Class 3 waves during June snowmelt; put in along CO 145 at Roaring Creek/milepost 34 and go 14 miles to Stoner/milepost 21. Beware of logs and fallen cottonwoods. Easier but still swift with possible hazards, Class 2 reportedly continues along CO 145 for 15 miles from Stoner to the town of Dolores.

The section now flooded by McPhee Dam was once beautifully lined by ponderosa pines with campsites, swift flows, and several good rapids—a now-forgotten reach that I fortunately got to canoe in 1978 before the dam was filled.

Though diversions from McPhee prevent boating below there on most years, historically this was one of the finest rivers in the western canyonlands for an extended float trip. The recommended 1,000 cfs for rafting now occurs only once every three to five years and for little duration. For kayaks, 200 cfs may be enough to squeak through. During dam releases, four sections can be boated April through June.

First, the Snaggletooth reach runs 47 miles, Class 3-4 through pine and dryland canyons. Put in at the Bradfield launch; from Cortez go west on US 491, at Cahone turn right (east) on CR R, go 3 miles, turn right on CR 16, go 1.5 miles, and turn left on CR S to the ramp. For the Slick Rock takeout, on US 491 go west through Dove Creek, turn north on CO 141 to Slick Rock, and head downstream from the CO 141 bridge on river left, open for access when the dam is releasing. Or use a BLM ramp 13 more miles downstream in Big Gypsum Valley: Drive east on CO 141 from Slick Rock 10 miles, turn northwest on 20.5 Road north of Gypsum Gap, and go 10 miles west to the ramp. Though the Bradfield–Slick Rock reach is mostly Class 2-3, it's principally known for a few larger rapids; two appear roughly halfway through, followed quickly by the infamous Class 4 Snaggletooth. Scout left and portage if necessary.

Next, Slick Rock to Bedrock is a Colorado Plateau gem of 50 miles, Class 2+ as an easy raft and kayak trip or canoe adventure. Sandstone cliffs include impressive overhangs—one large enough for a sizable group to camp beneath. Put in at Slick Rock or the BLM Big Gypsum Valley ramp 13 miles downstream and take out at Bedrock; drive northwest from Naturita on CO 141, soon turn left (west) on CO 90, go through Paradox Valley, at the Dolores bridge turn upstream on river left, and go 1 mile.

Bedrock to Gateway is a lesser-run 44 miles of Class 2 and some 3+ with a road alongside, but a fine canyon journey, especially if linked with the Slick Rock–Bedrock reach above. For the Gateway takeout, from Bedrock drive CO 90 east, within 1 mile turn left (north) on gravel River Road/Y11, continue to the San Miguel confluence, and turn left on CO 141 to Gateway and its ramp, river-right above the bridge.

Last and somewhat vexed, Gateway Canyon is mostly Class 2 but after 8 miles the canyon narrows and Stateline Rapid, on the Utah line, curves sharp right. Stop above the diversion wall protruding from the right and scout. Ugly in high water, the wall forces you left toward the suck of a bristling, splintering logjam that can clog the entire

The upper Dolores River rises with snowmelt as it trends westward through Engelmann spruce forests toward drier country below.

From Slick Rock to Bedrock, the Dolores cuts through its classic red-rock canyon.

left channel of the river, requiring a flawless move back right after the diversion. This is the only portage I've ever done with a fully loaded raft, during an early season solo trip in 1984. Since then the drop has reportedly been both easier and harder. After 24 more relatively uneventful miles, the Dolores enters the Colorado River with the Dewey Bridge takeout on the left.

But don't stop! Best to keep going down the Colorado 33 miles on big Class 2 with spectacular desert scenery to US 191 and a river-right ramp above the bridge at Moab. Thus, a 206-mile trip is possible from Bradfield to Moab. Or a relatively carefree but elegant 94 miles can be run from Slick Rock to Gateway without the uncertainties of Snaggletooth and Stateline Rapids.

Eagle River

Length: 61 miles plus 9 of the East Fork, total 70	**Boating:** Kayak, canoe, raft, tubes after early summer, day trips
Average flow: 573 cfs	**Whitewater:** Class 2-4
Watershed: 971 square miles	**Gauge:** Minturn, Wolcott
Location: West of Vail	**Highlights:** Fast mountain whitewater, easy access
Hiking: Headwater day hikes and backpacking, bike trails	

Though unsung as such, the Eagle with its East Fork is the longest river in Colorado's Rocky Mountains without a dam. But it's not wild. With roads the whole way, this is one of the most accessible mountain streams flowing through one of the most developed corridors. The South Fork from Tennessee Pass meets the East Fork, and then the main stem picks up Gore Creek from Vail and descends through a valley shared with I-70 to the Colorado River at Dotsero.

South of Minturn, abandoned mines caused the river to run orange in 1984 at a Superfund site where abatement of heavy-metal drainage cost $60 million and continues at a maintenance charge of $1 million per year. Meanwhile an economy shifting to recreation, along with ease of access on I-70 west of Vail, brought a development boom to the Eagle valley. Through it all, this stream remains a brilliant whitewater passage, and planning required of new developments has made some of the urbanized sections accessible for walking and biking. Seizing an opportunity for river sports, the town of Eagle opened its Whitewater Park in 2019, with constructed rapids and access near the fairgrounds.

 ## FISH

Rare native Colorado cutthroat and whitefish appear here at times, and the recovering Eagle supports brown, rainbow, and brook trout as a popular fishery.

 ## ACCESS

Below Gore Creek several I-70 exits feed to US 6 and riverfront roads.

 ## HIKING

Bike and pedestrian trails follow alongside the river as it passes through commercial, condominium, and golf course areas, and a 63-mile trail from Vail Pass to Glenwood Canyon is planned for the entire length of the basin. From the I-70 bridge east of Avon to below Edwards, 10 bike trail miles are completed, as are 22 lower river miles, Eagle to Dotsero. Other sections remain along US 6.

 ## PADDLING

Here are 40 miles of excellent Class 2-4 whitewater complete with bike trails for shuttles much of the length and with boating to mid-July, and longer on the lower river. High flows with continuous turbulence in the upper river through June are for expert paddlers; difficulty eases with lower runoff and below Edwards. Though ubiquitous, nearby

The lower Eagle River riffles in an autumn sunrise at Wolcott. PHOTO BY HOLLY LOFF

development is not overbearing from most perspectives along the Eagle's cottonwood shores, embedded within a shallow sheltering gorge much of the way.

Expert kayakers run Class 3-4 rapids from Gilman (south of Minturn) to Edwards through June.

The "lower Eagle" run from Edwards to Eagle is 18 miles of Class 2-3 rapids but mostly Class 2, runnable into July. To put in, go west on I-70 to Edwards/exit 163, drive south to US 6, turn right (west), go 1 mile to Hillcrest Drive and its Eagle River bridge, and park on the north side across the road from the water treatment plant. To take out, drive west on US 6 or take I-70 to exit 147 and Chambers Park near the fairgrounds on the west side of Eagle, with access both above and below Whitewater Park. For the upper half of this run, take out at a BLM access; take I-70 exit 157 and follow US 6 west of Wolcott 0.5 mile.

Finally, 15 miles of Class 2 riffle from Eagle to Dotsero near the Colorado River confluence. To take out use I-70 exit 133 and drive east on US 6 to the "Duck Pond" landing south of the freeway. For a shorter run, access at Gypsum avoids the lower 6 miles of slower water; take I-70 exit 140 and follow US 6 east to the ramp at the Eagle River bridge.

Though 40 miles of the Eagle can be run dam-free, camping opportunities are poor and the river, for now, is rarely done as an overnight trip.

Elk River

Length: 34 miles plus 15 of the North Fork, total 49
Average flow: 555 cfs
Watershed: 469 square miles
Location: Northwest of Steamboat Springs

Hiking: Headwater day hikes and backpacking
Boating: Kayak, canoe, day trips
Whitewater: Class 2-3
Gauge: Clark
Highlights: Mountain headwaters, whitewater

From Mount Zirkel at 12,180 feet, the North and Middle Fork Elk plunge westward to form the main stem. In another 8 miles, at Glen Eden, the river leaves Routt National Forest and embarks through ranches with cottonwoods for 25 miles to the Yampa confluence at US 40.

As the largest tributary of the Yampa, the Elk River is Colorado's third-longest dam-free stream but, more impressive, the Elk's water flows into the Yampa, then the Green and the Colorado, together comprising the longest continuous dam-free river mileage in the West—587 miles to Powell Reservoir. However, this is not a viable long-distance river trip owing to the heavy rapids of the Yampa's Cross Mountain Gorge and also the need for early season runoff.

The Elk was among twelve Colorado rivers studied for National Wild and Scenic status in the 1970s—a designation that would preclude Hinman Park Dam, once proposed 4 miles upstream from Glen Eden. The Forest Service recommended inclusion from the headwaters to Glen Eden, but Congress never acted.

 ## FISH

The upper Elk is a cold steep-gradient stream with rainbow, brown, cutthroat, and brook trout, plus mountain whitefish. Though the best habitat occurs in lower reaches, public fishing is precluded by private land below Glen Eden.

 ## ACCESS

From Steamboat Springs drive 7 miles west on US 40, turn north on Elk River Road/ CR 129, at Glen Eden turn right on gravel FR 400, and go to Box Canyon Campground and road's end.

 ## HIKING

Trails ascend the North and South Forks, plus the Middle Fork's source of Gold Creek to upper flanks of Mount Zirkel. See the Routt National Forest map. The gravel road for 10 miles above Glen Eden is great for biking.

 ## PADDLING

From the bottom of the box canyon—below the North-Middle Fork confluence—continuously swift Class 3 runs in early summer, 8 miles to Glen Eden with few technical challenges but no eddies or letup of waves, holes, and demands to evade big

Trails follow the Elk River's headwater branches, reached on skis here in springtime, which lingers into June. Lower, the main stem pushes westward with continuous breaking waves in early summer runoff bound for the Yampa River.

breaking waves by powering quickly toward one side or the other. Put in at Box Canyon Campground; end at Glen Eden bridge.

Rarely done, the lower 20 miles of riffling Class 2 can be run through ranches, but avoid trespassing, watch for fences, and don't expect a welcoming committee. It's possible to take out west of the US 40 bridge over the Elk above its mouth, 7 miles west of Steamboat and upstream of Milner.

Green River

Length: 775 miles total in Wyoming, Colorado, and Utah; 428 at the lower Colorado-Utah line
Average flow: 5,302 cfs at mouth
Watershed: 44,143 square miles total
Location: Northwestern Colorado
Hiking: Day hikes from trailheads and river camps

Boating: Raft, kayak, day trips and overnights
Whitewater: Class 1-4
Gauge: Greendale, Utah (Flaming Gorge Dam)
Highlights: Desert canyon river, whitewater, fishing, long trip

Comprehensively epic, the Green River below Flaming Gorge Dam offers an extended outing unmatched in the dryland regions of the West—far longer even than the Colorado through the Grand Canyon. Only a short section loops through Colorado, but it connects to mileage below, so a larger portion of the river is covered here as it enters the Colorado Plateau. See also the Wyoming chapter for 323 miles above Flaming Gorge Dam.

The Green is usually boated as a series of discrete yet substantial trips, but I gravitate to the larger picture: Outside Alaska, only the Salmon River is longer for total length of undammed and boatable flow in the American West. Few rivers offer similar qualities of sublime canyon depths, arid wilderness, side-canyon hikes, ancient pictographs, and moderate rapids.

After its Wyoming headwaters the Green pools into Flaming Gorge Dam west of the Colorado-Utah line, then arcs through pine-dotted drylands at northwestern Colorado's interface between the Rocky Mountains and Colorado Plateau. It creates Lodore Canyon's incision through the eastern runout of the Uinta Mountains, then proceeds as an extravaganza of deep canyons, meeting the Colorado River in Canyonlands National Park before the combined waters eddy into Powell Reservoir.

 ## FISH

The Green has long been a mainstay for imperiled warmwater fishes of the Colorado River basin: bonytail chubs, Colorado pikeminnows, humpback chubs, and razorback suckers—all displaced by Flaming Gorge Dam and below it by cold releases, altered flows, and predacious introduced fish. In place of natural warmwater habitat, the dam's chilled tailwater has become one of the West's most popular fisheries for introduced rainbow trout, drawing anglers worldwide—a bitter fate for native fish but a recreational phenomenon to fly casters.

For 8 miles from Flaming Gorge to Little Hole, brown and rainbow trout number up to an astounding 20,000 per mile—perhaps the highest such number anywhere. The Green transitions back to warm water through Brown's Hole.

 ## ACCESS

To reach the outflow of Flaming Gorge Dam from Vernal, Utah, take US 191 north, cross the dam, and turn right to the river ramp. A steep rough road reaches Echo Park and the Green-Yampa confluence: From US 40 east of Jensen, Utah, turn north at Dinosaur

Below Flaming Gorge Dam the Green River coasts through Brown's Park with placid waters.

National Monument's visitor center on Harpers Corner Road, and in 25 miles turn right, shift into low, and descend the dusty washboard 13 miles.

 HIKING

Busy with anglers, the Little Hole Trail follows the northeast bank from Flaming Gorge Dam downstream 8 miles to Little Hole and road access. Below, Brown's Park National Wildlife Refuge has fishing paths; from Colorado take CO 318 northwest from Maybell.

The Gates of Lodore Trail, 1.5 miles out and back, offers a view to the entrance of a great American canyon. From CO 318 turn west at the Lodore sign. Through Lodore, hiking is good in cross-country routes up ridgelines and in tributary canyons reached only by boat.

In Dinosaur National Monument, the Harpers Corner Trail, 3 miles out and back, offers one of the Colorado Plateau's classic views where Whirlpool Canyon lies 2,500 feet below. From US 40 at Dinosaur National Monument's visitor center, turn north and take Harpers Corner Road 34 miles to the end.

The Ruple Point Trail, 10 miles out and back, has views to the river in Split Mountain Canyon. From Dinosaur's visitor center, take Harpers Canyon Road 27 miles north to the Island Park Overlook trailhead.

 PADDLING

The runnable Green extends 377 miles from Flaming Gorge Dam to the river's mouth, and boaters can continue on the Colorado River through Cataract Canyon's 15 miles of Class 3-4 followed by 32 miles of reservoir to Hite Marina. That entire run is second only to Idaho's Salmon River as the longest dam-free western river trip. Permits in advance are needed for Lodore and Split Mountain Canyons in Colorado and for Desolation-Gray, Labyrinth, and Stillwater Canyons downstream in Utah. Numbers are limited, but for a one-raft and one-kayak trip I've managed to line all these up without much trouble through applications and mostly other boaters' cancellations.

The first reach, from Flaming Gorge Dam through Red Canyon, appeals to day-trippers and anglers—thousands of them. They and flocks of beginner rafters mob the summertime put-in. No permit is needed, but at busy times rafts must be inflated off-river and driven to the ramp. I was nearly busted by the Forest Service's contracted security forces for simply topping off my boat on a sizzling hot day (the Forest Service now administers this site with its own staff, which is a good thing). Clear water runs 8 miles with Class 2 riffles and world-renowned trout fishing in chilled tailwaters down to Little Hole.

Next, Little Hole to Indian Crossing is 9 miles of Class 2 with still-excellent fishing. Completing the tailrace trout water, Indian Crossing to Swallow Canyon is 12 miles with mostly Class 1 riffles and campsites reached by boat or car. Another 17 miles of Class 1, often buggy, continue through Brown's Park to Lodore Canyon.

To reach these runs, drive north from Jensen, Utah, and approach from upstream at the dam. If coming from Colorado, take US 40 west to Maybell, go northwest on CO 318/Brown's Park Road, and 45 miles west of Maybell turn left on CR 34N to Lodore Canyon. Farther on CO 318, cross the state line into Utah, continue on gravel Brown's Park Road, and at the sign turn left to Swallow Canyon, or 5 miles farther turn to Bridge Hollow ramp. For Flaming Gorge Dam, continue on Brown's Park Road to US 191 and turn left to the dam and river ramp below.

Downstream from the gentle waters of Brown's Park, the famed Lodore Canyon awaits as one of the most spectacular red-rock journeys in the West. For 20 miles cliffs tier up 2,000 feet from Class 2 rapids and three Class 3-4 drops cleaving the Uinta Mountains—the largest east–west range in America outside Alaska. The National Park Service at Dinosaur National Monument requires permits and reserved campsites; see www.recreation.gov.

Lodore Canyon's terminus at Echo Park and the mouth of the Yampa River—5 miles upstream from the Green River's reentry into Utah—marks the site of one of America's most notable dam fights. Here David Brower and the Sierra Club in 1956 defeated a proposal to flood both the Green and Yampa in Dinosaur National Monument, saving those canyons and more broadly safeguarding the national park system from further dam-ming. Unfortunately the reservoir proposal was moved downstream to the unprotected but sublime Glen Canyon on the Colorado and built.

Looming over Echo Park, Steamboat Rock rises vertically 800 feet—one of the most dramatic landforms towering over any river in America. Takeout is possible there with a rough road (see above), but I recommend continuing downriver. Lodore blends seam-lessly into Whirlpool Canyon for 17 miles and then into Split Mountain Canyon's 9 miles of big-volume Class 2-3 where the antecedent river predated the Uinta range's uplift, giving boaters a tour of the excavated center of a mountain with craggy outcrops and bold ridgelines. The classic Lodore–Whirlpool–Split Mountain trip of 46 miles ends at Dinosaur National Monument's ramp north of Jensen, Utah, where the Park Service strictly enforces permit requirements.

Entering the Colorado Plateau, the Green River carves upturned sandstone in Lodore Canyon, which ends in a vertical climax at Echo Park, just downstream from this high perch.

Though few do it, the entire 92 miles from Flaming Gorge Dam to the Split Mountain takeout make for a fabulous canyon expedition spanning from Rocky Mountain foothills to the Colorado Plateau.

And much more awaits on the Green River downstream. Below the Split Mountain ramp lies 100 miles of gentle water—astonishingly buggy, even in the desert. Springtime flows crest and recede, leaving stagnant water on the floodplain with insect-breeding habitat lasting until autumn. Below Sand Wash, Desolation and Gray Canyons' Class 2–3 rapids stretch 84 miles, followed by placid water for 129 miles past the town of Green River and onward through Labyrinth and Stillwater Canyons to the Green and Colorado River confluence. From there 15 miles of foaming Class 3-4 in Cataract Canyon of the Colorado, and finally 32 miles of windy mud-ringed reservoir to Hite Marina, altogether make for a remarkable sojourn from the Rocky Mountains and onward through some of the finest canyonlands of the Colorado Plateau.

Gunnison River

Length: 164 miles plus 48 of the Taylor River, total 212
Average flow: 2,514 cfs
Watershed: 8,012 square miles
Location: Southeast of Grand Junction
Hiking: Day hikes

Boating: Kayak, canoe, raft, day trips and overnights
Whitewater: Class 2-3
Gauge: Below Tunnel (upper), Grand Junction (mouth)
Highlights: Remarkable canyon, whitewater gorge, gentle drylands float

The Gunnison is the largest tributary to the Colorado River above the Green River, and below three large upper basin dams it carves one of the most exceptional gorges in the West at Black Canyon of the Gunnison National Park.

Beginning in foothills of the Elk Mountains at the confluence of the East and Taylor Rivers, the Gunnison riffles 15 miles through a broad valley to the town of Gunnison. Downstream it soon meets slackwater of three back-to-back reservoirs—Blue Mesa, Morrow Point, and Crystal—impounding 45 of 56 miles that had been the incomparable Black Canyon, as extraordinary in its way as the Grand Canyon of the Colorado. In 1933 the lower canyon was designated as Black Canyon of the Gunnison National Monument, whose upper limit was already constrained by the Denver & Rio Grande Railroad, built in the upper canyon in the 1880s, and the Gunnison Tunnel of 1909 that diverts water to neighboring Uncompahgre Valley farms, reducing Gunnison flows downstream. Upstream from the tunnel, the big three-dam complex was built in the 1960s.

Below the dams, diversion, and former railroad alignment, 11 free-flowing, wild miles churn through what's left of Black Canyon—now Black Canyon of the Gunnison National Park. On a depth-to-narrowness ratio, this mind-blowing feature may be the West's ultimate canyon: At 2,800 feet beneath the rim, the bottom in some places measures only 40 feet wide.

Below the park, a less-extreme canyon continues in a 14-mile reach that seems longer, administered by the BLM and accessible only by trail. River runners pack boats and hike in for excellent rapids, awesome scenery, and rainbow trout fishing.

From there the river flows gently through Delta, irrigated farmland, and the BLM drylands of Dominguez Canyon, where the water sweeps beneath rocky bluffs to Redlands Diversion Dam, a few miles up from the Colorado confluence at Grand Junction.

Additional depletions were proposed for hydropower in the 1980s at the upriver dams, but agreements in 2008 established base flows precluding the worst diversions. On the lower river near Dominguez, another hydropower dam, considered in the 1970s, would have flooded the gorge but was stopped.

Heavily impounded, the Gunnison remains remarkable with a unique canyon, a long stretch of free-flowing water, and habitat for endangered warmwater fish in its lower reaches.

 FISH

The Gunnison is one of Colorado's "gold medal" trout-fishing streams for 20 miles below Crystal Dam, with excellent angling for introduced brown and rainbow trout.

After packing their gear down a mile-long trail, boaters negotiate the Gunnison Gorge's wonderland of tight rapids and towering cliffs like this one midway through the two-day trip.

Most of the targeted water is reached only by boat; commercial guides pack gear to the river on horses.

Farther downstream, the US Fish and Wildlife Service designated Dominguez Canyon as critical habitat for imperiled razorback suckers and Colorado pikeminnows. In 1996 fish passage was added at the lower river's Redlands Diversion Dam, which had blocked migration since 1918.

 ## ACCESS

Reach the upper river with CO 135 north of Gunnison. For Black Canyon of the Gunnison National Park, take US 50 east of Montrose, then north on CO 347 to the South Rim visitor center and twelve overlooks. The North Rim is reached at six overlooks but requires a longer drive via Crawford and 10 miles of gravel.

Below the canyon and subsequent wild gorge, roads reach a BLM landing next to a private resort called the Pleasure Park. Take CO 92 for 15 miles east of Delta or 6 miles west of Hotchkiss and turn south at the sign for the Gunnison Forks Day Use Area. The lower river is reached by bridges off US 50 at Escalante and Whitewater.

 ## HIKING

At Black Canyon of the Gunnison National Park, short trails lead to the rim. See the Painted Wall, considered the tallest vertical rock in Colorado at 2,250 feet. Start at the

South Rim visitor center with a map. The long drive to the North Rim reaches Chasm Overlook and others.

Hikers descend to river level in Black Canyon only with extreme difficulty. From near the visitor center a steep, unmarked route drops 3,000 feet; first get a wilderness permit and advice from rangers. Follow the ravine—precipitous, rock clogged, and not for the faint of heart. Remember the route, which might be vague on return. Beware of rockfall from hiking partners and of poison ivy seemingly on steroids. Avoid the hike in hot weather, as temperatures soar on the black rocks.

Downstream from the national park, the Gunnison Gorge Trail switchbacks nicely for 1.5 miles to the river and cool refreshment.

 ## PADDLING

The upper river's Class 2 riffles meander 12 miles through cottonwoods and ranches, doable summerlong. Drive north from Gunnison on CO 135 to the East and Taylor River confluence and put in on the road's east side near Almont. Take out at McCabe's Lane; on CO 135 southbound through Gunnison, turn west on US 50, drive to the edge of town, and after the bridge turn left to the landing.

The gradient in Black Canyon National Park tops 240 feet per mile, making this 11-mile pitch one of the most extreme whitewater descents anywhere for expert kayakers prepped for waterfall problems and extensive portaging with rock-climbing gear.

Gunnison Gorge below Black Canyon is a stellar Class 3 technical boulder run of 14 miles—a great day trip but better with camping. The put-in is the catch: You must hike the steep trail reached via four-wheel drive. From Montrose drive north on US 50 for 9 miles, turn right (east) on Falcon Road, continue 4 miles to where Falcon becomes Peach Valley Road, then 10 miles including steep ruts, impassable when wet, to the BLM's Chukar trailhead/campground. From there pack by horses or carry 1.5 miles. Take out at the BLM access next to the Pleasure Park off CO 92 below the North Fork Gunnison confluence. I recommend the Pleasure Park's professional shuttles. I-Ks are a logical choice here, or horse packers for rafts.

Changing the pace, an 18-mile reach of uneventful dryland Class 2 can be run from the Pleasure Park to Delta. To take out, drive to Delta's CO 92/US 50 junction, go north on 50, and quickly turn left to a landing on the river's south side.

From Delta to Whitewater, Dominguez Canyon is a 39-mile Class 1–2 with one rock weir, most of it a national conservation area through remote drylands 800 feet deep and shared with a railroad. The BLM requires self-issue permits at the put-in, portable toilets, and fire pans for this multiday tour. Put in at Delta; take out west of US 50 at the CO 141 bridge in Whitewater.

Shorter by 10 miles, put in lower at the Escalante bridge; from Delta drive 10 miles north on US 50, turn west at the BLM's Escalante sign, and take gravel Road 6.5 to the bridge. Do not leave valuables in cars, and prep for summertime bugs. Additional regulations may apply in the future; check with the BLM's Montrose office.

Long-trip aficionados can maximize by paddling the whole 57 miles, Pleasure Park to Whitewater. Through June, another 15 miles of Class 2 can be added at the top with the North Fork Gunnison, Paonia to Pleasure Park. Drive east on CO 92, turn right at Stahl Orchards, and put in at the North Fork bridge.

Alder trees green the banks of the Gunnison in a quiet interlude within its gorge.

Below Whitewater, another 10 miles of Class 2 are possible to the Colorado River in Grand Junction; however, 2.3 miles upstream from the Colorado a 9-foot dam and Redlands Diversion canal must be portaged 500 yards—a doable slog with a canoe but hardly worth it unless you're continuing down the Colorado; another 47 miles of Class 1-2 end at the head of Westwater Canyon, with a BLM permit required for camping in Ruby-Horsethief Canyons (see Colorado River).

Platte River, South

Length: 439 miles plus 50 of the Middle Fork South Platte, total 489; 125 miles at Denver, 348 at the Colorado-Nebraska line
Average flow: 4,039 cfs, 224 at Denver
Watershed: 135,320 square miles
Location: Denver area

Hiking: Day hikes, bike trails
Boating: Kayak, canoe, day trips
Whitewater: Class 2-3
Gauge: Cheesman Dam (Deckers), Englewood (below Chatfield Dam)
Highlights: Fishing, paddling, urban trails

The sprawling South Platte basin drains the east side of the Rockies southwest of Denver and delivers 75 percent of the urban area's water supply. Dammed seven times and augmented by trans-basin diversions from west of the Continental Divide, the South Platte's a water-supply machine, yet several recreation reaches serve Colorado's urban population well.

High-elevation reaches flowing from Pike National Forest collect behind Cheesman Dam—at 221 feet the world's tallest when built in 1905 upstream from a CO 67 wide spot called Deckers. The river then flows through scenic Cheesman Canyon with the South Platte road (CR 67 and 97) alongside—one of the finest near-urban recreational river canyons in the West.

The North Fork South Platte joins on river left, and 2 miles downstream the river pools in Strontia Springs Reservoir, followed by Waterton Canyon, then Chatfield Reservoir, then the river's urban path through Littleton and Denver. Downstream from the city the South Platte winds across the plains with diversion dams and withdrawals, finally joining the North Platte in Nebraska.

In the 1980s the Denver Water Board proposed the 615-foot-tall Two Forks Dam above Strontia Springs, slated to flood Cheesman Canyon, where the National Park Service reported "outstandingly remarkable" recreation, fish, historic, and endangered species values. After approval by the Army Corps of Engineers, and nationwide controversy, the federal Environmental Protection Agency called the plan an environmental "catastrophe" and vetoed it in 1990—one of the last major dam fights undertaken in the United States, as of 2020, and a milestone exhibiting the EPA's ability to halt a dam based on environmental considerations.

Denver and other cities instead wisely instituted water conservation programs, installed water meters, increased groundwater pumping, and acquired farmland in order to transfer water rights to urban growth. The next, unexpected chapter of this saga is unfolding as downstream irrigation districts propose coupling new off-channel dams with pumping water back up to Denver suburbs, aiming to prevent the city from transferring more downstream runoff from irrigation to municipal use. Opponents of the lower-basin dams and pumping argue that wildlife including imperiled sandhill cranes are at risk.

 FISH

Though native fish have been largely eliminated from the South Platte, sport fishing here is some of the state's best—Cheesman Canyon a "gold medal" trout fishery with

Below Deckers the South Platte winds through Cheesman Canyon with lively paddling and a road alongside the river, seen here on an icy winter morning.

year-round angling for brown and rainbow trout. Lower reaches have warmwater species including catfish.

 ACCESS

Within Denver many streets cross the South Platte, urban parks have been established, and pedestrian and bike trails built. Cherry Creek joins the South Platte at a centerpiece called Whitewater Park; leave the car near REI (1416 Platte Street), off I-25 near 15th Street, and walk to the river.

For Waterton Canyon, take CO 121 in Lakewood or CO 75 south to Chatfield Reservoir, then 121 to the busy trailhead.

For higher reaches, take US 285 west from Denver and Lakewood, at Conifer turn south on CR 97, descend to the North Fork South Platte, continue 4 miles down it to the South Platte confluence, turn right, and ascend the South Platte to Cheesman Canyon's pullouts.

 HIKING

Denver and Littleton have miles of trails along the stream—see city maps.

Waterton Canyon has a bike/hiking trail for 12 miles round-trip to Strontia Springs Dam. Watch for bighorn sheep. This is also the north end of the 486-mile Colorado Trail—a Rocky Mountain ultra-hike to the west.

In Denver the South Platte features whitewater ledges with a paved trail alongside at Confluence Park.

Upstream, CR 97 makes excellent biking through Cheesman Canyon, best when traffic is light.

 PADDLING

The upper South Platte and its North Fork have a few sketchy whitewater runs. Dependable paddling starts at Deckers with 11 miles through Cheesman Canyon, Class 2 with a bit of 3 and the road alongside for access, boatable all summer. From Denver take US 285 west (see above) or from the south drive to Woodland Park and northward.

The Littleton run is 4 miles of Class 2 with some Class 3, runnable year-round below Chatfield Dam and through suburbs with trails alongside. From I-25 exit 207 go south on US 85, cross Mineral Avenue, turn right into South Platte Park, and continue west to the put-in. To take out, from I-25 exit 207 turn right onto US 85/Santa Fe Drive southbound, cross Oxford Avenue, turn right (west) on Union Avenue, cross the river, turn right, and park east of the ballfields. On this run beware of dam remains. The Union Chutes surfing waves are modified ledges, Class 3 when high; scout from the river-left trail.

In Denver, Confluence Park features constructed ledges and urban surfing holes, but don't swallow the water. Park near REI.

Rio Grande

Length: 1,885 miles, 197 at the Colorado–New Mexico line
Average flow: 433 at the state line, depleted at the mouth
Watershed: 173,333 square miles, 4,668 in Colorado
Location: Southwestern Colorado
Hiking: Headwater trails, day hikes

Boating: Canoe, raft, kayak, mostly day trips
Whitewater: Class 2-3 (Class 4-5 downstream in New Mexico)
Gauge: Wagonwheel Gap, Del Norte, New Mexico line
Highlights: Mountain headwaters, Class 2-3 paddling

With headwaters in southwestern Colorado's San Juan Mountains, the Rio Grande becomes the fifth-longest river in America before it ends in the Gulf of Mexico, though diversions deplete flows acutely.

Beginning at 13,478-foot Mount Canby east of Silverton, headwaters drop eastward to Rio Grande Reservoir and then flow semi-wild through Rio Grande National Forest, across ranchland centered in Creede, and onward to meet the South Fork. Farmland and diversions follow to Del Norte and a meandering route across San Luis Valley. Irrigation desiccates the river in summer as it reaches volcanic hills and nears the New Mexico line, where flows are recharged by the Conejos River and groundwater from porous volcanic rock at the upper end of the Rio Grande's passage through northern New Mexico's extraordinary canyonlands.

 ## FISH

The river in San Juan National Forest is good trout habitat, with angling for brown trout downstream to Del Norte. In San Luis Valley, 15 miles upstream from New Mexico, 17,000 acres with 5 riverfront miles were bought by a conservation coalition in 2018 to reinstate flows for imperiled Rio Grande chubs, Rio Grande suckers, and Central Flyway birds.

 ## ACCESS

For headwaters, from Gunnison take US 50 west to CO 149 and go south over Spring Creek Pass. For lower reaches, continue down 149 to the community of South Fork, then east on US 160 to Alamosa.

 ## HIKING

National forest trails reach source waters above Rio Grande Reservoir.

 ## PADDLING

Lively whitewater lies below Rio Grande Dam with 10 miles of Class 3 rapids in early summer, dependent on dam releases. Put in at River Hill Campground; from CO 149 west of Creede, take FR 520 toward the dam and turn into the campground. To take out, go to the FR 520/CO 149 intersection, turn right on 149, drive 3 miles to FR 522, turn right, and continue 1 mile to the bridge. The first half of this run is a beautiful

High in the San Juan Mountains of southern Colorado, the Rio Grande forms rocky rapids downstream from Rio Grande Dam.

forested canyon with clear, fast, rocky water. The second half enters ranchland. On my raft trip years ago, an unexpected dangerous cable spanned the river at chest height near the takeout.

Wagon Wheel Gap lies below Creede with 12 miles through a forested valley with CO 149 alongside—an easy bike shuttle. Put in 7 miles southeast of Creede above FR 600. Take out at the 149 bridge above the South Fork. Class 2 rapids ease to gentler water.

Roaring Fork River

Length: 68 miles	**Hiking:** High country at headwaters
Average flow: 2,000 cfs below the Crystal River	**Boating:** Kayak, raft, canoe, day trips
Watershed: 1,455 square miles	**Whitewater:** Class 2-4
Location: West of Aspen, south of Glenwood Springs	**Gauge:** Aspen, Glenwood Springs
	Highlights: Road-accessible boating and fishing

The Roaring Fork of the Colorado starts with snowmelt of Independence Pass at exhilarating heights above timberline. The river speeds through the north fringe of Aspen, grows with the Fryingpan River from the north, matures with the Crystal River from the south at Carbondale, and pushes onward in a broad valley to Glenwood Springs and the Colorado River. The entire corridor has faced booming development from Aspen to Glenwood Springs.

This is Colorado's largest river with no main-stem dams, but it's missing a lot of water; a Bureau of Reclamation trans-basin diversion takes flows from the tributary Fryingpan River and tunnels them eastward to the Arkansas River. Additional water from headwaters is piped beneath Independence Pass to Twin Lakes Reservoir and the Arkansas, reducing Roaring Fork flows in Aspen 30 percent.

 ## FISH

Below Aspen this is one of Colorado's "gold medal" fisheries, with rainbow and brown trout plus native mountain whitefish. Though the stream flows through a busy tourist corridor, scarce public land limits fishing from shore; anglers use rafts or drift boats below Carbondale.

 ## ACCESS

CO 82 follows the Roaring Fork the entire way, with public landings in Basalt, Carbondale, and elsewhere.

 ## HIKING

CO 82 east of Aspen tops Independence Pass with a large parking lot and hiking above timberline—some of the most spectacular western high country that's just a step outside the car along a major paved highway. Two miles west of the pass a trail climbs north to the Roaring Fork source, Independence Lake.

West another 7 miles, intimate waters of the upper Roaring Fork plunge over waterfalls and swirl into green pools rimmed by granite—a busy but extraordinary swimming spot called the Grottos, named for an adjacent cavernous enclave with a floor of ice smoothened by repeated freeze-and-thaw and persisting incredibly into summer. From Aspen drive east on CO 82 for 8 miles (0.9 mile past Weller Campground), turn right on a dirt lane, cross the footbridge, and follow the larger path upstream. Watch for the grotto in a rocky depression.

The Rio Grande Trail for bikers and walkers runs 42 miles—Aspen to Glenwood Springs—and is one of the West's longer rails-to-trails conversions, built on the retired

Southeast of Aspen the Grottos of the Colorado River's Roaring Fork draw swimmers to deep green pools.

Denver & Rio Grande Railroad's right-of-way, connecting with the Colorado River bike trail at Glenwood Springs.

PADDLING

Expert kayakers only should launch on the Slaughterhouse Run—Class 4 for 5 miles below Aspen.

Downstream, Class 3 rapids run 6 turbulent miles through July. Start at Lower Woody Creek Bridge off CO 82 at milepost 31; take out at milepost 25.

From Basalt to Glenwood Springs the river calms to Class 2 summerlong with some big-water wave trains for 25 miles through mostly private land among cottonwoods. Beware of irrigation headgates. Start in Basalt at the Fryingpan confluence. Take out halfway down at CO 133 in Carbondale or continue to Glenwood Springs landings, including Veltus Park; from CO 82 (Grand Avenue) go west on Eighth Street, cross the river, and turn left. Or continue into the Colorado to Two Rivers Park on river right.

San Juan River

Length: 251 miles plus 18 of the East Fork and Elwood Creek, total 269; 59 miles in Colorado	**Location:** Above Pagosa Springs
	Hiking: Headwaters
Average flow: 3,889 cfs at the mouth in Utah; 925 at the Colorado–New Mexico line	**Boating:** Canoe, kayak, day trips
	Whitewater: Class 2-3
	Gauge: Pagosa Springs
Watershed: 18,147 square miles	**Highlights:** Urban stream at hot springs, mountain whitewater

This second-largest tributary to the entire Colorado begins at Wolf Creek Pass. The East and West Forks join 10 miles above Pagosa Springs, and the main stem flows southwest into a piney canyon followed by desert country in New Mexico and a reservoir behind 402-foot-high Navajo Dam. At Farmington the Animas adds substantial flows. The lower river crosses Utah to meet the Colorado in Lake Powell.

 FISH

The upper reaches of the East and West Forks support Colorado River cutthroat, while lower sections have rainbow and brown trout. The San Juan's noted fishing is at chilled

At Pagosa Springs the San Juan passes through the center of town, with hot springs and recreational shorelines.

tailwaters below Navajo Dam, with up to 15,000 trout per mile—among the highest such numbers anywhere.

 ## ACCESS

US 160 follows the lower West Fork from the south side of Wolf Creek Pass to the East Fork confluence, while FR 667 tracks the East Fork. US 160 then follows the main stem into Pagosa Springs, with access at city parks. Downstream the San Juan enters remote canyon country followed by gravel roads through the Southern Ute Indian Reservation.

 ## HIKING

The upper West Fork has a 20-mile out-and-back from its trailhead to Piedra Pass in the Weminuche Wilderness. Take US 160 northeast from Pagosa Springs 12 miles to FR 648 and go left for 2 miles to the trailhead.

Pagosa Springs has swimming, hot springs, and waterfront walkways—the centerpiece of the town.

 ## PADDLING

The West Fork is Class 2 for 5 miles through July. Put in at West Fork Campground; take out at the US 160 bridge near the mouth.

Above Pagosa Springs, 10 miles of Class 2-3 riffle through July across private land from the East–West Fork confluence to town.

Below Pagosa Springs, the river flows 16 miles through Mesa Canyon, Class 2-3 to Trujillo, but much of this crosses the Southern Ute Reservation, where access is not allowed.

Beyond the Rocky Mountains, the lower San Juan crosses the Colorado Plateau with an outstanding canyon trip, Class 2-3 for 84 miles from Bluff, Utah, to Clay Hills at the upper end of Powell Reservoir's backwater, best in spring and early summer. BLM permits are required and limited.

San Miguel River

Length: 83 miles
Average flow: 341 cfs
Watershed: 1,554 square miles
Location: Northwest of Telluride
Hiking: Headwaters trails
Boating: Kayak, raft, canoe, day trips

Whitewater: Class 2-3
Gauge: Placerville, Nucla, Uravan
Highlights: Nearly dam-free, Class 2-3 paddling, cottonwood corridor

This Dolores tributary is largely intact as a natural river, though with abandoned mines, withdrawals below Norwood, and several diversion dams but no storage reservoirs. Because of major diversions that are exported from the Dolores southward, the San Miguel carries more than half the flow at the confluence.

The river begins with Bridal Veil Creek plunging from headwalls of the San Juan Mountains into the valley of Telluride—former mining town now upscale ski resort. Abandoned mines remain a legacy of the past, evident in brightly colored tailings on mountain slopes.

The river picks up its South Fork and rushes northwest paralleled by CO 145 for 25 miles to Norwood Bridge, then another 29 miles including 14 through a roadless canyon to Naturita. Beyond several diversion dams and a defunct power plant, the San Miguel runs its final 18 miles with CO 141 alongside, ending at Uravan and the Dolores confluence.

With three preserves, the Colorado Nature Conservancy regards the San Miguel's riparian habitat as some of the Colorado basin's best.

 FISH

Native fish in the upper basin included Colorado cutthroat trout and mottled sculpins, largely extirpated, though cutthroats survive or have been reintroduced here and to selected tributaries.

The upper half of the San Miguel supports rainbow and cutthroat hybrids. Brown and brook trout appear on lower reaches, transforming to warm water, where the BLM lists native roundtail chubs, flannelmouth suckers, and bluehead suckers as sensitive species.

 ACCESS

CO 145 parallels the river below Telluride with heavy traffic, followed by CO 141.

 HIKING

Headwater trails ascend the San Juan Mountains east of Telluride. Riverfront roads look tempting for biking but have fast traffic and poor shoulders.

 PADDLING

Class 2-3 rapids are typically good through June or July, though the climate is getting drier and runoff season shorter. Much of the San Miguel is continuously swift with breaking waves, few eddies, and log hazards possible, especially until mid-June. Lower

As the Dolores's largest tributary, the San Miguel tracks west from Telluride and grows with runoff through semiarid foothills and cottonwood forests.

flows remain swift, with rocks exposed. Through substantial mileage crossing private land, watch for barbed wire, pass-through fences, hanging PVC pipe barriers to cattle, a notorious hanging pallet fence with a center opening, and hazardous low bridges during peak flows.

The Sawpit run, 7 miles of swift Class 2–3, starts 4 miles below Telluride at South Fork Road and ends at Fall Creek Road, 2 miles above Placerville, with CO 145 alongside.

From Fall Creek to the Specie Creek recreation site, *Paddling Colorado* lists 5 miles along CO 145 as swift Class 2.

The most-run section, Specie Creek to Norwood Bridge on CO 145 east of Norwood, is 8 miles of Class 2–3, commercially rafted May and June.

The roadless Norwood Canyon is 16 miles of Class 2–3 starting at Norwood Bridge. After 6 easy miles a low dam is reportedly runnable on the far left. To take out, drive CO 145 west from Norwood to CO 141; half a mile farther west on 141, turn right on EE 30, stay right, and go northeast and upriver 6 miles to Pinyon and FR 540's "Green Truss" bridge.

These four runs total 36 continuous miles of swift Class 2–3, typically run as day trips owing to roads, private land, and lack of campsites.

Separated by diversion dams from the reach above, the lower San Miguel has 18 miles of swift Class 2+ to the Dolores through June. Put in near Naturita's CR 97 bridge and the CO 141/CR 97 intersection. To take out, follow 141 west to Uravan, turn left, cross the bridge, and stay right on gravel downstream to the Dolores confluence.

Taylor River

Length: 48 miles
Average flow: 328 cfs
Watershed: 476 square miles
Location: Northeast of Gunnison
Hiking: Headwaters trails

Boating: Kayak, raft, canoe, day trips
Whitewater: Class 2-4
Gauge: Taylor Park Reservoir
Highlights: Technical Class 3 paddling

The Taylor takes shape in the Collegiate Peaks Wilderness of Colorado's Sawatch Range, gathers with tributaries in Taylor Park Reservoir, then bubbles southwestward to join the East River and form the Gunnison River.

 FISH

With steady cold flows from its upstream dam, the Taylor is a rainbow trout fishery with pullouts; also accessible in Gunnison National Forest campgrounds.

 ACCESS

From Gunnison drive north on CO 135 to Almont, and turn right on Taylor River Road/FR 742. If coming from the east, the Cottonwood Pass gravel road over the Continental Divide is fine for cars after midsummer.

Gathering waters from the west side of Colorado's tallest range—the Sawatch—the Taylor River is a playground of rock-studded rapids before meeting the East River and forming the Gunnison.

HIKING

The paved Taylor River Road is lightly traveled, offering 20 miles of riverfront biking.

 PADDLING

The Taylor is a textbook whitewater playground of rocky mazes, tight chutes, abrupt pour-overs, and swirling eddies. Forgiving at low-medium levels, stair-step drops end in recovery pools of clear water. Dam controlled, flows hold fairly steady at boatable levels through midsummer or later and often flow well when other rivers run too high or low for paddling.

Personally, the middle and lower Taylor is my favorite among Colorado's technical runs for whitewater canoeing—also great as an intermediate kayak outing or lively day in a small raft.

Advanced paddling begins a few miles downstream from Taylor Park Dam and below Lottis Creek Campground and extends 6 miles with Class 3-4 to an access below White-water Resort. *The Floater's Guide to Colorado* warns of several weirs and fences.

Another 6 miles of Class 3 run from below Whitewater Resort to the FR 742 bridge below Beaver Creek.

From the FR 742 bridge to the mouth is 5 miles of Class 2. Take out on the East River along CO 135.

While there, the lower East River has Class 2 paddling through its cottonwood corridor from Cement Creek to the Taylor confluence. The combined Taylor and East continue as the Gunnison River with 12 miles of Class 2.

White River

Length: 196 miles in Colorado and Utah plus 39 of the South Fork; total 235, including 60 in Utah
Average flow: 614 cfs
Watershed: 4,990 square miles
Location: Northwest Colorado
Hiking: Headwater day hikes and backpacking

Boating: Canoe, raft, day trips and overnights
Whitewater: Class 1-2
Gauge: Rangely, Meeker
Highlights: Long, remote desert canoe trip, endangered fish

With mountain headwaters, miles of cottonwoods through an otherwise spare desert, long stretches of roadless and rarely visited riverfront, and prime habitat for imperiled warmwater fishes, the little-known White is one of Colorado and Utah's most varied and significant semi-natural rivers. It ranks among the least dammed and least developed major tributaries to the Colorado, its length split between mountain, foothill, and desert terrain.

The South Fork gathers runoff from the aspen-clad Flat Tops massif and runs 8 wilderness miles followed by 15 that are trail accessible. The river then plunges through a 2,000-foot-deep canyon incised in the White River Plateau. The final 13 miles are paralleled by a dirt road through private land surrounded by national forest.

Shorter and road accessible, the North Fork descends the north side of Flat Tops Plateau to Trappers Lake, then runs west 23 miles with a road and recreation sites to the South Fork confluence.

Significant in environmental history, Trappers Lake is where Forest Service landscape architect Arthur Carhart in 1919 was tasked with developing cabin sites but instead conceived the idea for a national program of wilderness preservation, later advanced by biologist Aldo Leopold and conservation visionary Robert Marshall. Congress ultimately enacted their proposal as the National Wilderness Preservation System, which has grown to 109 million acres in 762 areas but still totals less than 2 percent of the lower forty-eight states.

From the North and South Forks confluence, the main stem runs 21 miles through a roaded valley of private land with diversions for pasture, ending at Meeker. It then meanders 85 miles through quiet water and hay fields with several diversion weirs, and upstream from Rangely hits the backwater of its only dam, Taylor Draw, built in 1983 for the unusual purpose of intercepting ice jams before they cause local flooding and wash ashore in large chunks threatening town properties. The Rio Blanco Water Conservancy District expanded the dam in 1991 for hydroelectric power; however, on this extremely turbid river the reservoir lost half its surface area to siltation in just twenty years. The pool was projected to fill with silt by 2028 in spite of 750 sediment "traps" built upstream. The district has proposed a new dam up to 260 feet tall and a related dam on adjacent Wolf Creek, but the efficacy, economy, legitimacy of water rights, and outcome of this quirky proposal are unknown as of 2020.

Below Rangely the White flows another 23 miles in Colorado and about 60 in Utah to the Green River, crossing an arid desert with high bluffs and cliffs where a lush but thin band of cottonwoods and willows line waterfronts. Exotic tamarisk took over

Below Rangely the White River winds through its semi-wild desert corridor.

floodplains but may be fading due to predatory beetles that have been released along the Green. Occasional dirt roads meet or cross the river, but no major roads parallel the stream's course.

The BLM owns much of the riverfront in Utah down to the lower 20 miles, which pass through the Uintah and Ouray Indian Reservation. Within the oil, gas, and oil-shale zone of western Colorado/eastern Utah, public land in the lower basin has been leased by the BLM for oil production, and additional public acreage has been slated for fossil fuel extraction.

Though harsh in its arid path from the Rocky Mountain plateau to the Green River, milky brown with silt from its starkly erodible basin, and secluded in a corner of the West beyond reach of recreational enthusiasts and, for that matter, almost everybody, the White remains lightly developed, distinctive in its remaining wildness, and important to native fish.

 FISH

Small tributaries of the North and South Forks support rare Colorado River cutthroat trout. The forks are also habitat for rainbow, brown, and hybrid trout, plus native whitefish.

From its mouth at the Green River up to Taylor Draw Dam above Rangely and previously beyond, the White provides key habitat for endangered Colorado River pikeminnows, humpback chubs, bonytail chubs, razorback suckers, and other native warmwater fishes, all imperiled throughout the Colorado Plateau owing to dams, lost habitat, and reduction of free-flowing mileage needed for migrations. With the exception of Taylor Draw Dam, the White offers excellent connectivity between aquatic habitats for these fish, and critical populations maintain migration routes combining contiguous undammed reaches of the White, Colorado, and Yampa Rivers.

ACCESS

Headwaters of the North Fork at Trappers Lake are reached east of Buford on CR 8, then gravel FR 205. The lower South Fork—principally private land—is reached south of Buford on CR 10 and upstream via White River National Forest trails.

From Buford down, Flat Top Road/CR 8 follows the main stem west to Meeker. Then CO 13 and CO 64 continue downstream through the ranching valley to Rangely, where local CR 2 continues down the valley 10 miles and ends. The lower river flows into Utah with nominal access surrounded by dirt roads serving the oil industry.

Southward from Vernal, Utah, paved UT 45 bridges the White south of a remote intersection called Bonanza. Farther downstream, Fuel Line Bridge crosses 12 miles east of the Green River. Also coming from Vernal's outskirts but farther west, paved UT 88 crosses the White just above its Green River confluence.

HIKING

At the North Fork, trails climb into the Flat Tops Wilderness from Trappers Lake. At the South Fork, national forest trails begin at the end of CR 10.

The White River enters a harsh dryland of buttes, bluffs, and bottomlands on its way to the Green River in Utah.

Trails do not follow the main stem; however, off-trail walking through desert and mesa country of the lower river in Utah is good from river campsites on BLM land.

PADDLING

While Class 1–2 paddling is possible for 77 miles from the North and South Forks confluence below Buford to Rangely, boating and camping is complicated by private land and Taylor Draw Dam.

Below Rangely, river travel is excellent as the gentle flow enters wilder country in 600-foot-deep canyonlands with no development and little road access after the first 10 miles. The river winds past unvisited bluffs, mesas, and cottonwood floodplains for 70 miles—one of the longer essentially wild desert canoe trips in the West. It's the longest reach I've paddled in Colorado or Utah and seen no people. Flows drop too low after June, but prep for mosquitoes before then. The lower 20 miles leaves canyon country and enters lowland terrain of the Uintah and Ouray Indian Reservation.

Shorter trips are possible by taking out at UT 45's Bonanza bridge southeast of Vernal or Fuel Line Bridge—which I recommend—another 18 miles west of Bonanza and south of Vernal via UT 88 to Ouray and then east. A BLM map helps for the maze of oil-industry roads. I took out at Fuel Line Bridge, short of the wetland flats of the reservation, where a tribal permit is officially required.

Yampa River

Length: 243 miles plus 19 of the Bear River, total 262
Average flow: 2,005 cfs
Watershed: 8,168 square miles
Location: Steamboat Springs and westward
Hiking: Flat Tops headwaters, urban trail in Steamboat

Boating: Raft, kayak, canoe, day trips and overnights
Whitewater: Class 1-5
Gauge: Steamboat Springs, Deerlodge Park
Highlights: Canyon expedition, whitewater, cottonwoods

The Yampa courses from the Flat Tops Wilderness to the Green River in Dinosaur National Monument, passing through some of the West's finest cottonwood forests and across crumbling badlands down to magnificent canyons of the Colorado Plateau.

The Yampa's upriver extension as the Bear River is dammed twice with irrigation reservoirs. Then in 1978 Catamount Dam was built on the upper main stem as part of a real estate scheme, and 7 miles farther upstream the taller Stagecoach Dam, 145 feet, was completed for hydroelectric power and water supply in 1988 after a heated battle and narrow local vote. The Yampa has been called the last major undammed Colorado River tributary—not quite true considering these impoundments and those of the Bear River, which is the upper Yampa in everything but name.

Hot summer days bring out the crowds along the Yampa in Steamboat Springs.

From its headwaters on the northeast side of the Flat Tops Wilderness, the river flows east and then northwest through ranches to Steamboat Springs, where the rushing water has become the bustling tourist town's delight.

From there westward for 73 miles to Maybell, the Yampa nourishes one of the finest riparian corridors in the West—a nearly continuous riverfront band of narrowleaf and Fremont cottonwoods in an unusual mix of box elder, red osier dogwood, and willows, together prime habitat for songbirds, beavers, and elk. Only about 7 percent of the river is diverted—rare for a major ranchland river.

Below Maybell the Yampa enters the Colorado Plateau, and at Cross Mountain Gorge heavy whitewater pounds through an inaccessible vertical-wall canyon.

Flattening momentarily above Deerlodge Park, the Yampa next enters one of the West's classic river retreats, disappearing in sinuous bends with thousand-foot sandstone walls and winding 46 miles within Dinosaur National Monument—one of the longer river reaches protected within the national park system. This is also Colorado's longest section of stream totally lacking both dams and roads.

Waters flowing from tributaries to the Yampa—and then in the subsequent continuous path down the Green and Colorado Rivers in Utah to Powell Reservoir—constitute the longest unbroken free-flowing river mileage in the West: The North Fork Elk flows into the Elk, Yampa, Green, and Colorado for a dam-free length of 587 miles. Nearby, the main-stem Yampa below Catamount Dam merges with the Green and Colorado Rivers for 540 dam-free miles. However, neither of those lengths appeal as a doable river trip for most boaters, as Cross Mountain Gorge is for experts only and early season flows are needed upstream from the Green and especially in Cross Mountain and on the Elk.

In the 1970s a local water district and electric association proposed Juniper Canyon and Cross Mountain Gorge hydropower dams on the Yampa between Maybell and Deerlodge. Those were halted and the BLM subsequently found the river suitable for Wild and Scenic designation, but it still lacks protection above Dinosaur National Monument.

 FISH

In the upper basin, small tributaries flowing from the north as Elkhead and Fortification Creeks provide habitat for imperiled Colorado River cutthroat.

Along with the White, Colorado, and Green Rivers, the lower Yampa is among the most important streams for endangered warmwater fishes of the Colorado basin. Some migrate hundreds of miles down the White, up the Green, then up the Yampa to spawn, making all three rivers essentially one from ecological perspectives.

Middle and lower reaches support introduced bass, catfish, and also pike, planted as a sport fishery but decimating native fish.

 ACCESS

US 40 enters the Yampa basin from the east and runs down the valley until the river veers north. At Maybell 40 crosses again, then bends conclusively away from the river with only side-road access.

HIKING

Outstanding trails at headwaters of the Bear River climb to the "Devil's Causeway," an enthralling thin ridge of rock separating the Yampa basin eastward from the White River watershed to the west. Drive south from Steamboat Springs on US 40, go right on CO 131, at the village of Yampa turn right on CR 7, and continue to the trailhead at the end.

In Steamboat, 8 miles of popular paved pedestrian and bike trails follow the river.

For remote views into Cross Mountain Gorge, take US 40 west of Maybell to milepost 44, turn north on Deerlodge Park Road, go 2 miles, and turn right on CR 123. In half a mile go left on a four-wheel-drive track, drive or walk 2 miles to the trailhead, and hike 1.5 miles to the rim.

In lower canyons, off-trail hiking from boat-in campsites includes a spectacular trail on the south side to cliff tops at Harding Hole.

 PADDLING

Above Steamboat Springs, 8 miles of Class 1 meander through meadows and ranches. Drive south on US 40 and go right on CO 131 to a landing near the bridge. Take out upstream of Steamboat on the west side of 40 at Yampa River Park.

Through downtown Steamboat, 2 miles of Class 2-3 have been enhanced with rock placements and rapids enjoyed by kayakers, canoeists, paddleboarders, tubers, inflatable dinosaurs—you name it. Put in at Yampa River Park or anywhere along the river's urban path. To take out, drive west on US 40, turn south on 20 Mile Road, and park across from the library or continue to the town's transit center.

Below Steamboat the Yampa meanders out of the Rocky Mountains, through foothills, and onto the Colorado Plateau, with one of the West's finer cottonwood forests amid ranchland along the US 40 corridor and through foothill canyons—altogether 134 miles from Steamboat to the top of Cross Mountain Canyon with mostly Class 1 riffles runnable April to mid-June or so. Various landings appear past Hayden, Craig, and Maybell, and a number of small diversion dams and low bridges require caution.

The first 40 miles are private land with three normally runnable diversion dams to Yampa River State Park headquarters, 2 miles west of Hayden. Another 26 miles go to South Beach near Craig; on US 40 west of Craig, go south on CO 13, cross the river, and turn right.

The 32-mile Little Yampa (Duffy) Canyon runs from South Beach to Duffy Mountain; to take out, drive west from Craig on US 40 for 19 miles, turn south on CR 17, then left on CR 181 to Duffy Mountain landing. Carry a portable toilet for this section of BLM, state, and private land; no permit is required. See Friends of the Yampa's online *Little Yampa Canyon Recreation Guide*.

Duffy Mountain to Juniper Springs is 12 miles, followed by the 8-mile Juniper Canyon, ending at the US 40 bridge above Maybell. A few miles above the bridge a gnarly diversion dam may require portage, as it did for me on a high-water canoe trip many years ago.

Another 29 miles go to the East Cross Mountain takeout. This must-do exit for the middle Yampa lies on river left; Cross Mountain Canyon looms ahead. Cross Mountain Canyon is a Class 4-5 tumult of steep continuous rapids run by experts in early summer for 4 miles to Deer Lodge.

The lower Yampa ranks among the classic river trips of the Colorado basin, here at cliffs below Harding Hole.

Below Deer Lodge the lower Yampa flows through one of the most exquisite boatable canyons of the Colorado Plateau. Take US 40 west from Maybell 17 miles and turn north on Deerlodge Park Road to the ramp. From there the Yampa runs 44 miles to the Green River at Echo Park, but most boaters continue on the Green for 27 miles of excellent water to the National Park Service's Split Mountain ramp upstream of Jensen, Utah—71 miles altogether.

Through the Yampa's lower canyon Weber sandstone veers high and rapids swell with early summer runoff. Upstream from the Green River 4 miles, a 1965 flood-induced debris flow created the run's big Class 3+ drop, Warm Springs. Scout and run far right for this pushy flush with a hole that can instantly flip, calming to Class 2 at low flow when the hole can more easily be avoided. Rafters embark May and June, or July with a heavy snowpack. By midsummer flows are low for rafts but suitable for kayaks and experienced canoeists. National Park Service permits, with substantial fees year-round, are in heavy demand until July. See www.recreation.gov.

Rivers of Idaho

With mountains deeply cut by waterways, abundant snow and rainfall in high terrain and northern reaches of the state, and more remote country and designated wilderness than almost anywhere else in the nation, Idaho is regarded as America's premier region for free-flowing rivers both wild and long. This reputation owes principally to four rivers: the Salmon, Middle Fork Salmon, Selway, and Snake River in Hells Canyon. But the state has 107,000 miles of streams, and 3,100 of them are considered good for rafting, kayaking, or canoeing according to *Paddling Idaho*.

Fine waters can be found all over the Rocky Mountain region, but the Northern and Middle Rockies in Idaho and Montana get the most rain and snow, and Idaho has five among the Rockies' ten largest rivers: the Snake, Pend Oreille/Clark Fork, Kootenai, Clearwater, and Salmon.

The state's hydraulic system is understood most fundamentally by knowing the route of the Snake River. This artery receives all the state's water except for three river basins in the far north plus the Bear River, which loops through the southeast corner of Idaho and becomes the principal source of landlocked Great Salt Lake. The Snake enters Idaho after maturing with generous runoff of eight sub-ranges of the Rockies in the Greater Yellowstone region of Wyoming. It flows onto the arid Snake River Plain, crosses southern Idaho's potato empire, then bends north to define the boundary with Oregon in Hells Canyon before angling west to the Columbia River at Pasco, Washington.

The North Fork Clearwater River flows from forested heights of the northern Rocky Mountains.

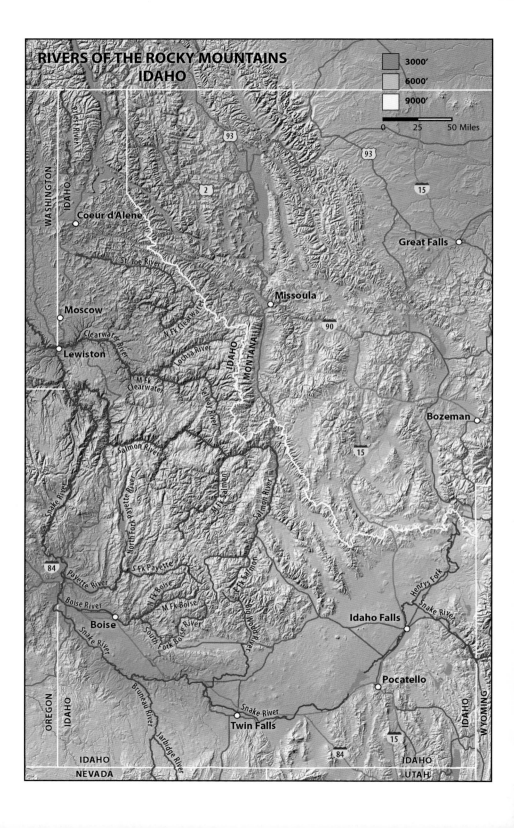

RIVERS OF THE ROCKY MOUNTAINS
IDAHO

3000'
6000'
9000'

0   25   50 Miles

WASHINGTON
IDAHO

Priest River

93

2

Coeur d'Alene

St. Joe River

Moscow

Great Falls

Missoula

90

Clearwater River
N Fk Clearwater

Lewiston

Lochsa River

M Fk Clearwater

IDAHO
MONTANA

Selway River

15

Bozeman

Salmon River

North Fork Payette River

M Fk Salmon

Salmon River

Snake River

84

S Fk Payette

Payette River

N Fk Boise

M Fk Boise

E Fk Salmon

Big Wood River

Boise River

Boise

South Fork Boise River

Snake River

Idaho Falls

Henrys Fork

Snake River

Pocatello

15

OREGON
IDAHO

Bruneau River

Jarbidge River

Snake River

Twin Falls

IDAHO
WYOMING

15

IDAHO
NEVADA

84

IDAHO
UTAH

Along the way the Snake receives a stellar collection of rivers draining highlands to the north and east. Centerpiece is the Salmon River system—lifeline to the mountainous heart of Idaho and legendary among all rivers in the West. Other tributaries include the Henry's Fork, Big Wood, Boise, Payette, and Clearwater. From the south and west, the Snake absorbs lesser flows of the Blackfoot and then the Bruneau and Owyhee, flowing not from the Rockies but deserts of the Columbia Plateau. Idaho's relatively small but water-rich panhandle north of the Snake basin includes the Spokane, Pend Oreille, and Kootenai Rivers.

Many of Idaho's Rocky Mountain rivers support one or more of the state's native coldwater fish species: chinook salmon, sockeye salmon, summer steelhead, mountain whitefish, bull trout, and redband trout, plus westslope, Yellowstone, and Bonneville cutthroat trout. Salmon and steelhead here were once among the most plentiful of their kind in the world, but dozens of distinct runs have been reduced to remnants or driven to extinction owing to downstream dams. Bull and cutthroat trout reside in native streams without going to sea but they too need long, cold, free-flowing reaches of clean water and are indicative of lotic qualities; a map of their survival is a map of healthy streams in the Northern Rockies.

With the Salmon River, Idaho boasts the longest undammed waterway in the West. For the past twenty years, a series of scientific assessments have confirmed that Idaho's once magnificent runs of salmon and steelhead can be recovered if downstream dams on the lower Snake River are eliminated, and to do this has been one of the most intense and prolonged efforts undertaken for river conservation in our nation's history.

While several other states have more mileage of streams protected in the National Wild and Scenic Rivers system, Idaho can claim some of the most cherished and significant from a nationwide perspective. The Middle Fork Salmon and the Middle Fork Clearwater, including its sources the Selway and Lochsa, were among the prestigious first twelve rivers and tributaries to be safeguarded with this gold standard of river protection. The Snake in Hells Canyon followed in 1975 as one of the most significant additions to the Wild and Scenic system because it halted imminent plans to build what would have been one of America's tallest dams above the mouth of the Salmon River. In 1978 the upper St. Joe was added, and in 1980 a long-sought 119 miles of the Salmon were included along with its tributary, the Rapid River. Portions of the Owyhee, Bruneau, Jarbidge, and tributaries were designated in 2009 in the desert of southwest Idaho.

The state Department of Fish and Game requires invasive species permits—bought at sporting stores, visitor centers, and online—for nonmotorized craft except inflatables under 10 feet long. Fees support efforts to prevent introduction of exotic plants and animals.

IDAHO RIVERS

Big Wood River
Boise River
Boise River, North Fork
Boise River, Middle Fork
Boise River, South Fork
Bruneau and Jarbidge Rivers
Clearwater River, Middle Fork
  and Main Stem
Clearwater River, North Fork
Henry's Fork of the Snake River
Lochsa River
Payette River
Payette River, North Fork
Payette River, South Fork
Priest River
Salmon River
Salmon River, East Fork
Salmon River, Middle Fork
Selway River
Snake River, "South Fork"
Snake River in Southern Idaho
Snake River in Hells Canyon
St. Joe River

Big Wood River

Length: 137 miles plus 12 of the Malad, total 149; 31 at Ketchum
Average flow: 439 cfs
Watershed: 1,972 square miles
Location: North and south of Ketchum
Hiking: Paved bikeways, headwater trails

Boating: Class 1 on tributary Silver Creek, canoe, kayak
Whitewater: Not recommended
Gauge: Hailey
Highlights: Cottonwood corridor, trout waters

The Big Wood, or "Wood River," is the waterway of Ketchum, Sun Valley, and Hailey, taking shape below Galena Summit in the Sawtooth National Recreation Area. The North, West, and East Forks join at the Boulder and White Cloud Mountains interface north of Ketchum. The Big Wood eventually meets the Little Wood, where the name changes to "Malad" River, with waters that push through stark blackened lava fields to the Snake River below Hagerman.

Eastward, the Little Wood flows through ranchland and dry volcanic terrain. Its tributary, Silver Creek, is a legendary trout stream with a Nature Conservancy preserve.

 ## FISH

Anglers cast for rainbow and introduced brook and brown trout all along the Big Wood River. Silver Creek is a world-renowned fishing destination for brown and rainbow trout.

 ## ACCESS

For the scenic upper river, take US 93 north from Twin Falls to Shoshone, then ID 75 north. The lower river can be seen from US 20 west of the ID 75 intersection at Sheep Bridge access, upstream from Magic Reservoir, and, below, at Malad Gorge State Park.

 ## HIKING

Trails ascend the North, West, and East Forks in the Boulder Mountains. Along upper reaches of the main stem, local angler paths lead out from Forest Service campgrounds and picnic areas. Below Easley Campground a short path enters a fine riverfront cottonwood grove 13 miles north of Ketchum. The BLM's Sun Peak picnic area and paths lie 1.5 miles north of Ketchum. In Ketchum, Hailey, and Bellevue 30 miles of bike and walking trails follow along or near the Wood River.

At the 874-acre Silver Creek Preserve a nature trail loops from the visitor center. From Ketchum drive south on ID 75 for 26 miles, turn east on US 20, and in 7 miles turn right on Kilpatrick Bridge Road.

The Malad River, with white foam in a black basalt canyon, can be seen from trails at Malad Gorge State Park; from I-84 at Bliss, go east on US 26 for 5 miles, south on 1200 E, and east on 2000 S.

Riffling among cottonwoods and willows, the Big Wood River speeds from its headwaters at the intersection of the Sawtooth and Boulder Ranges in central Idaho.

 PADDLING

Some of the Wood can be kayaked or canoed above and below Ketchum, but fallen cottonwoods make paddling hazardous. I've dragged over a lot of logs here and don't recommended it.

Silver Creek's Class 1 float runs 3 miles from Stalker Creek Bridge above the Nature Conservancy's visitor center to Kilpatrick Bridge, with an easily biked shuttle. Avoid anglers by paddling before Memorial Day; register at the visitor center.

Boise River

Length: 103 miles plus 102 of the South Fork, total 205
Average flow: 1,578 cfs
Watershed: 3,909 square miles
Location: In and near Boise
Hiking: Day hikes

Boating: Canoe, kayak, tubes, day trips
Whitewater: Class 1-2
Gauge: Glenwood bridge in Boise
Highlights: Urban greenway

In the city of Boise, this river is centerpiece to one of America's finest urban recreational greenways from the Warm Springs Golf Course to Ann Morrison Park and beyond. Envisioned with a progressive plan in 1964, the city pieced the greenway together by acquisitions and park improvements spanning decades.

The main-stem Boise begins at the South and Middle Fork confluence in the pool of Arrowrock Dam, built 351 feet high in 1911—the highest dam in the world then and fictional centerpiece of Wallace Stegner's greatest novel, *Angle of Repose*. Below, the river is re-impounded by Lucky Peak Dam, then released into the urban area. Several low dams appear upstream from Barber Park; below there the river runs with only minor diversion structures through much of the city. Farther downstream at least eight low dams require short portages.

 ## FISH

In the cold tailwaters of Lucky Peak Dam anglers cast for hatchery rainbow and brown trout. Below Boise, warming water supports channel catfish, largemouth bass, and smallmouth bass—all exotic fishes here.

 ## ACCESS

Julia Davis Park lies upstream of Capitol Boulevard on the southwest edge of downtown, across a footbridge from Boise State University. Other parks also have trails and boating access. See the city's Greenbelt map.

 ## HIKING

The paved riverfront trail draws walkers, runners, bikers, and roller-bladers even in winter—typically snow-free. The Bethine Church River Trail, 1.6 miles, is good for birding, with 150 species sighted; off East Parkcenter Boulevard and downstream from Barber Park the trail lies on river left.

 ## PADDLING

At the upstream (southeast) end of the city, put in at Barber Park; from downtown drive east on Warm Springs Avenue/ID 21 for 5 miles, turn right on South Eckert Road, cross the bridge, and go right into the park. Float 6 miles past twelve city parks to Ann Morrison Park—river left upstream of a low dam.

Through the heart of the state's capital the Boise River has become a community centerpiece since restoration and riverfront open-space initiatives were launched in the 1960s.

Novice floaters drift here in a festive atmosphere every summer day, though all should beware of shoreline snags and water sharply chilled by bottom-draw from the dam upstream—wetsuits are advised for tubers when it's not hot. Small Class 2 rapids appear at three diversion structures; the first may require portage at low flows. To miss the crowds go early, on weekdays, and in autumn. Avoid high-water hazards above 1,500 cfs.

From Morrison Park to Glenwood Bridge is another 5 miles of Class 1, but either embark below a dam located upstream from Americana Bridge or portage left. Three low dams follow. To take out, from downtown drive northwest on State Street 5 miles, go left on Glenwood, left at Plantation Shopping Center, and turn right before the bridge.

Also below Morrison a whitewater park with a formidable surfing wave lies west of downtown at 3400 West Pleasanton Avenue, 2 blocks north of Jefferson Street.

Downstream from Boise and neighboring Garden City the river splits into the North and South Channels for several miles around Eagle Island. *Guide to Idaho Paddling* describes a 13-mile Class 1 reach from Glenwood Bridge, past Eagle Island in the south/ left channel for more water and fewer logjams, and to Star Road Bridge, halfway between Eagle and Caldwell. This includes log blockages and three dams or diversions with at least one portage; beware of all and be ready to portage. The Star Bridge takeout is just above another hazardous dam.

Farther downstream, 14 miles of Class 1 flow with good birding and no diversion dams reported, but be alert to hazards. Start at Old Highway Bridge in Caldwell; take out on US 95 downstream of Wilder Bridge on river left.

Irrigation diversions shunt the lower river into ditches that return silty remains. At Old Fort Boise historic park, this Idaho artery joins the Snake River.

Boise River, North Fork

Length: 50 miles
Average flow: 555 cfs
Watershed: 379 square miles
Location: East of Boise
Hiking: Day hikes

Boating: Kayak, raft, day trips
Whitewater: Class 2-4
Gauge: See the Middle Fork's Twin Springs gauge and divide by two
Highlights: Whitewater day trip

Near Idaho's largest population center, this is the least developed of three Boise River branches and runs entirely through Sawtooth and Boise National Forests. Headwaters gather from 8,000-foot peaks and flow through 8 miles of the Sawtooth Wilderness. The westbound river then runs 11 miles partly accessible by four-wheel drive and another 16 miles by gravel road, ending at a 10-mile canyon with no road or trail down to the Middle Fork. The basin is recovering from a fire in 1994, followed by landslides.

 FISH

Here are native Idaho redband, bull trout, whitefish, and westslope cutthroat but also introduced rainbow trout.

The North Fork of the Boise flows from the Sawtooth Wilderness and then with a Forest Service road alongside for 15 miles between Deer Park and Black Rock Campground.

 ACCESS

From Boise take ID 21 northeast to Idaho City and 1 mile beyond turn right on FR 327, then onward to the North Fork's Black Rock Campground.

 HIKING

Most frontage has either dirt roads or no trails at all. A 1-mile path on river right lies below Black Rock Campground.

 PADDLING

From Barber Flat Campground to Black Rock Campground a beautiful 4-mile Class 2-3 run has the gravel FR 327 alongside, good for bike shuttles.

From Black Rock to Troutdale at the North-Middle Fork confluence, 10 miles of roadless Class 3-4 technical whitewater flow until midsummer. Watch for logs. To take out, from Boise drive ID 21 east 17 miles, and after Lucky Peak Dam and the Mores Inlet bridge, turn right on gravel to Arrowrock Dam and onward up the Middle Fork to the North Fork confluence at Troutdale Campground. For the North Fork put-in, continue up the Middle Fork on FR 268 for 5 miles, go left on FR 376, then climb and drop 7 miles on rough road to the North Fork at Barber Flat. Put in there or turn left and go 4 miles downstream to Black Rock.

Boise River, Middle Fork

Length: 52 miles
Average flow: 572 cfs
Watershed: 381 square miles
Location: East of Boise
Hiking: Day hikes and backpacking
Boating: Kayak, raft, canoe, day trips and overnights

Whitewater: Class 2-3+
Gauge: Twin Springs (which includes the North Fork) and divide by two
Highlights: Day trip and overnight boating, headwater hiking

From the lake-studded mountain crest at the Boise-Salmon River divide, the Middle Fork Boise flows 14 wilderness miles south to the backwoods community of Atlanta, where Kirby Dam—a low-head blockage built for mining in 1905—was replaced in 1992 at public expense of $2 million to contain toxic mining residue. Subsequent restoration of the mill site in 2006 reduced arsenic and mercury pollution. Below Atlanta a gravel road follows the Middle Fork.

 FISH

Natives include redband rainbow trout, cutthroat, bull trout, and whitefish; anglers cast for brook and cutthroat trout. The water is cold and unproductive but supports good numbers of fish.

Early summer runoff makes for an intricate raft run on the Middle Fork Boise below Lake Creek.

ACCESS

From Boise take ID 21 northeast, pass Lucky Peak Dam and the Mores Inlet bridge, turn right, drive the length of Arrowrock Reservoir, and continue on gravel up the Middle Fork to Atlanta, 50 slow miles from ID 21.

 HIKING

Tributary Queens River flows from high country of the Sawtooth Wilderness southward with a trail alongside, meeting the Middle Fork 4 miles downstream from Atlanta. The Roaring River and Sheep Creek also have backcountry trails. The Middle Fork road below Atlanta is good for riverfront biking on gravel but sometimes dusty.

 PADDLING

A stellar boating reach of 30 miles runs from a roadside put-in near the Queens River to Badger Creek—one of my favorite sections of accessible but lesser-known river in Idaho. I've done this as a small-raft, multiday trip after snowmelt of early summer but before flows bottom out—a terrific intimate-channel, low-volume option to Idaho's popular overnight trips that require permits. Tight water with Class 2-3+ rocky rapids, scenic cliffs, and forested mountains appear throughout, with occasional small campsites. For kayak or whitewater canoe outings of any length, the riverfront shuttle is easy by car or mountain bike.

The popular lower Middle Fork from Troutdale (just above the North Fork–Middle Fork confluence) down to Badger Creek Campground (above Arrowrock Dam's backwater) is a fine 11-mile Class 2 run through July.

Boise River, South Fork

Length: 102 miles plus 9 of the Ross Fork, total 111
Average flow: 958 cfs
Watershed: 1,306 square miles
Location: Southeast of Boise
Hiking: Day hikes and backpacking

Boating: Kayak, canoe, day trips and overnights
Whitewater: Class 1-3
Gauge: Anderson Ranch Dam
Highlights: Wild canyon, accessible float, camping in upper reaches

Longest and largest of Boise's forks, this river tours a scenic valley of Sawtooth and Boise National Forests. Below the Big Smoky Ranger Station, 22 miles riffle to Featherville with cottonwoods, ponderosa pines, and campgrounds alongside. In another 10 miles the river pools into Anderson Ranch Reservoir. Below it, the South Fork runs through a roaded and then wild canyon to backwaters of Arrowrock Reservoir, where the main stem begins.

 FISH

Natives include redband, bull trout, and whitefish. Anglers cast for brook and rainbow trout, especially in the cold tailrace of Anderson Ranch Dam through 10 roadside miles, heavily fished.

Below the Big Smoky Ranger Station the South Fork of the Boise transitions through forest to sagebrush terrain on its way to Featherville and lower whitewater runs.

ACCESS

For the upper South Fork, from I-84 at Mountain Home take US 20 east 31 miles to FR 61, go north to Featherville, then east on Shake Creek Road/FR 227/Big Smoky Road. See the paddling section for lower sites.

HIKING

Streams above the Big Smoky Ranger Station have trails alongside and extend across the Boise-Salmon River divide. The Big Smoky Creek Trail runs 18 miles to the mining site of Vienna. A gravel road from Big Smoky down to Featherville is good for riverfront biking.

PADDLING

An 11-mile Class 2-3 run from Anderson Ranch Dam to Danskin Bridge, boatable all summer, appeals to paddlers and anglers. Landsides in 2014 concentrated some rapids, amping this run up to Class 3 with pushy water for canoeists. The gravel road makes shuttling easy. To reach the dam, take I-84 to Mountain Home/exit 95, go east on US 20 for 20 miles, turn north on FR 134/Anderson Ranch Dam Road, and continue 5 miles to the dam. To take out, drive downriver past Cow Creek Bridge and 10 gravel miles total to Danskin Bridge.

Immediately below, with more of a whitewater scene, the South Fork's roadless Class 4+ Canyon Run starts at Danskin and flows 17 miles with takeout above Neal Bridge upstream from Arrowrock Reservoir. Rapids intensified after landslides in 2014; runnable all summer through the arid basalt-cliff canyon, easing from Class 4+ to Class 3-4 at midsummer flows. To reach the takeout from Danskin, drive north on FR 113 for 8 miles to Prairie, and go left (west) on FR 189 for 11 miles to the bridge—also reached from Boise via I-84 exit 64 and Blacks Creek Road. The combined Anderson Dam–Neal Bridge run totals 28 miles of Class 2-4+ all summer with no permit requirement—not much used as an overnighter, but the narrow corridor would require management attention if it was.

Bruneau and Jarbidge Rivers

Length: Bruneau, 153 miles; Jarbidge, 80 miles
Average flow: Bruneau, 374 cfs at Hot Springs; Jarbidge, 176 cfs (modeled)
Watershed: The Bruneau is 3,378 square miles including the Jarbidge, which is 472
Location: Southwest Idaho desert

Hiking: Canyon rim overlook, no trails
Boating: Kayak, small raft, overnights
Whitewater: Class 4-5 with portages
Gauge: Bruneau
Highlights: Vertical wall canyon, wilderness whitewater

The Bruneau, its tributary the Jarbidge, and the neighboring Owyhee River in southwestern Idaho carve America's largest and finest concentration of sheer-wall basalt and rhyolite canyons, 700 to 1,200 feet deep. New Mexico's upper Rio Grande basin has the only comparable entrenched and boatable volcanic canyons in the West. The yawning depths of these canyons are not even imagined from the featureless plateau topography until one steps to the edges of rimrocks.

These rivers are not geologically in the Rocky Mountains but are briefly included here as key Idaho rivers in the adjacent Columbia Plateau province. The Bruneau also has a 60-mile-long East Fork and 70-mile-long Sheep Creek. Owyhee forks lie in Idaho, but the river's more popular main stem in Oregon offers big, short-season whitewater.

Remote desert lifelines, these rivers provide habitat for mule deer, mountain lions, and peregrine and prairie falcons, plus the world's largest population of California bighorn sheep. The Bruneau hot springs snail—endangered by groundwater pumping—is endemic to 5 miles of the lower Bruneau on the Snake River Plain.

Congress designated the Bruneau, Jarbidge, and portions of the upper Owyhee in Idaho plus fourteen tributaries in the National Wild and Scenic Rivers system in 2009 following a decade of negotiations between Idaho Rivers United and ranchers who ultimately supported the reservation of water rights protecting both ranchers and instream flows. Most of the canyon corridors are public land administered by the BLM.

 FISH

Upper mountainous reaches of the Bruneau support rare native redband trout. Remnant bull trout persist in the Jarbidge—exceptional among desert rivers running cold and clear rather than warm and silty. A reduction of grazing within the canyons and headwaters has improved fish and riparian habitat, according to BLM managers.

 ACCESS

From I-84 at Mountain Home take ID 51 south to Bruneau, turn left on Hot Springs Road, at Hot Springs bear left on Clover Three Creek Road, and in 7 miles turn right at the Bruneau Overlook sign. Other roads are remote and when wet turn to grease that's troublesome even with four-wheel drive, even on flats, so rain or snowmelt—common during springtime boating season—limits access.

With its demanding and remote rapids deeply entrenched, the Bruneau River sculpts its canyon in southwestern Idaho's desert, seen here from an overlook 15 miles south of Bruneau.

HIKING

Perpendicular walls limit access to the Bruneau and tributaries. Short rim-walking strolls are possible at the Bruneau Overlook (see above). These canyons reach sizzling temperatures in summer. And don't forget rattlesnakes—it has never taken me long to stumble upon a camouflaged coil here.

PADDLING

Forty miles of the middle Bruneau, 30 miles of the Jarbidge, and 20 miles of lower Sheep Creek, with Class 4-5 rapids and portages, are run by expert boaters during high flows, usually in May depending on snowfall on mountains above, which in some years scarcely occurs at all.

Prepare for a maze of roads to reach any put-in; see the BLM's *Owyhee, Bruneau and Jarbidge Wild and Scenic Rivers Boating Guide* online. I recommend professional shuttles listed with the BLM. In addition to dozens of challenging rapids, two weirs are encountered. Commercial outfitters offer trips in the limited and potentially cold springtime season. Prepare for all weather possibilities.

Clearwater River, Middle Fork and Main Stem

Length: Middle Fork, 23 miles; main stem, 75; plus 100 of the Selway; total 198
Average flow: Middle Fork, 7,555 cfs; main stem, 15,001 cfs
Watershed: Middle Fork, 3,411 square miles; main stem, 9,384
Location: East of Lewiston
Hiking: Short walks

Boating: Canoe, raft, drift boat, day trips and overnights
Whitewater: Class 1-2, big volume
Gauge: For the Middle Fork add together the Lochsa and Selway at Lowell, Orofino (middle main stem), and Spaulding (lower river)
Highlights: Big river, Class 2 rapids, summerlong and autumn flows

Formed where the Selway and Lochsa meet at Lowell, the Middle Fork Clearwater is one of the cleanest large rivers in the West. After 23 miles it's joined by the South Fork at Kooskia to form the main stem—the third-largest river in the Rocky Mountains of the United States where it meets the Snake at Lewiston.

With the combined flows of the Selway and Lochsa, the Middle Fork of the Clearwater is one of the clearest rivers of its size in the Rockies. Here it riffles through its wooded corridor near Swan Creek.

The main-stem Clearwater drops through several strong Class 2 rapids in its road-traversed canyon between Kalmia and Orofino.

In 1968 the Middle Fork along with the Selway and Lochsa were among twelve charter members of the National Wild and Scenic Rivers system, banning Penny Cliffs Dam on the Middle Fork above Kooskia at Maggie Creek. Together these streams remain among the most outstanding members of this prestigious group of American rivers.

 ## FISH

Native salmon were blocked at the lower Clearwater by the Washington Water Power Dam in Lewiston until its elimination in 1973—perhaps America's first celebrated removal of a dam when Governor Cecil Andrus pushed the plunger and welcomed salmon back home. The native run had gone extinct, but without the dam, the Nez Perce tribe introduced chinook from other streams, and they now migrate upriver in summer.

Steelhead had surmounted the dam at Lewiston, and the Middle Fork remains one of the nation's top rivers for those anadromous trout, fished mostly in fall with a run lasting through March, though in 2019 there was no season owing to poor returns. Anglers use drift boats in this large river and target resident trout May through July.

 ## ACCESS

Take US 12 east from Lewiston 96 miles or west from Missoula 121 miles.

HIKING

US 12 runs alongside the Middle Fork and main stem, with heavy traffic. For a short stroll, visit Clearwater National Forest's Wild Goose Campground, 2 miles west of Lowell, and in another mile Three Devil's picnic area at the base of a beautiful rapid.

 PADDLING

With 1,000 to 15,000 cfs in summer, the Middle Fork is a superb big-water Class 2 river with excellent rapids, clear water, and cedar-lined woodland scenery. Strong flows continue after other rivers have dropped. Don't think it's just riffles seen at the put-in— several drops can challenge canoeists. The first 9 miles to Swan Creek through national forest are ideal, offering summertime paddling, tubing, paddleboarding, and swimming. In late summer all this emerges in its full glory of lucid pools, sandbars, and sharper drops. The river abruptly enters the Columbia Plateau of lava flows 17 miles below Lowell. Take out near the mouth at the US 12 Kooskia bridge.

Longer runs can be continued in big volume down the main stem 8 miles to Kamiah, with access at the US 12 bridge there. Below, the Clearwater continues 22 miles with intermediate landings to the Orofino bridge, passing through pines, grasslands, and striking basalt layers in an impressive canyon, though cramped by the road and railroad tracks. My favorite reach is 7 miles, Long Camp access (6 miles below Kamiah) to Five Mile access, with four Class 2 big-volume rapids and long pools.

Another 43 miles of Class 1 and occasionally 2 continue through the Nez Perce Reservation and private land to Lewiston with ramps off US 12. The lower Clearwater passes the industrial bulwarks of Potlatch and terminates in backwaters of the Snake River's Lower Granite Dam. Take out in Lewiston's Clearwater Park, east of the impounded Clearwater–Snake River confluence, off US 12 on the north side of Memorial Bridge— altogether 96 miles from Lowell, Class 1-2, July through October. Another 9 miles of Class 2 can be added at the top with the Selway River from Boyd Creek Campground.

Even with traffic and development, the Middle Fork–main stem offers one of the Rockies' epic long-distance river trips. Springtime flows on the lower river reach a Mississippian 100,000 cfs, to be avoided.

Clearwater River, North Fork

Length: 135 miles
Average flow: 5,980 cfs, 3,453 at Canyon Ranger Station above Dworshak Reservoir
Watershed: 2,444 square miles
Location: Northern Idaho

Hiking: Tributary day hikes and backpacking, biking
Boating: Kayak, raft, day trips and possible overnights
Whitewater: Class 2-4
Gauge: Canyon Ranger Station
Highlights: Semi-wild woodland river

Dworshak Dam flooded the lower 54 miles of this remote river in 1973 before opposition to large dams gained momentum in the politics of conservation. Even Interior Secretary Stewart Udall regretted not being able to stop the 717-foot-tall dam—third-highest in the United States—according to interviews with me in 1983. The reservoir eliminated one of the finest steelhead streams anywhere. Much of the near-wilderness valley had escaped logging, and free-flowing mileage of the 135-mile-long artery was rarely equaled anywhere in the nation.

Upstream from the reservoir, 81 miles of exquisite river remain—a major stream in its own right. Both the investment in driving and the river length justify an exploratory

The swift, pure North Fork Clearwater flows through its remote forest before hitting the backwaters of Dworshak Dam in northern Idaho.

For 81 miles the upper North Fork Clearwater flows dam-free—a haven for native cutthroat and bull trout.

week—or two. Fill up the tank and check your spare tire for this gravel-road marathon to a universe of delectable rapids, rocky shores, and forested canyons. Local people toting four-wheelers in the pickup and fly fishers come to camp, but this remains a lightly visited outpost even by Idaho standards on weekdays and in early autumn.

In my opinion, the North Fork Clearwater tops the nationwide list of rivers worthy of National Wild and Scenic designation but not yet included.

 FISH

Steelhead and salmon are gone, but the upper North Fork and pristine tributaries have some of the West's finest bull trout and westslope cutthroat populations. Rainbow trout and kokanee are still stocked in Dworshak Reservoir and migrate upriver into native fish territory, the brilliant red-and-green kokanee making quite a show in early autumn.

 ACCESS

If you want a driving tour of one of the more beautiful rivers anywhere, look no further. Every mile holds me rapt—once you get there, which is no small undertaking. Take US 12 east from Lewiston to Orofino, go east on Michigan Avenue/Grangemont Road to ID 11, angle north to Headquarters, then follow FR 247, enduring miles of clear-cut hell through industrial forests to Clearwater National Forest and Aquarius Campground, 4 miles upstream from Dworshak's backwater. Pavement continues upriver 6 miles, turning

Though fires have seared mountainsides like they have nearly everywhere through the Rockies, an expanse of deep green forest blankets many of the North Fork Clearwater's shores.

to gravel FR 247 and becoming FR 250 above Orogrande Creek; get a Clearwater National Forest map.

Farther upstream, FR 250 climbs through Black Canyon for 14 miles, while FR 255 bears right to ascend Kelly Creek and later reconnect with FR 250 above Black Canyon. After snowmelt cars can continue northeastward on FR 250 over Hoodoo Pass to I-90 at Superior, but be ready for a lot of rattling washboard.

 ## HIKING

No trails follow the North Fork but the riverfront road makes for excellent mountain biking, including Black Canyon, though I avoid the dust of weekends. Tributary trails ascend Weitas, Kelly, and Cayuse Creeks.

 ## PADDLING

The North Fork is an athletic Class 3-4 for kayaks or rafts at medium and moderately high flows, mostly Class 3 as levels drop. Peak runoff is extremely pushy, with log hazards. In July levels fall too low for boaters seeking a good flush, but I've found the lower 10 miles from Quartz Creek to Aquarius a fabulous technical run even in September—an outrageously beautiful nirvana for whitewater canoeists with a Class 3 kicker finale at Aquarius Campground. With promising runs upstream as well, I can't think of a finer place to spend a one- or two-week whitewater retreat.

From Deep Creek to Aquarius Campground the remote North Fork Clearwater offers an outstanding 16 miles of Class 3 whitewater.

The key North Fork demarcation is Class 5 Irish Railroad Rapid (milepost 39), unrunnable for many boaters and a stopper for all at some levels. Above this colossal boulder-drop, boating is good from Weitas Creek Campground for 14 miles of Class 3-4 (3 when low) with takeout at Deep Creek above Irish Railroad; flag this sweet little beach. Below Irish Railroad, use the milepost 38.9 access path for the Class 3-4 run of 6 miles to Quartz and on to Aquarius—Class 2-3 at low flows. Seldom run as such, the reaches above and below Irish Railroad would make great overnight trips if you don't mind the road. Above Kelly Creek, the upper North Fork's Black Canyon run rates Class 4 through early summer, while tributaries Kelly and Cayuse Creeks are Class 3-4.

Shuttles are a breeze on the waterfront road. The river gets little paddling use and virtually no overnights, but think Selway with a gravel road and no permit requirement. If these runs were in Alaska, many of us would want to fly there to do them.

Clear water, green shores, and rocky rapids make the 10-mile reach of the North Fork Clearwater from Quartz Creek to Aquarius Campground a whitewater gem.

Henry's Fork of the Snake River

Length: 130 miles
Average flow: 2,098 cfs
Watershed: 3,021 square miles
Location: North of Idaho Falls
Hiking: 1-mile and 4.4-mile hikes
Boating: Canoe, kayak, day trips

Whitewater: Class 1-3 with unrunnable sections
Gauge: Ashton
Highlights: Trout fishing, geology, waterfalls

Renowned for trout, the Henry's Fork of the Snake also has thundering waterfalls, unusual wildlife habitat, unique geology, and good paddling, both easy and hard.

The river rises with robust springs within a few miles of the Continental Divide west of Yellowstone National Park. Tributaries feed Henry's Lake, which was raised by a dam. Below it the river meanders and rushes through wetlands and forest to Island Park Reservoir, managed for lower basin irrigation. Six miles below it the river curves glassy through Railroad Flat at Harriman State Park—Idaho's first state park, legendary among anglers. Farther down the river plunges over three waterfalls including Lower Mesa—relatively unknown but in my opinion one of the showiest falls in the West.

The entire upper river occupies the Island Park Caldera—a 25-mile-diameter basin where volcanism left a broad depression perched in Rocky Mountain highlands. This collapsed bowl of volcanism is similar to that of Yellowstone National Park, as its genesis is the same. Both calderas resulted from the North American plate of lithosphere, or continental crust, tectonically migrating westward over a stationary "hot spot" deep beneath the earth's surface. A subterranean magma vent—imagine a stationary torch aimed upward at the surface of the earth from underground—produces volcanic activity by melting the hardened continental plate as it floats slowly westbound like a migrating geological skin overtop the underlying semi-molten layers of earth. Yellowstone's boiling pots and geysers now occupy the hot-spot position held earlier by Island Park.

Though wildness is diminished by development, roads, logging, and two dams, the upper basin is our closest cousin to another Yellowstone caldera; management, not intrinsic qualities, defines the major difference between the two. Here at Targhee National Forest, aerial views, for example, show that clear-cutting stretched to the horizon in the 1980s.

Besides trophy trout, moose, elk, and eagles reside, plus rare trumpeter swans with 6-foot wingspans. The elegant white birds depend on warm spring flows of the Henry's Fork—ice-free all winter in a frigid, but warming, climate.

After plunging through canyons at the caldera's margin, the river enters its intensively irrigated lower basin. Bridging the natural and fishery values of the upper Henry's Fork with agricultural traditions below, the Henry's Fork Foundation works with farmers, striving for better water-use efficiency.

After gliding through glassy upper miles known as some of the finest trout-fishing water, the Henry's Fork of the Snake thunders over Lower Mesa Falls.

 ## FISH

Fly Fisherman editor John Randolph called the upper Henry's Fork "the premier dry fly fishing stream in the entire world." Few waterways have this combination of clean and cold spring-fed flows, low gradient, and insect life. The mirror-like surface at Railroad Flat supports introduced rainbows, but native cutthroat also survive in the upper river.

 ## ACCESS

From Idaho Falls drive north on US 20 to Ashton, then east on ID 47 to the waterfalls, or continue on 20 to the upper river.

 ## HIKING

For Lower Mesa Falls, drive to Ashton, turn east on ID 47/Mesa Falls Scenic Byway, pass Bear Gulch Ski Area, park at Grandview Overlook, and walk to the 65-foot drop. Northward on ID 47 another mile, turn west on FR 295 to the Upper Mesa Falls visitor center and a mile-long trail to the 114-foot falls.

Continue north and reconnect with US 20 at Harriman State Park. For the Coffee Pot Rapids Trail, proceed north on 20, bridge the Buffalo River, in 2 miles turn left (west) on FR 030, go 1 mile, turn right on Flat Rock Road/FR 130, go 2 miles, and turn left on FR 311 to the trail, 4.4 miles out and back.

PADDLING

For a gentle cruise, paddle 3.6 miles of Class 1 all summer from Big Springs to US 20 at Mack's Inn, negotiating a log or two. Take US 20 north of the Buffalo River almost to Mack's Inn, turn right on Big Springs Loop Road/FR 059, go 4 miles to Big Springs, and turn north to the Big Springs Water Trail. To take out, drive from Mack's Inn north on US 20 across the Henry's Fork bridge, take an immediate right, and go 0.4 mile to a pullout. No fishing allowed here!

Downstream from Mack's Inn and US 20, the Coffee Pot Rapids run of 6 miles continues through July. Don't be fooled by the stream's gentle demeanor thus far; here a gorge-bound Class 3 section runs half a mile. Put in upstream at Mack's Inn. To take out, drive from there southward on US 20 3.5 miles, turn west on FR 030, and go 2 miles to McCrea Bridge Campground. Class 3 rapids can be avoided by taking out before them at Upper Coffee Pot Campground, river left.

A separate 4-mile Class 2 run with rock gardens through Box Canyon flows downstream all summer from the Buffalo River confluence. To put in, take US 20 south from Mack's Inn 5 miles, turn west, and go 1 mile to the base of Island Park Dam. To take out, drive US 20 south from Mack's Inn 10 miles, turn west on Old Highway 191, and go to the Last Chance ramp. Paddle midday and avoid anglers in this popular fishing reach.

Lochsa River

Length: 60 miles plus 27 of Crooked and Brushy Forks, total 87
Average flow: 2,829 cfs
Watershed: 1,182 square miles
Location: Northeast of Lowell, 121 miles west of Missoula
Hiking: Day hikes, backpacking up wilderness tributaries

Boating: Kayak, raft, day trips
Whitewater: Class 3-4+
Gauge: Lowell
Highlights: Rapids, whitewater canyon without development, tributary wilderness

Like the famed Selway River, the twin but northerly Lochsa flows with mint-tinted whitewater through evergreen forests to the confluence, together forming the Middle Fork Clearwater. This is one of the West's most intact and undeveloped rivers that also has a major road through its corridor, much of it lined with magnificent western redcedars on the road-free south side. The entire main stem down from the Powell Ranger Station is designated Wild and Scenic.

A fly fisherman casts for cutthroat trout in the Lochsa River near the Split Creek footbridge.

High water during the snowmelt of late spring through midsummer makes the Lochsa River a national and international destination for expert whitewater paddlers.

At declining flows in late summer the lower Lochsa makes a great Class 2-3 canoe run, here below Knife Edge Campground.

Runoff begins in Lolo Pass at the Idaho–Montana border—enshrined as the forbidding heights where Lewis and Clark ate horses to avoid starvation in September snowstorms.

Attempting to cross the same route but in a remarkably different way 209 years later, industrial "mega-loads" of Alberta-bound oil-drilling equipment 300 feet long and 30 feet high were halted in 2014 on the Lochsa highway—not by snowdrifts but by Idaho Rivers United and today's Nez Perce Indians standing in the road and objecting to the industrial priority given to the Lochsa's Wild and Scenic corridor. Their precedent-setting case argued that the Forest Service obligation under the Wild and Scenic Rivers Act included addressing threats involving a major highway, and the industrial transports were stopped.

 FISH

Native steelhead spawn in the Lochsa and tributaries, and introduced chinook have somewhat replaced the native run extirpated by the now-removed Washington Water Power Dam at Lewiston. However, all anadromous runs are sharply reduced by down-stream dams on the Snake River. The Lochsa is now known as a westslope cutthroat stream and supports rainbow trout, bull trout, and mountain whitefish. Snorkeling in the transparent pools is a good way to see these fish.

 **ACCESS**

Take US 12 east from Lewiston 97 miles to Lowell at the Lochsa-Selway confluence. Another 78 miles ramp up the western front of the Bitterroot Range while the Lochsa churns through the conifer canyon. Among all Wild and Scenic Rivers, this may be the one most seen from a road.

 HIKING

While only angler paths touch the shores here and there, trails ascend wooded tributaries in Clearwater National Forest. The DeVoto Grove's interpretive path among 2,000-year-old western redcedars, highly deserving of reverence, lies 12 miles west of Lolo on US 12. Another 10 miles downstream the trail to Jerry Johnson Hot Springs crosses a Lochsa footbridge and leads 1 mile south to the thermal pool along Warm Springs Creek. I would now visit this renowned soak only off-season.

 **PADDLING**

The upper Lochsa, for 20 miles from Papoose Creek to Grave Creek, is mostly Class 3 boating at medium-low flows with continuous gradient. Downstream it claims some of the West's most outstanding road-accessible rapids for 25 miles to Knife Edge Campground and attracts expert kayakers to Class 5 on high flows of early summer, Class 3-4 through midsummer, and low-water but still-difficult runs lingering later. Other accesses are available.

Finally, 11 miles of Class 2-3 continue where I've had great canoeing even in late summer to the Lochsa's end, with takeout at Three Rivers Resort—no fee, so be generous at the store. Or take out 2 miles upstream at the Pete King Creek pull-off.

Payette River

Length: 83 miles plus 110 of the North Fork, total 193
Average flow: 2,958 cfs
Watershed: 3,311 square miles
Location: North of Boise
Hiking: Short strolls at access areas

Boating: Kayak, raft, canoe, day trips
Whitewater: Class 2-3+
Gauge: Horseshoe Bend
Highlights: Lively whitewater all summer with easy access

The main-stem Payette flows from the North and South Forks confluence at Banks. Below there excellent whitewater is followed by gentler currents to the backwater of Black Canyon Dam. The lower river's braided channels with diversions weave through farmland to the Snake River.

 FISH

In 1924 Black Canyon Dam upstream from Emmett halted rich runs of salmon and steelhead to the upper river, and in the 1960s Hells Canyon dams on the Snake terminated all salmon on the Payette, now a rainbow trout fishery upstream of Horseshoe Bend, also

The Payette River below its North and South Forks juncture at Banks is Idaho's most popular Class 2-3 whitewater, with strong flows all summer and fall.

with brown trout and native whitefish. From Emmett downstream, exotic smallmouth and largemouth bass, channel catfish, and black crappie do well.

 ## ACCESS

From Boise take ID 55 north to the Payette at Horseshoe Bend and on to Banks. The lower river lies off ID 52 between Emmett and Payette.

 ## HIKING

Some access areas and pullouts have short walks; see the South Fork for headwater hikes.

 ## PADDLING

Idaho's most popular whitewater run is the "Main"—8 miles of Class 3–3+ along ID 55 from Banks to a pullout, Beehive Bend, prime for kayakers and expert canoeists when low, boatable summerlong with a festive weekend scene. A small fee is charged for Forest Service access at Banks and other Payette ramps.

Below Beehive, Class 2+ appeals to whitewater canoeists for 6 miles to a takeout along ID 55 north of Horseshoe Bend by 1.8 miles.

Separated from that run by a diversion dam (portage left if paddling through), 10 miles of easier Class 2 run from ID 55 to Montour Road Bridge. At mile 5 stay right past a runnable rock dam. To put in, drive just south of the ID 55 bridge below Horseshoe Bend (first bridge coming from Boise), and turn west on Old Emmett Road to a pullout. To take out, from ID 55 at Horseshoe Bend turn west on ID 52, go 9 miles, turn left on Monture Road, and go 1 mile to river left at the bridge.

Payette River, North Fork

Length: 106 miles plus 4 of Trail Creek, total 110
Average flow: 1,292 cfs
Watershed: 928 square miles
Location: North of Boise
Hiking: Headwater trails

Boating: Canoe, kayak, day trips
Whitewater: Class 1-5
Gauge: Banks
Highlights: Varied upper reaches including quiet meadow meanders, extreme rapids below

Though principally known for its lower reach—a world-class tumult of Class 5 whitewater—moderate and easy flows of the North Fork Payette lie upstream near McCall and Cascade.

Lower reaches were threatened by the Gem Irrigation District's 1980s hydroelectric diversion plan that would have depleted flows below Cascade, fought by paddlers and ultimately dropped.

 FISH

The lower North Fork is not good fish habitat owing to channelizing effects of the railroad and highway, plus Cascade Dam's warm releases. Headwaters support rainbow trout.

Gentle flows of the North Fork Payette downstream of McCall wind through wetland meadows for 9 miles from Sheep Bridge to Smylie Lane.

At an abandoned mill site in the town of Cascade, Kelly's Whitewater Park has been constructed with waves and rapids for kayakers and surfers.

 ACCESS

From Boise take ID 55 north to Banks and upstream to McCall.

 HIKING

Minor paths reach the water from pullouts. A trail from Upper Payette Lake climbs 3 miles to headwaters of Twentymile Creek.

 PADDLING

The North Fork has the unusual paddling distinction of offering fine Class 1 beginner boating and also the most extreme Class 5 torrent of whitewater regularly kayaked in the Rockies.

Moderate in comparison, a McCall "town run" of 4 miles, Class 2-3, runs to Sheep Bridge through July or so; park and start at the Payette Lake dam along ID 55 in McCall. Take out at Sheep Bridge; drive busy ID 55 to the south end of town, turn west on Deinhard Lane, go 0.5 mile, turn left on Mission Street, and in 0.3 mile turn oblique right on gravel to Riverfront Park at Sheep Bridge.

Next, 9 miles of serpentine Class 1+ flow through July below Sheep Bridge. For the takeout, follow ID 55 south from McCall 8.6 miles, turn west on Smylie Lane, go 3 miles on washboard gravel, cross the bridge, and turn right. Watch for logs.

The lower North Fork Payette draws extreme whitewater boaters to a continuous escalator of Class 5 gradient.

In the town of Cascade, Kelly's Whitewater Park's suite of Class 2 drops with Class 3 waves and holes was constructed at an abandoned sawmill site, with good flows all summer. Approaching Cascade from the south, cross the North Fork bridge and turn right at the sign.

South of Cascade, 10 miles of Class 1 summerlong offer mountain views to the west, good birding, and nominal development but a lot of cows. One of few runs in this book that's totally Class 1 without rapids, it's great for novice paddlers and a favorite among local stand-up paddleboarders who don't mind the distance. Launch from the town park by the ID 55 bridge at the south end of Cascade. To take out, drive ID 55 south 7.7 miles, turn west on Carbarton Road, and go 1.6 miles to the bridge.

From Carbarton Bridge to Smith's Ferry, 10 miles of popular Class 3 run strong all summer. To take out, drive ID 55 south from Carbarton Road 9.5 miles to a pullout near Cougar Mountain Lodge.

The famous 16-mile Smith's Ferry–Banks maelstrom with eighteen named Class 5 rapids drops 110 screaming feet per mile, structurally squeezed part of the way by road and railroad riprap on either side, and kayaked only by experts through late summer when Cascade Reservoir releases warm water. Roadside pullouts appear throughout. Forget pool-drop—this foaming extravaganza defines continuous big whitewater in the West.

Payette River, South Fork

Length: 80 miles
Average flow: 1,087 cfs
Watershed: 1,189 square miles
Location: Northeast of Boise
Hiking: Headwater day hikes and backpacking

Boating: Kayak, canoe, raft, day trips
Whitewater: Class 2-4 plus a portage
Gauge: Lowman (upper), Lowman plus Deadwood (lower)
Highlights: Scenic mountain river, spectacular canyon, whitewater

The upper South Fork Payette rushes through the Sawtooth Wilderness and continues with sharp rapids, intimate gorges, and thickets of willows to Lowman. Another 15 miles drop through an awesomely rugged canyon with a major waterfall. Lower reaches both rush and riffle, then steepen to the North Fork confluence.

 FISH

Though not highly productive, the South Fork has rainbow trout and is important for native redband and bull trout.

The South Fork Payette emerges from wilderness and descends through forests of the Sawtooth Mountains' west slope, here 3 miles above Lowman.

At Oxbow Bend, where the South Fork Payette begins to pitch steeper through its gorge, a hydroelectric dam and diversion were proposed but defeated in the 1980s, giving rise to the organization Idaho Rivers United.

 ACCESS

For the upper river, from Boise drive ID 21 northeast to Lowman, then upstream along the South Payette 21 miles to a right turn on gravel FR 524, which continues along the river 6 miles to Grandjean Campground and the Sawtooth Wilderness beyond. For lower sections, take ID 55 north from Boise and turn east on Banks–Lowman Road, paved the whole way.

 HIKING

Sawtooth sources lie east of Lowman, up South Fork Road to Grandjean Campground and on to 16 miles of trail reaching headwater lakes at the Payette–Salmon River divide— classic western high country. Downstream but still above Lowman, angler and campground paths appear along ID 21, and lower access areas have short paths to the river.

 PADDLING

From the Wapiti Creek bridge 2 miles below Grandjean Campground, 28 river miles of beautiful, mostly Class 2-3 water with a few steep drops run to Mountain View Campground, 1 mile upstream from Lowman. Logs create hazards in upper reaches and sometimes in Kirkham Gorge, above Mountain View. The lower third of this reach—8 miles from Helende Campground to Mountain View—is boated the most, through June or

Big Falls requires portage in the remarkable canyon of the South Fork Payette, 8 miles downstream from Lowman.

later if you like low, intimate flows. The entire reach is worth a week's paddling vacation for competent boaters through forests and mini-gorges with good biking on the roadside shoulder, many campgrounds, and streamside paths.

Below there, and from the Deadwood River confluence, the South Fork Canyon's formidable Class 4 challenge of 12 miles is for experts only, with mandatory portage of 40-foot Big Falls, seen in the distance upstream from a Banks-Lowman Road pull-off. With tantalizing views from the highway, this relatively little-known, narrow, crag-rimmed canyon is among the most spectacular in the West.

Next, the Class 3 "Swirly Canyon" runs 8 utterly enchanting miles deep within an inner gorge that seems to belong to another world and features some big waves and holes. Start at Danskin Creek Bridge 21 miles east of Banks; take out 14 miles east of Banks across from Hot Springs Campground.

Class 1–2 rapids resume for 7 miles summerlong from Alder Creek, in 5 miles passing the Middle Fork confluence (alternate access) to Deer Creek ramp. Drive 12 miles east of Banks, turn right on Alder Creek Road, and put in river left at the bridge. Deer Creek takeout is 4.6 miles east of Banks.

Finally, the Class 4 rocky "Staircase" is well named and offers 5 miles of popular kayaking all summer, Deer Creek ramp to Banks (ramp access fees charged).

Priest River

Length: 71 miles plus 28 of the Upper Priest River, total 99
Average flow: 1,718 cfs
Watershed: 981 square miles
Location: West of Sandpoint
Hiking: Day hikes and backpacking in upper reaches

Boating: Kayak, canoe, day trips and overnights
Whitewater: Class 2-3
Gauge: Priest River
Highlights: Semi-wild river of northern Idaho

The Priest River enters Idaho from British Columbia's Selkirk Mountains, flows 16 miles south into 4-mile-long Upper Priest Lake, then 3 miles into 19-mile-long Lower Priest Lake, followed by 42 swift miles to the Pend Oreille River in its reservoir behind Albeni Falls Dam near the Idaho-Washington line.

In northern Idaho the Priest River flows in late summer with rocky rapids below Priest Lake.

FISH

Below Priest Lake the river supports brook, rainbow, and cutthroat trout but is not a good fishery owing to warm releases from the dam upstream and to introduced non-native fish where bull trout, cutthroat, and whitefish once thrived. In a classic case of mismanagement, kokanee were introduced to Priest Lake followed by lake trout as a lure to fishermen, and then mysis shrimp were added as food for kokanee but they served ravenous lake trout better, which then decimated the kokanee, native trout, and whitefish.

 ACCESS

Drive west of Sandpoint to the town of Priest River, turn north on ID 57, and continue to the lakes and riverfront.

 HIKING

The Idaho Centennial Trail follows the upper river from Canada to Upper Priest Lake and along its wild east shore, then along Lower Priest Lake before veering east.

 PADDLING

With early summer runoff the river downstream of Lower Priest Lake is a technical Class 3 whitewater run or a rocky Class 2 when low, winding through Panhandle National Forest with undeveloped shorelines and only occasional road access among rolling conifer-clad mountains for 38 miles. This is generally considered too low by midsummer, but I've enjoyed a fine rock-picking Class 2 overnight canoe trip in August.

From the town of Priest River, take ID 57 north to the put-in at Priest Lake State Park's Dickensheet Campground, 4 miles south of Lower Priest Lake. Paddle to the town park in Priest River.

Also gracing northern Idaho, east of the Priest the Moiye River flows from Canada into the Kootenai with Class 4 whitewater in early summer.

Salmon River

Length: 425 miles
Average flow: 11,140 cfs
Watershed: 13,480 square miles
Location: Central Idaho
Hiking: Day hikes and backpacking
Boating: Raft, kayak, canoe, drift boat; day trips, overnights, and extended expeditions

Whitewater: Class 2-4
Gauge: Sunbeam (upper), Shoup (mid-river), White Bird (lower)
Highlights: Wilderness, rapids, campsites, best ultra-long river trip in America

The Salmon River has charismatic wildlife, whitewater, seductive campsites, hot springs, hiking trails, delectable summer weather, and good flows through autumn for nearly 400 miles—all that one might desire in a wild river vacation, extended expedition, and free-flowing haven to revisit again and again. Surviving salmon and steelhead are among the most critical in the West, and healthy spawning runs could be restored.

The Salmon's Path

The river can be divided into four sections. Headwaters in the Sawtooth Mountains, which rise west of the upper river, gather from some of Idaho's loftiest and snowiest country, yielding abundant cold water. With the White Cloud Mountains likewise contributing streams from the east, the river winds north between the two great

The upper Salmon riffles downstream from Redfish Creek with Mount Heyburn rising at the crest of the Sawtooth Mountains in the background.

ranges. Dozens of chilled tributaries are increasingly important to imperiled salmon as the climate warms.

The second section, flowing east then north from Clayton to North Fork, includes one of the longest nearly continuous cottonwood forests in the West through private ranchland with dozens of diversions for irrigating pasture, but the river's aquatic habitat and riparian woods are reasonably intact or restorable.

The third section cuts westward from North Fork to Riggins for 150 miles through the wild mountainous heart of Idaho. This legendary whitewater artery picks up the wilderness Middle Fork, the remote South Fork, and a flock of tributaries draining peaks a vertical mile above. An 80-mile roadless stretch offers one of the most sought-after river trips in the West where the Salmon borders the Frank Church–River of No Return Wilderness. In recent decades wildfires have seared this canyon, transforming it into a mosaic of burned and wooded slopes.

Finally the lower Salmon penetrates America's third-deepest canyon, behind only the Kings River of California and Hells Canyon of the Snake, which the Salmon joins at the confluence.

Natural Qualities

The Salmon may evoke more superlatives than any other river in the West. Dam-free and boatable mileage of the Salmon and Snake together total an unequalled 416 miles from the Sawtooth Valley hatchery weir to Lower Granite Dam's backwater on the Snake River upstream from Lewiston.

Tributary basins form the second-largest designated wilderness in America outside Alaska—only the ultra-spare Mojave Desert's Death Valley Wilderness with its 2019 additions is larger. A north–south distance of 155 roadless miles across the Salmon basin is one of the longest road-free spans in the West. No other river in America transects so much mountain country—continuous for the Salmon's entire length and 7,000-foot descent from alpine peaks to Hells Canyon desert, the hottest place in the Rockies.

All sections of the Salmon offer some of Idaho's most important habitat for bighorn sheep, elk, mule deer, mountain lions, mountain goats, black bears, and bald eagles.

The Salmon is the wildest and cleanest river of its size in the West, offering excellent habitat for imperiled salmon and steelhead. Water quality is excellent, and tributaries offer criterion spawning habitat for anadromous fish where natural barriers, such as waterfalls, do not occur.

Dozens of tributaries are important to the river's health and the stocks of fish that persevere. Among the larger contributors, the Pahsimeroi and Lemhi Rivers—once overflowing with spawning salmon—have been degraded with diversions and riparian damage, but better care and restoration has begun. Indian, Owl, Horse, Chamberlain, Sabe, and Bargamin Creeks join the Salmon as excellent tributaries in middle reaches.

Meeting the main stem in its wild midsection, the 90-mile-long South Fork is a renowned Class 4-5 early summer paddling run that meets the Salmon 24 miles above the Carey Creek takeout, so a permit is needed to continue on the main stem below the mouth of the South Fork. This tributary is like a smaller, steeper Middle Fork (see separate write-up) with habitat for native fish, including 20 percent of Columbia basin chinook. Logging of the South Fork basin triggered widespread erosion and landslides in the 1960s, still limiting the once-abundant runs of fish, and fires have charred large areas.

Hancock Rapids sieves through rock gardens in the midsection of the main-stem Salmon River. Recent forest fires have created a mosaic of burned and unburned mountainsides through much of the river's Rocky Mountain corridor.

Facing another siege, Idaho Rivers United and Save the South Fork Salmon have thus far fended off gold-mining proposals for the East Fork of the South Fork.

Conservation

Efforts to add the middle reach of the main-stem Salmon to the National Wild and Scenic Rivers system date to that program's inception and culminated in 1980 with inclusion of a 125-mile reach from North Fork down to Long Tom Bar above Riggins. This banned a concrete plug proposed in the heyday of big-dam building at a cliff-bound site called Crevice. In 1988 Congress passed a more limited law barring other hydroelectric developments that had threatened the lower 112 miles of river.

If four existing dams downstream on the Snake River were removed, the magnificent runs of salmon and steelhead would return, according to two decades of biological reports. Those dams are the least useful and most wasteful among eight on the Snake and Columbia below the mouth of the Salmon.

In 2016, and incredibly for the fifth time, a federal district judge ruled that the Army Corps of Engineers must revise plans to prevent the lower Snake River dams from driving salmon toward extinction, which some estimates project by 2040 if decisive action is not taken. The new plan must consider elevated water temperatures and elimination of the lower Snake River dams. Drafts of the plan in 2020 were widely criticized for inadequate consideration of dam removal (see the Snake River in Hells Canyon for more on this issue).

On another front, additional protection of open space and restoration of flows from current ranchland diversions could improve riparian and aquatic habitat and restore outstanding fish and wildlife values. The Idaho Fish and Game Department has worked to minimize effects of diversions along upper reaches since the 1950s, but more remains to be done. In 2018 Advocates for the West sued the Forest Service for failure to act on twenty-three diversions from headwater tributaries. In a lukewarm response, the agency agreed a year later to review the problem.

If riparian open space protection and in-stream flow improvements were combined with removal of the four lower Snake River dams downstream, the Salmon would become the most remarkable exemplar of river restoration and conservation in America and perhaps the world.

 ## FISH

The Salmon River's chinook population was likely the most abundant on earth before the Columbia and Snake River dams were built. Remnant runs still migrate 900 miles upstream from the ocean—one of the longest anadromous journeys anywhere. The fishes' headwater destinations are the highest-elevation salmon-spawning streams on the globe. However, all salmon and steelhead runs here are imperiled. The red and green sockeye of the Salmon headwaters in aptly named Redfish Lake survive by the frayed thread of a captive breeding program; one sockeye returned in 1992, seventeen in 2019, with year-to-year threats of extinction continuing.

Lacking the problem of downstream migration past the dams, many Salmon tributaries remain strongholds of bull trout and westslope cutthroat.

 ## ACCESS

To reach the upper basin, take ID 75 north from Twin Falls, or drive ID 21 northeast from Boise. The eastern basin is reached by US 93 north of Challis. For the lower river, take US 95 north of McCall.

 ## HIKING

To start with the headwaters, from Galena Summit on ID 75 north of Ketchum, drive 4 miles northwest, turn south on dirt FR 215 for 3 miles, and walk 2 miles to the modest woodland source at the Sawtooth and Smoky Mountains interface.

The Sawtooth Mountains on the west side of the upper Salmon's passage include some of the most spectacular craggy mountain landscape in America, and Sawtooth National Recreation Area is renowned for its stellar 700-mile trail system. For one highlight, hike the popular 18-mile Petit-Alice-Toxaway-Farley loop. Farther north, Sawtooth Lake is another memorable high-country destination.

Dozens of lower-elevation valleys and canyons offer excellent trails; along the middle Salmon, try Owl, Horse, Chamberlain, Bargamin, Indian, and Sheep Creeks, all best reached from raft-in sites on the river. A main-stem trail follows the Salmon's north shore 12 miles from road's end at Corn Creek downstream; from US 93 at North Fork drive 46 miles west to Corn Creek and the trailhead. Discontinuous sections of riverfront trail are reached by boat through the roadless reach between Corn and Carey Creeks.

 **PADDLING**

Peak flows up to 100,000 cfs on the lower river occur mid-May through June, and even normal high water makes many rapids harder than listed by a full class. Snowmelt wanes through July as runoff clears and settles into elegant pool-drop rapids. Levels remain adequate for boating all summer from the upper river in Sawtooth Valley to the mouth, while good weather persists into October at lower reaches.

Though seldom run as such, the Salmon is America's best ultra-long river trip without dams; a 425-mile journey is possible from Sawtooth Valley to the backwater of Lower Granite Dam on the Snake River in Lewiston. The only trip of comparable mileage in the West is the Colorado Plateau's Green River for 392 miles from Flaming Gorge Dam to Powell Reservoir on the Colorado River in Utah—a vastly different sojourn through the Great American Desert.

Portable toilets and fire pans are required from Corn Creek to Carey Creek and on the lower river. See Forest Service and BLM regulations.

For details about boating on the Salmon River and helpful mile-by-mile maps, see *The Upper Salmon River Boating Guide* by the Idaho Department of Fish and Game, Sawtooth National Forest, and BLM for 150 miles from Sawtooth Valley to North Fork. For the following 105 miles, North Fork to Riggins—the River of No Return section—see the Forest Service's *The Salmon: A Wild and Scenic River.* For the lower river—Hammer Creek (32 miles below Riggins) to Heller Bar on the Snake River—see the BLM's *Lower Salmon River Boating Guide.* Gaps between the coverage of these booklets are covered in other guidebooks and here.

Sawtooth Valley paddling features striking views of the Sawtooth Range immediately west. Flows above Redfish Creek drop low in late summer, and passage is blocked at the Sawtooth fish hatchery. Nonetheless, flows through midsummer below Decker Flat are a swift, twisting, willow-crowded, beautiful Class 2 paddle of 9 miles. Drive ID 75 for 45 miles north of Ketchum to Sawtooth Valley and turn west on Decker Flat Road to the bridge. Downstream I've carried river-left around the hatchery weir, but to get out above it, drive on ID 75 north from the Decker intersection for 6 miles to Gold Creek fishing access, where you park 350 feet from the river. Definitely flag this nondescript takeout. A wide shoulder makes shuttle biking good through Sawtooth Valley in spite of heavy summer traffic.

Next, put in a mile below the hatchery at Buckhorn ramp—6 miles upstream from Stanley. However, to protect spawning salmon, boating is closed August 15 to September 22 from the hatchery to Snyder Springs ramp, 20 miles below Stanley. In any event, here and elsewhere avoid disturbing spawning redds identified by oval-shaped mounds of clean gravel in riffling water (other gravel tends to be darkened by brown algae in late summer).

From Buckhorn to Mormon Bend Campground (7 miles northeast and downstream of Stanley) 12 miles of Class 2 offer breathtaking views back to the Sawtooth Mountains. Swift, rocky rapids run continuously for the first few miles to Stanley—Class 3 when high, receding in late summer to a tamer Class 2 maze of rounded glacial boulders.

Below Mormon Bend, 15 miles of Class 2-4 run to Torry's Hole ramp. Shotgun Rapids, Class 3-4, appears 4 miles below Mormon Bend, followed in 2 miles by the intimidating remains of Sunbeam Dam—a quick dogleg to the right but Class 4 with hazardous rebar exposed on the left. Road-scout and run right-center. Most boaters avoid this by putting in below Sunbeam at Yankee Fork access or below. Two Class 3

Rafts drift downstream on the middle section of the Salmon River in this evening view from a high perch on the Warren Creek Trail.

rapids follow in the 5 miles below Sunbeam. Snyder Springs Campground appears 12 miles below Mormon Bend and is the first put-in possibility below the spawning reach that's closed in late summer. Torrey's Hole cement ramp awaits 2 miles downstream.

Below Torrey's, delightful Class 1-2 water flows with mountain scenery, wildlife, frequent landings, cottonwood forests, ranchland, and remarkably few boaters after the first few miles. The East Fork enters from the White Cloud Mountains (see separate description). Rock-rubble wing dams, bulldozed up annually as diversions by ranchers, are dead ends if unscreened for salmon and can be troublesome to boaters; stay in the main current or favor the opposite side.

Unrecognized as such, this section of the Salmon is perhaps the West's finest extended length of Class 2 paddling water—excellent as an easy raft trip or a canoe journey for experienced paddlers. The river passes through downtown Salmon at 105 miles below Torrey's; resupply downtown with a quarter-mile walk eastward on Main Street. Another 23 miles of Class 1-2 go to North Fork, and then 4 miles to Deadwater Spring access. From Torrey's ramp to Deadwater makes a fabulous 132-mile road-accessible Class 2 trip all summer and autumn with no permit required and many access points.

From Deadwater to the Snake River the Salmon includes Class 4 whitewater, though most large rapids are fairly uncomplicated high-volume Class 3 drops. Jet boats ply lower parts of the middle reach and the lower Salmon near the Snake confluence.

The first big turbulence comes at Pine Creek, 20 miles below the North Fork—likely the hazard that dissuaded Lewis and Clark from following the Salmon's route to the Pacific and prompted them to name this the "River of No Return." The drop is worth a scout from the bridge just upstream.

At 46 miles below North Fork, the Corn Creek ramp marks the end of riverfront roads for the next 80 miles and the beginning of the most popular overnight floating reach—typically six days to Carey Creek, though the 46 miles upstream from Corn Creek are essentially wild and offer exceptional boating directly above the usual section. From Corn Creek down, Forest Service permits are required, in high demand and limited numbers, June 19 to September 8. I make a point of putting in above and passing Corn Creek after the reserved permit season ends; the weather is usually fine through September. Register at the ramp. Below there occasional riverfront resorts appear but most is wild.

The Middle Fork (see separate description) has joined from the south, forming a big waterway and powerful main-stem rapids in this quintessential Rocky Mountain river tour with idyllic campsites along the lucid green stream.

Most boaters scout the Salmon's larger drops: Black Creek, Big Mallard, Chittam, and Vinegar Creek; see the Forest Service's guide. Gnarly Black Creek comes 21 miles from Corn Creek and just below the former Salmon Falls Rapid, which is now flooded out by the landslide that created the Black Creek drop in 2011. Changing conditions at this freshly deposited bedload sourced in Black Creek—immediately upstream on the right—warrant a river-left inspection every time. At Big Mallard, 37 miles below Corn Creek, the unintuitive route at lower flows lies in an extreme left chute, pinched there by a rock and pour-over.

The South Fork enters at mile 56 below Corn Creek, and at mile 80 boaters take out at Carey Creek—the first good landing since the road to once-popular Vinegar Creek ramp, 3 miles upstream, has deteriorated. However, this eventful river has miles to go.

No reservations are needed to float the rest of the Salmon, yet the boating is exceptional, making the lower 110 miles a great option for rafters who don't plan their vacations

A gentle reach of the lower Salmon below Riggins reflects golden light of autumn; other sections of the lower river have rollicking big rapids.

ahead of time or fail to score a permit for the coveted River of No Return section or other classic western river trips. However, *avoid* the lowest reach of the Salmon during high flows (see below).

First, the lower Salmon winds 25 miles from Carey Creek to the town of Riggins, where long-distance boaters can resupply from a midtown ramp.

With 82 miles from Riggins to the Snake River, prepare for big-wave rapids. The first 30 miles to Hammer Creek ramp have US 95 alongside, long pools, straightforward but powerful Class 3 drops, sandy beaches, and intermediate access at nine sites including Lucile, 9 miles below Riggins.

Self-serve BLM permits are available at Hammer Creek where—favoring wilder terrain—many boaters choose to start their lower Salmon outing. Drive there on US 95 north of Riggins 26 miles, before the White Bird Grade turn west onto Old Highway 95, and follow signs.

Below Hammer Creek, through mostly roadless country, strong flows connect four linked canyons in the desert. I scout Snow Hole Rapid, Class 4, on either side, 28 miles below Hammer Creek. Big wave trains interspersed with campsites continue.

At 45 miles below Hammer Creek and 4 miles above the Snake confluence, Slide Rapid does not exist at low-medium flows, but at 20,000 cfs and higher this otherwise innocuous constriction produces a wave that without exception flips boats of any size. And portage is virtually impossible. Even the Grand Canyon of the Colorado has no such obstruction to river travel. All boaters should unconditionally avoid the lower Salmon at

The Selway River Trail is one of the West's finest long-distance riverfront hiking routes, here 5 miles up from its lower trailhead.

3.2-million-acre Frank Church–River of No Return Wilderness southward in the Salmon basin. Combined, they would easily form the largest block of wilderness in the lower forty-eight states.

The Selway's designation in the original Wild and Scenic Rivers Act halted the Penny Cliffs Dam proposal on the Middle Fork Clearwater from flooding far up the Lochsa and Selway. Instead, this is one of America's longer rivers protected in the Wild and Scenic program from source to mouth.

Hiking and campsites are premier, and snorkeling for fish is great in transparent water. The river is fed by wild tributaries including Moose Creek, which can double the flow about halfway through the float trip.

 FISH

Cutthroat populations are excellent, and bull trout thrive. A small number of salmon and steelhead that surmount eight deadly dams downstream on the Snake and Columbia Rivers make their way back to rich spawning grounds here. Superb habitat in this basin would be repopulated if the four Snake River dams downstream were removed (see Snake River in Hells Canyon).

 ACCESS

For the lower Selway, take US 12 east from Lewiston 96 miles or west from Missoula 121 miles to Lowell, turn south, and continue 18 miles up the lower river to Selway Falls—an

Massive boulders congest the lower river's channel at Selway Falls.

impressive extended boulder-jammed cataract—and another mile to road's end and the rafters' takeout.

Pack a lunch or two for any drive to the upper river: From Missoula head south on US 93 for 67 miles to Darby, in 4 more miles turn right on MT 473/West Fork Road, go 14 miles, turn right on Nez Perce Road, and continue 40 gravel miles to the end at Paradise Campground—one of the remotest road-accessible spots in the West.

 HIKING

The Selway Trail runs 50 wilderness miles from road's end at Paradise down to Meadow Creek above Selway Falls—among the West's finest riverfront backpacking routes, with dozens of white sand beaches, green pools, and foaming rapids in view. Summer is hot and the trail is known for resident rattlesnakes, though I saw none on my last hike of 7 splendid miles up from the lower trailhead. On the road to it, definitely stop for an eyeful of Selway Falls.

 PADDLING

Among seasoned river runners, a special awe surfaces at the simple mention of the Selway. Some value this trip even more than the Grand Canyon and Middle Fork Salmon. Lucid water roars in Class 3-4 rapids with gripping challenges through the 47-mile journey.

Recognizing that a range of river experiences are needed, and that the Selway's pristine nature could easily be marred, the Forest Service rations trips to one daily—America's only river so regulated for near-solitude. The downside is that independent boaters'

Exquisite wilds of the Selway River alternate in steep, rocky drops catching both sunlight and shadows with accumulating thunderheads overhead.

chances of scheduling a trip are less than one in forty. Along with the Grand Canyon, this is the hardest permit for noncommercial boaters to score.

Snow keeps the road to Paradise closed through May. Early June brings high flows with some of the most continuously difficult whitewater regularly run as a multiday trip in the West. Facing severe outcomes in the event of a flip and a long swim, early season boating is only for experts in strong teams. If the gauge at Paradise reads 6 feet, it means a thundering 20,000 cfs on the lower river and Class 5; 3 to 6 feet means really pushy Class 4; 1 to 3 feet means 1,500 to 8,000 cfs and Class 3-4 rapids with big water persisting until the bottom end of that spectrum. Popular raftable levels come in late June through early July, with intricate rapids and beautifully complex routing at lower volumes.

The reservation requirement is lifted after July, so an athletic low-water trip is an option for skilled boaters in hard-shell or inflatable kayaks. If flows are adequate to drag or carry over tight spots of the upper river, runoff is adequate much later for paddling below Moose Creek—also a pack-raft option via the trail. Others who want to see this wild passage can consider bypassing the permit requirement by going with an outfitter or by hiking.

The most challenging drops appear 26 miles below Paradise at Moose Creek, where flows can instantly double, and extend 5 miles.

See *Guide to the Selway River* by Duwain Whitis and Barbara Vinson. Shuttle for the 47-mile trip is 255 miles one way—one of the worst such ratios. Don't forget your take-out car keys! Professional drivers can save two days of time.

Below Selway Falls a splendid Class 2-3 outing summerlong runs 8 miles to Boyd Creek Campground. Another 9 miles of Class 2 run to the mouth, easily shuttled by bike. Though rarely run as such, the lower Selway makes a fine road-accessible overnight trip, with options to continue down the more developed Middle Fork Clearwater.

Snake River, "South Fork"

Length: 60 miles from Palisades Dam to the Henry's Fork
Average flow: 4,169 cfs
Watershed: 5,680 square miles
Location: East of Idaho Falls
Hiking: Day hikes

Boating: Canoe, drift boat, raft, day trips and overnights
Whitewater: Class 1-2
Gauge: Heise, Lorenzo
Highlights: Cottonwoods, cutthroat trout, wildlife, large canoeing river

From Palisades Dam, 270 feet high near the Wyoming border, the Snake flows to the Henry's Fork confluence in summerlong runoff through one of the West's finest cottonwood forests and outstanding habitat for Yellowstone cutthroat trout and wildlife.

Though this is the main-stem Snake—the same river that's famously scenic upstream in Grand Teton National Park and then rushing through Alpine Canyon—this section is locally called the "South Fork." Of course, a "main stem" cannot flow into a "fork," but the South Fork title distinguishes this from the river above and also from the Henry's Fork, which joins from the north and is sometimes called "North Fork" by Idahoans.

Geology here has transitioned from the Rockies to the volcanic Snake River Plain, but the mountain character of the Snake continues to the topographic outpost of the Menan Buttes at the Henry's Fork mouth. There the Snake ranks seventh-largest among rivers within the Rockies in the United States, but by the time it reaches the Columbia River the Snake grows to be the largest Rocky Mountain river south of Canada, by far.

Frosty nights of late September turn narrowleaf cottonwoods yellow and gold as the Snake River's "South Fork" makes its elegant passage through Swan Valley and beyond.

Here at the mid-Snake's upper end, the 11 miles below Palisades Dam traverse Swan Valley ranchland. Below, in Conant Valley, the road departs at mile 14 below the dam, and for the next 48 miles the Snake riffles through magnificent cottonwoods with gravel bars beneath basalt cliffs. Engelmann spruce in shaded pockets transition westward to drier terrain and then irrigated farms perched on bluffs. At mile 40 below the dam, river-size diversions are withdrawn, and then farmland encroaches with levees as the river curves toward the Henry's Fork and then to Idaho Falls.

The riparian corridor supports 126 bird species including half of Idaho's bald eagles plus ospreys, moose, elk, and beavers—all in precious habitat, as 80 percent of the Snake's total mileage across four states has been lost to dams, diversions, and development.

The wild section with cottonwood forests through Conant Valley was once threatened by the Lynn Crandall Dam proposal and then by golf course and housing developments— all rejected after contentious discourse.

 FISH

One of few high-volume, low-gradient rivers in the Rocky Mountains, this is excellent for Yellowstone cutthroat; 4,000 trout per mile draw anglers nationwide. However, the Bureau of Reclamation stores water upstream at Palisades Dam in winter, reducing flows to 900 cfs on average when 1,800 would be better for rearing trout. A revised release program is under consideration as of this writing. Introgression and crossbreeding of imported rainbow trout is the major threat to native cutthroat, and the Idaho Department of Fish and Game has placed weirs in key tributary spawning streams to block rainbows.

 ACCESS

From Idaho Falls drive east on US 26 to ramps at Byington, Conant Valley, Palisades Dam, and other landings.

 HIKING

The BLM's Canyon Rim Trail tours basalt bluffs from Black Canyon upstream 6 miles to Dry Canyon. On US 26 drive 18 miles east of Idaho Falls, turn left, cross Heise Bridge, and continue up the north shore to the trail. For the upper trailhead, take ID 33 to Victor and turn west on ID 31.

 PADDLING

Most boaters and anglers launch day trips here, but this section of the Snake is also one of the West's finest for overnight canoeing. Early summer flows are high but doable for experienced boaters. Summer is good, but autumn is great with cottonwoods turning gold. Free overnight permits require a portable toilet, fire pan, and small fee; camp at designated sites.

From Palisades ramp—river-right below the dam—16 miles riffle to Conant ramp, 2 miles below the US 26 bridge on river left. One mile above the bridge, cling extreme left and eddy-out to see the tiered cascade of Fall Creek as it tumbles into the Snake.

Below the US 26 bridge, the river arcs away from paralleling roads. For this stellar reach, put in at Conant, where commercial guides host a lot of anglers in drift boats.

Forty islands downstream are eligible for wilderness designation; 220 in all invite strolls among cottonwoods and gravel bars. Sloughs appeal as back channels for canoeists and might carry an intimate 100 cfs instead of the main channel's several thousand, but beware of snags. Waves and strong eddy lines can build with dam releases; tie boats when beaching. Take out 25 miles below Conant at Byington ramp on the left; from Idaho Falls drive east 17 miles on US 26, turn north on 175E, and right on Ririe Highway to the ramp. See the BLM's *South Fork of the Snake River Boating Guide* for multiple landings.

Below Byington, avoid three diversion structures blocking right-side canals, but otherwise favor the Snake's right side. Once beyond the diversions, 1.5 miles below Byington, assiduously stay right to avoid the "Great Feeder," coming ominously into view on the left. This 8-foot-tall cement headgate sucking off one-third or more of the river creates a serious hazard to be avoided at all costs; no warnings were posted at this potentially fatal obstruction when I last ran this stretch years ago.

Below Byington 21 miles, and just beyond the mouth of the Henry's Fork, boaters can beach at the base of the 800-foot Menan Buttes and walk the strikingly bare black lava slopes to the summit for a view of the river's exit from the Rocky Mountains and its entry onto the volcanic Snake River Plain. In another 2 miles the Menan Buttes ramp appears on the left; from Rexburg drive ID 33 west, cross the Henry's Fork, continue 2 miles, turn south on Twin Buttes Road, and go to the Snake River bridge.

Springtime below Conant Valley on the Snake River bursts with cottonwoods' new green leaves along the waterfront.

The "South Fork" of the Snake, at the bottom of this photo, meets the Henry's Fork, on the right, at the edge of the 800-foot-tall Menan Buttes—two of the world's largest cones of volcanic tuff.

For those who want the longest trip lacking dams, another 16 miles with increasing farmland but mostly BLM frontage continues to the ID 48 bridge and left-side Mike Walker ramp. From Palisades to there makes a 78-mile trip without major rapids or dams, canoeable all summer. Below ID 48, three low but portageable dams block the Snake through another 19 miles to Idaho Falls and its dammed rapid at center city.

Snake River in Southern Idaho

Length: 475 miles from Idaho Falls to Brownlee Dam backwater
Average flow: 17,582 cfs at Brownlee
Watershed: 54,202 square miles to Brownlee
Location: Southern Idaho
Hiking: Short walks

Boating: Canoe, kayak, raft, day trips and overnights
Whitewater: Class 1-5 and unrunnable
Gauge: Milner
Highlights: Geology, waterfalls, whitewater

The Snake's midsection below the Henry's Fork is severely affected by diversions, agriculture, and development across the Snake River Plain, including sixteen of the entire Snake's twenty-four dams that impound half the river's full mileage. However, some reaches on the plain still offer important natural values and a hint of what was once among the most extraordinary hydrologic and biological phenomena in the West. This section of the Snake lies outside the Rocky Mountains, but within Idaho, so I cover it here but only briefly. See my book *The Snake River: Window to the West* for more on this fascinating but vexed length of river.

A splendid cottonwood reach of 12 miles, the Fort Hall Bottoms, lies upstream of the 52-mile-long American Falls reservoir. Put in at Blackfoot, upstream from the US 26

At Star Falls basalt bedrock squeezes the Snake River into a narrow passage. Though normally diverted to a trickle here, springtime snowmelt can reach 12,000 cfs.

bridge. Beware of a canal to the right, also a rock dam (drag boats) and two other diversions. The river then enters the Fort Hall Bottoms, with many sloughs. Paddle to the Ferry Butte/Tilden bridge southwest of Blackfoot; to get there, drive US 91 south and turn right on Ferry Butte Road.

Rarely seen, and an Idaho secret that's scarcely known beyond the local area, Milner Dam is a monument to untempered water diversions in the West. At this antiquated structure nearly all the flow is taken from a river whose upstream mileage is longer than Pennsylvania's entire Delaware River, but with flows shunted into river-size canals left and right. Here the Snake is America's largest waterway that's virtually all diverted at one site, leaving a parched riverbed much of the year.

But, in late spring of years when the Snake overflows its upriver dams, a 1.3-mile maelstrom of Class 5 whitewater below Milner becomes the most intense rapid of its volume and length west of Niagara Gorge. A few expert kayakers run this on 10,000 to 15,000 cfs, with portage at a river-wide hole at 8,000 cfs and below.

To see the dam—and either the depleted river channel through summer or a surge of whitewater in springtime—take I-84 east from Twin Falls to exit 194, go east on the frontage road, and south on Milner Road 4 miles. When last there I was able to walk across the dam and downstream for a good look at the canyon.

Star Falls, or "Cauldron Linn," follows 7 miles below Milner. This bedrock slot in the plain is nearly dry most of the time but at peak runoff churns through a 30-foot slanted drop. From I-84 exit 194, go west on the frontage road 4 miles, then south on Murtaugh Road.

Murtaugh Gorge follows for 14 miles. When flowing in springtime it contains astonishing whitewater at 8,000 to 20,000 cfs, attracting expert kayakers to a Class 4+ run, with a likely portage. Hansen Bridge, east of Twin Falls, offers a bird's-eye view; take I-84 exit 182 and drive to the bridge immediately southward. A walk across this height reveals a geologic and hydrologic phenomenon no one would expect to see from surrounding lava flats. In its natural state, the sheer-wall Murtaugh would be among the more extraordinary canyons of the West with its Niagara of whitewater instead of sun-baked bedrock.

Twin Falls comes next. The north side of this 180-foot drop is diverted for hydropower, and the south side reduced to an algae-scum trickle most of the time. But for a remarkable eyeful during springtime crests, take US 93 to Twin Falls, turn east on US 30, go 5 miles, and turn north at the sign.

Downstream 2.5 miles, Shoshone Falls drops 212 feet. For views from the rim, from US 93 in Twin Falls go east on CR G2 for 3 miles, then north on E4000N/Falls Avenue.

Much of the Snake River's oceanic volume diverted upstream bubbles back into the river through Thousand Springs—the biggest groundwater discharge basin in the West. The springs riddle the north side of the river upstream of Hagerman, and virtually all are affected by hydroelectric turbines tapping the vertical drops or by diversions for fish farms where nine in ten trout bought in restaurants nationwide are raised in concrete vats. At pocket refuges an imperiled sculpin and rare snails survive—chief reasons that additional diversions have not been piped aside.

Replenished, the Snake River's Hagerman Reach, big-volume Class 2-3, runs for 7 miles northwest of Hagerman. Rafters launch all summer for family trips just off I-84. Drive US 30 northwest from Hagerman 1 mile, and turn left to the ramp below the Lower Salmon Falls power plant. Take out at Bliss Bridge; from I-84 exit 141,

Seen from ID 50's Hansen Bridge, the Snake River in Murtaugh Gorge barely flows across bedrock that would be covered with water if it weren't for diversions upstream.

go west into Bliss, turn left on River Road, before the bridge go right, then right again to the ramp.

West of Glenns Ferry, Three Island Crossing State Park marks where Oregon Trail pioneers forded the Snake as it spread into three channels, now too deep to wade (I know!).

Farther downstream, Swan Falls is the last of the middle Snake dams, followed by 116 miles to Brownlee Reservoir. The first 32 miles to Marsing pass 300-foot-high basalt walls in the BLM's Birds of Prey Natural Area hosting the greatest concentration of nesting raptors in America. The river runs all year, but May is best to see fifteen species of hawks, eagles, and falcons. Below the first bridge avoid a right-side canal. To launch, take I-84 exit 44, go 8 miles south to Kuna, then 18 miles on Swan Falls Road to the dam. A 15-mile Class 1-2 paddle ends at Walters Ferry; from Nampa take 12th Avenue Road south 20 miles.

Beyond the canyons, 17 miles from Walters Ferry to Marsing supports white sturgeon, North America's largest freshwater fish, though they fail to reproduce because many miles of clean free-flowing water are needed for sturgeon eggs to tumble in the current.

From Marsing to Brownlee Dam's backwater near Weiser, I somehow managed to find doable campsites through 84 miles of Class 1 dominated by industrial agriculture, food processing plants, levees, and riprap, but the river also passes eighty-six islands of the Deer Flat National Wildlife Refuge—reserved for wildlife and, owing to a lack of flood flows, mostly thick with brush.

Snake River in Hells Canyon

Length: 105 miles in Hells Canyon, 1,080 for the entire Snake River
Average flow: 18,500 cfs at Hells Canyon Dam, 56,000 at the Snake's mouth far below Hells Canyon
Watershed: 109,000 square miles in the entire Snake basin
Location: West-central Idaho

Hiking: Day hikes and backpacking
Boating: Raft, kayak, drift boat, overnights
Whitewater: Class 3-4, very big volume
Gauge: Hells Canyon Dam
Highlights: Big whitewater, deep canyon

Flowing from headwaters in Wyoming and then across Idaho to Oregon and ending in Washington, the Snake is the Columbia's largest tributary and the twelfth-largest river in the United States. Half the flow enters via Idaho's Salmon and Clearwater Rivers, bringing Rocky Mountain runoff to the lower Snake. In length, this river exceeds the Columbia by 126 miles at the confluence of the two but drains drier country, delivering only 30 percent of the flow where the two meet in Pasco, Washington.

Typical of Snake River rapids in Hells Canyon, whitewater above Pittsburg Landing pushes powerfully as rafter Bill Sedivy negotiates a summertime flow of 14,000 cfs.

After traversing its midsection across southern Idaho, the Snake carves the depths of Hells Canyon—the river's last free-flowing reach before encountering four dams and back-to-back reservoirs to the Columbia and then four more dams to tidewater.

Natural History

Hells Canyon is a major landmark of the West, with thunderous rapids and wild shorelines beneath basalt walls and arid slopes tiered up to forests, meadows, and peaks. Altogether it is a museum of biological diversity spanning a mile-and-a-half vertical rise above continental cleavage separating the Seven Devils Mountains in Idaho from the Wallowa Range in Oregon—both geologically part of the Columbia Plateau, though in other respects, including plant life and general appearance, they might be considered western outliers of the greater Rocky Mountain chain.

The river scours America's second-deepest canyon. Cross-sections of topographic maps reveal that slopes drop 5,620 feet from the Oregon side and 7,900 from Idaho's Seven Devils—deeper than the Grand Canyon of the Colorado, though the full gulf of topographic extravaganza is unseen because cliffs and sub-peaks block the views. Only the Middle Fork Kings in California's Sierra Nevada churns deeper beneath summits—8,000 feet up on both sides there. But the Snake has more of a canyon feel—big river beneath steep walls—while the Kings is more a mountain stream among peaks.

The Snake River in Hells Canyon is joined by the Salmon River, entering in the center of the photo from the right. Cherry Creek runs north on the lower left; Divide Creek runs south on the lower right.

The Snake's geologic past was even more cataclysmic than its present. Hardened lava once blocked the water's passage north and dammed up the ancient Lake Idaho, which extended 300 miles upstream from today's canyon to present-day Hagerman. From this inland sea—longer than Lake Erie—the ancestral river amazingly spilled not north as it does today, but westward as a great waterway across today's southern Oregon to the Klamath basin in California and to the Pacific.

Faulting eventually fractured the north side of the lake's impeding lava deposit, and a Columbia-bound stream eroded into headwalls north of today's Pine Creek, eventually breaching them enough to unplug Lake Idaho and release it northward. This surgically down-cut the route of today's Snake in Hells Canyon by carving through a patchwork of volcanoes, Columbia basalts, and underlying sedimentary and igneous rocks earlier accreted by terranes that now variegate the inner gorge in gray and brown.

Another cataclysm descended 15,000 years ago when ice age Lake Bonneville—big as Lake Michigan—similarly broke free from bedrock constraints upstream in Utah and ripped through the Snake's corridor from Pocatello downward and across a whole state as a 400-foot-tall earth-moving tsunami.

Harsh volcanic slopes above the Snake's riparian shores now blend to ponderosa pines, Douglas firs, and grasslands. Lower elevations remain rocky, arid, and notoriously hot in summer, yet starkly lovely with spotty but appreciated shade of hackberry trees and their evaporation-resistant, sandpaper-like leaves along the shores.

Conservation

Hells Canyon was once a continuous wilderness chasm of 200 miles. This lacked the sheer-wall, red-rock sublimity of the Colorado River's Grand Canyon but was otherwise comparable in length, whitewater, and wilderness. However, by 1964 the Idaho Power Company had built three dams that flooded the upper half of the canyon and entombed five of seven great rapids, as recounted to me by legendary river runner Martin Litton, who ran some of the last trips through the upper canyon.

Below the dams the river still surges. Silt and pollution from the Snake's troubled agricultural odyssey across southern Idaho has accumulated as a green algal soup in the upstream reservoirs—big septic tanks—leaving the water that the dams release downstream green and clear.

This 104-mile length of river to Asotin—above Lewiston—was protected in one of the great sagas of river conservation history. First threatening it, the 700-foot Nez Perce Dam was proposed by the federal Bureau of Reclamation below the Salmon River in the 1960s and would have flooded that landmark stream as well as Hells Canyon of the Snake. Conservationists, oddly aligned with private power interests intent on building their own dam, halted the plan, but then the threat shifted to the 670-foot High Mountain Sheep Dam proposal, 1 mile above the Salmon and in the heart of Hells Canyon.

Ruin of the river was averted when Brock Evans—a now-notorious conservation veteran but then a start-up lawyer working for the Sierra Club—filed appeals to the Federal Power Commission moments before midnight of the due date, delaying approval long enough for conservationists to gain traction. Idaho Governor Cecil Andrus eventually declared that Hells Canyon Dam would be built only "over my dead body," as he repeated to me later in 1988, and Congress designated the Snake a National Wild and Scenic River in 1975. Momentously, this victory signaled the beginning of the end of

The Snake churns above the mouth of the Salmon River at the site where the High Mountain Sheep Dam was proposed but stopped through National Wild and Scenic River designation in 1975.

the big-dam building era in America. The same year, a proposal to build a lesser dam on the Snake downstream at Asotin was also halted.

Hydropower produced at the upper Hells Canyon dams might be regarded as inexpensive if external costs are ignored, which they are in a calculus that Idaho Power Company consumers enjoy. But before the power company arrived, millions of salmon and steelhead migrated up the Snake to the Boise, Payette, Malheur, and Owyhee; some swam the whole way to Nevada via Salmon Falls Creek. Dams throughout the basin now bar that enormous food supply from 368 miles of the Snake and 3,000 miles of Columbia basin spawning streams altogether.

The river suffers below the Hells Canyon dams as well. Because suspended silt settles to the bottoms of the upstream reservoirs, "hungry" water downstream erodes the banks more aggressively than before and fails to deposit silt the way free-flowing rivers do when balancing erosion with deposition. Furthermore, the Idaho Power Company manages the Snake for peak-hour use by dumping a lot of water at once through turbines in the afternoon and storing it at night. The combined effect has washed away a rich riparian belt of willows plus 80 percent of the spacious sandy beaches that had hallmarked the extraordinary place in Martin Litton's heyday. Below the mouth of the Salmon River—still dam-free—larger beaches prevail where one can see a marked difference between the manipulated and free-flowing river regimes.

Yet wildness remains in the awe-inspiring canyon, the main stem still supports spawning chinook, and it continues as a conduit for wild fish headed to the Salmon River. Federal law now requires updated licenses for the Hells Canyon dams, and with them, an opportunity for improvements. Renewals have so far been withheld pending resolution of water quality infractions; reservoir releases from the Idaho Power Company dams are too warm to meet modern standards.

The hotter current debate concerns the four lower Snake River dams below Hells Canyon that hinder salmon and steelhead on their journeys upriver and down. These and the four lower Columbia River dams below the mouth of the Snake have reduced some of the greatest runs of salmon in history to endangered species. Current numbers even in rare "good" years fall far below thresholds considered essential to the species' long-term survival. From the Columbia basin's historic high of 16 million salmon and steelhead, returns have fallen to a recent ten-year average of 2.2 million, down to 665,000 in 2018 and projected at 1.2 million for 2020. Even worse in future prospects, the great majority of these fish come from hatcheries, whose numbers are not sustainable without healthier wild returns, which are tapped as seed stock of superior genetic quality to supply the hatcheries.

The Army Corps of Engineers' fish passage facilities and downriver transport—ironically done by trapping young fish and motoring them like wood chips or wheat in barges to sea level—have failed to stem the decline.

Meanwhile, turbines at the four Snake River dams generate less than 4 percent of the Northwest's electricity—easily replaced through efficiency measures, according to the Northwest Power and Conservation Council—and much of that hydropower is generated in springtime when it's least needed. Though dam proponents argue that the dams are needed for power-generating flexibility, most Snake River hydropower is surplus to northwestern needs, and even the sales to California have been curtailed or stopped in recent years because of cheaper renewable options. Incredibly, much of the salmon-killing electricity generated at Snake River dams goes unused for lack of buyers.

To barge grain and wood products from Lewiston—450 miles from the ocean—was the boosters' primary impetus for building the dams. But the barging system, with commodities bound for Asia, would never survive without a nearly complete subsidization by American taxpayers, and only a tiny fraction of the Columbia River's total barge traffic goes the whole way up to Lewiston. If the four dams from there down to the Columbia were breached, railroads could fill the gap, as they used to do and increasingly do today.

Even in Lewiston, where people vociferously backed the damming of their river in the 1960s, support for removal has grown. Ironically the uppermost reservoir, lapping at town's edge, aggrades with dam-induced silt deposits, which inexorably raise the riverbed and promise to eventually threaten the town's levees and flood the community unless the dams are breached.

Touting economic as well as fishery benefits, Idaho Rivers United and the Save Our Wild Salmon Coalition argue for dam removal. Federal judges have declared five times in twenty-five years that the Army Corps must prepare a better plan, and a 2016 ruling specifically ordered consideration of dam removal. That has brought no change in federal policy, but the Corps' finding is being challenged. The outcome of this drama will become either one of the greatest river conservation stories in our history or one of the greatest ongoing tragedies of unnecessary loss.

Rafters, drift boaters, and kayakers nationwide still come to Hells Canyon, which is also popular among jet boaters, whose unrestricted numbers soared for decades while quotas sharply limited nonmotorized boaters. This became the West's most infamous conflict between motorized and nonmotorized river users, shouldering conflicts about noise, wakes, crowding, and inequities of management. After years of debate and inaction by the Forest Service, some restrictions were placed on jet boat use, with some motor-free days prescribed in upper Hells Canyon. Powerboat use remains heavy below Pittsburg Landing and on weekends.

 ## FISH

A mix of twenty-four native and introduced fishes in Hells Canyon includes not only chinook salmon and steelhead, but also bass, trout, catfish, black crappie, suckers, and pikeminnows. The lower end of Hells Canyon is critical to the imperiled steelhead and chinook returning to the Grande Ronde and Imnaha Rivers of Oregon and to Idaho's Salmon River. This is also some of the best habitat for rare white sturgeon, which grow as long as some of the boats on the river.

Much of the Snake has great bass fishing, and when steelhead and salmon runs are adequate, a sport season for them becomes a major sporting and regional economic event.

 ## ACCESS

What remains of Hells Canyon is mostly car-free. A steep gravel road leads to Pittsburg Landing; from US 95 at White Bird, cross to the west bank of the Salmon River and take gravel Deer Creek Road/FR 493 west 16 miles. On the Oregon side northeast of Imnaha, Dug Bar Road (four-wheel) rattles to the canyon's bottom. See below for paddling access.

 ## HIKING

Summertime is insufferably hot for hiking. May is ideal; autumn is pleasant. Beware of rattlesnakes throughout. From Pittsburg you can walk upstream on the east-side trail 30 miles to Brush Creek—2 miles below Hells Canyon Dam, which is isolated by canyon walls. From Dug Bar, the west-side Snake River Trail clings to canyon sides for 56 miles up to Battle Creek—4 miles below Hells Canyon Dam.

My favorite hike to the canyon is via the Imnaha River in Oregon; drive to Joseph, then northeast to Imnaha, northward to the Imnaha bridge, and walk down the west-side Imnaha Trail 4 miles to the Snake. Evade robust vines of poison ivy.

 ## PADDLING

Hells Canyon is second in the West only to the Colorado's Grand Canyon for enormous big-volume rapids. Typical summer flows of 12,000 cfs are thrilling for experienced rafters and kayakers. Challenging water occurs at 20,000 cfs, and springtime peaks of 60,000 create an otherworldly sense of scale. Boats of any kind in the wrong place (monstrous holes) can be flipped at any level, and long swims are especially hazardous early in the season.

Springtime boating in Hells Canyon thrills with its soaring sweep of green grasslands but may include high-water challenges. Summer sizzles with little shade but delightful conditions on the water. Fall is exquisite, with good weather lingering to October. Permits are required and numbers are limited; call Hells Canyon National Recreation Area.

Most boaters run 79 miles from Hells Canyon Dam to Heller Bar. Some exit after 32 miles at Pittsburg Landing to avoid a longer shuttle, jet boats, and gentler rapids. Though few do it, I recommend continuing on enjoyable water with nice campsites the whole way to Lewiston for a 104-mile journey. Headwinds, motorboats, and road encroachment increase below Heller.

For the Hells Canyon put-in, drive I-84 northwest from Boise, at Ontario take US 95 north to Cambridge, turn west on ID 71, and go 29 miles past Brownlee and Oxbow Dams to the base of Hells Canyon Dam.

To reach the Heller Bar takeout, from Clarkston, Washington, go south on WA 129 to Asotin, bear left at the light, and follow Heller Bar Road south. The longer float trip to Hellgate Park in Lewiston makes for a shorter shuttle.

The uppermost 17 miles of Hells Canyon present the biggest whitewater: Class 4 at Wild Sheep (scout left 6 miles from put-in), Granite Creek (2 miles farther, scout left or right), and then Lower Bernard Creek, Waterspout, and Rush Creek, plus scores of smaller but powerful drops. At 20,000 cfs in spring, Granite Creek Rapid's "Green Room" has the largest glassy green wave anywhere. See *The Wild and Scenic Snake River: Hells Canyon National Recreation Area* booklet by the Forest Service.

Wild Sheep Rapid is one of the two largest drops in Hells Canyon. The rafter's path here is left of center, then moving right.

Evening light warms the Snake River in Hells Canyon at Sulphur Creek Rapids below Pittsburg Landing.

Though most of the sand has disappeared with hydroelectric peaking, campsites remain. Beware of the dam release, which can rise and fall 5 vertical feet, ramping from 5,000 cfs to 20,000 in seemingly no time. On a solo trip, I once had to swim in heavy current to retrieve my raft, which I had pulled far onto the beach but foolishly forgotten to tie.

In the heart of Hells Canyon, boaters can access good hiking on the west- and east-side trails, plus paths up Battle, Granite, Saddle, Sluice, and Temperance Creeks. For cooler hiking weather, do this trip in autumn.

The shuttle for Hells Canyon is long, and the jet boats annoying for anyone not on them, yet this trip remains an American classic and the premier big-water voyage of the Rocky Mountain region.

St. Joe River

Length: 140 miles
Average flow: 2,928 cfs
Watershed: 1,833 square miles
Location: East of Saint Maries
Hiking: 1 mile or more out and back, 21 miles point to point

Boating: Canoe, kayak, raft, day trips and overnights
Whitewater: Class 1-4
Gauge: Calder (lower river)
Highlights: Wild headwaters, native trout, whitewater and also easy paddling

Scarcely known outside the region, the St. Joe is undammed except in its lowest miles and has one of the longest free-flowing reaches in the Rocky Mountains.

A checklist of local megafauna along the upper river includes elk, mule deer, moose, black bears, grizzly bears, wolves, mountain lions, and wolverines. Western redcedars elegantly line much of the river's southern shore, while the St. Joe Road has mostly preempted the north shore.

Northern Idaho is wetter than the Rockies to the south, with forests a lot like those of the Cascade Mountains and Pacific Northwest, though the 1910 Big Burn consumed

Hidden in the forests of Idaho's Northern Rockies, the St. Joe's remarkable course begins in wildness, drops through challenging rapids, and flattens into miles of quiet water. Morning mist clears here at the upper St. Joe.

The St. Joe riffles for miles on its route west to Coeur d'Alene Lake.

three million acres in this region. Legendary Joe Halm and his crew of twenty-four found refuge at a gravel bar where waters of the St. Joe barely saved their lives.

Above Avery a 67-mile reach in St. Joe National Forest is in the National Wild and Scenic Rivers system. Below, Potlatch and other forest industries own and intensively log most land. The 52 miles up from Avery to the road's end at Spruce Tree Campground are one of the Rockies' outstanding semi-wild rivers, having paved road access, exceptional beauty, clear water, constant riffles and rapids, and no development.

 ## FISH

Westslope cutthroat thrive in upper reaches, one of Idaho's "blue ribbon" trout fisheries. Trout Unlimited considers this one of the best cutthroat streams in the West—catch-and-release for native trout. Bull trout also depend on unlogged forests of the upper basin for clean shaded water. Rainbow trout are caught in lower reaches.

 ## ACCESS

From Saint Maries turn east on FR 50/St. Joe River Road, drive 16 miles upstream along flatwater backed up by Coeur d'Alene Lake, continue 45 miles through a forested but cutover valley, and pass the community of Avery, which in the past thirty years has transformed from a rough-cut logging burg to fly-fishing destination. Continue 40 more paved miles to road's end at Spruce Tree Campground. From an intersection 1.7 miles west of there, a gravel road climbs eastward over Red Ives Peak, then returns to the St. Joe upstream at Heller Creek, likely snowbound until June.

Or, for the upper river, drive 28 miles from I-90 at Saint Regis, Montana, on gravel FR 282 up Little Joe Creek, over Gold Summit, and down paved FR 50 to the St. Joe 12 miles west of Spruce Tree.

 HIKING

From Spruce Tree Campground the St. Joe Trail leads upstream 21 roadless miles to where the gravel road again touches down at Heller Creek Campground. Though tempting in its wild river corridor, the first few miles of the route are a dusty horse trail clinging to mountain slopes without many river views.

The entire St. Joe Road is great for biking on riverfront pavement, but much of it has heavy log truck traffic, which can be avoided on weekends and after noon in late-summer fire season.

 PADDLING

After the road to Heller Creek opens in late June, experts paddle the 18-mile Class 4 upper reach, Heller Creek to Spruce Tree, through a wild wooded valley. Higher flows can be too pushy to negotiate logjams.

From Spruce Tree down to Gold Creek, 12 miles of Class 2-3 run until August or so.

From Gold Creek to Bluff Creek, 8 miles of Class 4 flow strong through July, including possible log blockages, with levels dropping to a wonderfully rocky crystal-clear run in late summer.

The St. Joe drops through Skookum Canyon with a mile of Class 4 whitewater at high flows that eases into rocky maneuvering later in summer.

Alpine Creek, tributary of the St. Joe, invites exploration by wading upstream from its mouth in Skookum Canyon.

From Bluff Creek to Turner Flat Campground, 16 miles of Class 2 are runnable most of the summer.

From Turner Flat to Packsaddle Campground, rapids intensify to Class 3-4 for 1 mile through the striking Skookum Canyon. I found this to be a blast as a low-water Class 3 canoe run even in early September, with lining of the first rock-clogged drop. Packsaddle lies 5 miles east of Avery.

From Packsaddle to St. Joe City, with intermediate takeouts, 38 miles of Class 1-2 stay floatable all summer. Below St. Joe City the river is flatwater backup from Coeur d'Alene Lake and sees motorboat use.

The St. Joe's unique mouth west of Saint Maries features natural levees extending into Coeur d'Alene Lake like ribbons of land, supporting strips of cottonwood trees housing the largest colony of nesting ospreys I've ever seen. This odd feature resulted when Post Falls Dam, on the Spokane River downstream, raised the lake level in the lowland habitat.

At the South Fork Flathead's entrance to Meadow Creek Gorge, bedrock slants into the river while the passage narrows and deepens.

Rivers of Montana

Montana means "mountain" or "mountainous country" in Latin, and this largest state in the Rockies is surely that, but it's also a land of rivers with some of the finest free-flowing waters in the West drawing boaters, hikers, and anglers. Here are excellent whitewater streams for paddling, a few of America's best long river trips, legendary trout fishing, and extraordinary opportunities for streamside hiking and backpacking, especially in the exquisite wilds of the Greater Yellowstone region and the Northern Rockies of Glacier National Park and surroundings.

Picture Montana's river geography of 169,800 miles in two parts. Rivers west of the Continental Divide rush or meander toward the Columbia River through valleys and canyons of the Northern and Middle Rocky Mountain provinces, while rivers east of the crest drop swiftly from lofty summits but then ease with low gradient through hundreds of miles of Great Plains grasslands.

Here are some of the largest rivers by volume in the interior West. Topping the charts, the Clark Fork, including its downstream extension as the Pend Oreille River in Idaho, is the second-largest and second-longest river in the Rocky Mountain region of the United States, trailing only the Snake. The Yellowstone, Kootenai, Flathead, and Missouri are Montana's other big rivers.

With a direct relationship to river qualities, Montana can boast the third-largest block of wild and semi-wild land outside Alaska: the northern portion of the Greater Yellowstone Ecosystem. Only central Idaho and the linear expanse of the Sierra Nevada in California have larger tracts of wilderness. But not to split hairs: A comparably wild mountainscape lies in Montana's north as the Glacier National Park/Northern Continental Divide ecosystem, called the "Crown of the Continent," drained by the Flathead River plus the Swan and Blackfoot and upper portions of the eastbound Two Medicine, Teton, Sun, and Dearborn before they encounter dams and spill onto the Great Plains.

Montana has five rivers totaling 388 miles designated in the National Wild and Scenic Rivers system—the Flathead's three forks plus the longest wild section of the Missouri and 20 miles of East Rosebud Creek, which in 2018 became the first Montana stream added to the Wild and Scenic program in forty-two years. Conservation groups in 2020 proposed 600 more Montana miles for Wild and Scenic status.

With its coldwater streams, wild country, and abundant insect life along glassy currents, Montana has the finest reputation in America—and perhaps the world—for trout fishing. Catch-and-release on the Madison, Yellowstone, Bitterroot, Gallatin, Beaverhead, Big Hole, Big Horn, Smith, and Clark Fork draws anglers nationwide.

Instructively significant here, Montana ceased stocking all streams supporting native trout back in 1971 and found that wild fish rebounded dramatically in numbers and health without hatchery fish as competitors, vectors of disease, and genetic compromisers. With lessons that don't seem to be learned in other states, discontinuing stocking, in fact, made trout fishing a backbone of the state's annual $7 billion recreation economy.

Of course, there's bad news as well. Analysis by the state's Department of Environmental Quality found that 73 percent of Montana's stream miles suffered "impairment" from pollution—a statistic not much different than elsewhere, except discordant and

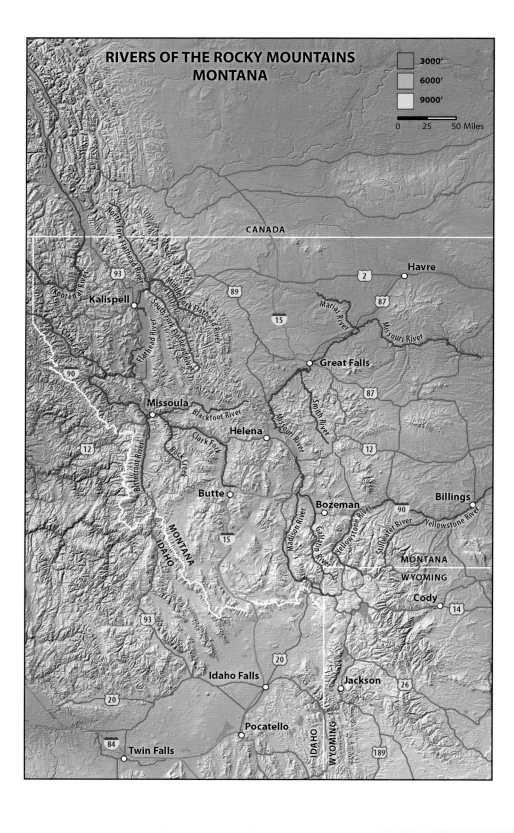

unexpected here where writer William Kittredge in 1988 proclaimed Montana "the last best place" in the West—a phrase Montanans heartily embraced.

The reputation of the state's "blue ribbon" trout waters—even without stocking for a half century—owes typically to introduced but "naturalized" rainbow and brown trout rather than to native fishes that more fully indicate ecological health. Rainbows are native only in the upper Kootenai basin, and elsewhere represent descendants of stocked fish. Meanwhile, cutthroat are limited to remote areas largely beyond reach of nonnatives. The westslope variety lives west of the Continental Divide and the Yellowstone cutthroat eastward. On the Pacific side and in the Belly River on the east side of Glacier National Park, bull trout indicate even wilder qualities with their need for clean cold water, fallen trees as woody habitat in streams, and unmuddied spawning gravels.

MONTANA RIVERS
Bitterroot River
Blackfoot River
Clark Fork River
Flathead River
Flathead River, North Fork
Flathead River, Middle Fork
Flathead River, South Fork
Gallatin River
Kootenai River
Madison River
Marias River
Missouri River
Rock Creek (Clark Fork Basin)
Smith River
Stillwater River (Yellowstone Basin)
Yellowstone River

Much of the biological degradation of Montana's streams owes to diversions depleting flows. Even famous trout streams such as the Big Hole are acutely affected by withdrawals for pasture and hay fields. Dams have likewise been built on nearly all the rivers and diminish natural qualities.

The invasion of exotic species, from the stocked brown trout that anglers covet to the universally despised knapweed as it displaces riparian plant life, affects most of Montana's habitats. Also exotic, the egregious whirling disease—a degenerative infection causing trout to spin in circles and die—was introduced and initially spread by hatchery fish and has diminished some of the state's finest rainbow trout streams and posed ominous threats to cherished trout waters throughout the West.

Hard-rock mining for silver, gold, and other minerals has long polluted Montana's rivers, with persistent degradation from abandoned mines. A survey by the organization Pacific Rivers found 6,000 abandoned mines in Montana—many leaking pollution no less than mercury and lead. The Clark Fork infamously happens to be the nation's longest Superfund toxic waste site—130 miles of the upper river, meaning not just a mountain of tailings but *the river itself*. Strip mining for coal and gas fracking on the east slope, along with suburbanization and trophy homes around booming recreational communities such as Big Sky, Bozeman, Kalispell, Livingston, and Missoula, all add threats to the state's waterways.

Nevertheless, significant portions of key rivers remain natural, and several waterways are truly exceptional from nationwide perspectives. Foremost are the Yellowstone and Flathead. Others retain important qualities, and lotic wealth can be restored if measures are taken to avoid further problems and to correct damage of the past.

Bitterroot River

Length: 86 miles plus 45 of the West Fork, total 131
Average flow: 2,300 cfs
Watershed: 2,832 square miles
Location: South of Missoula
Hiking: Day hikes and backpacking along tributaries

Boating: Canoe, kayak, raft, day trips and overnights
Whitewater: Class 1-2
Gauge: Darby (upper), Missoula (lower)
Highlights: Recreational and cottonwood corridor, long canoe route

Perhaps Montana's best example of a clean, scenic, recreational river within a developed valley, the Bitterroot flows to the Clark Fork just downstream from Missoula.

To be clear, this is not a wild river. US 93 runs the valley's length, while lesser roads track both sides. A chain of bustling towns rise with ranchland and riprap armoring too many banks in between, including miles of rock placed by the Northern Pacific Railroad in the 1960s (now a bike trail). Yet the river flows brightly with runoff of the Bitterroot Range—stacked up scenically along the west shore while the gentler Sapphire Mountains ramp eastward. Cottonwood lowlands stretch through this gentrifying ranch valley.

Stretching northward, the Bitterroot River offers a rare canoe trip of nearly 100 miles without major rapids or large dams. Cottonwoods line the shores here at Hamilton.

Irrigation diversions cause flows to be low, but several organizations are working with ranchers to improve late summer levels.

FISH

Westslope cutthroat and naturalized rainbow trout are the draws making this Montana's third-most-popular stream for anglers—behind the Madison and Big Horn—largely because of easy access. Tributaries remain refuges of westslope cutthroat and bull trout.

ACCESS

US 93 south from Missoula runs the length of the main stem, with a lot of frontage roads.

HIKING

The Bitterroot Trail is a 50-mile bikeway/rail-trail conversion that's mostly paved and off-road from Hamilton down, linking seven towns to the Milwaukee Trail near Missoula's McCormick Park (south side of the Clark Fork off Old Highway 93, or reached via the I-90 Orange Street exit and Cregg Lane), with camping, lodging, and restaurants.

Trails along tributary creeks climb the formidable Bitterroot Mountains ascending from Lake Como between Conner and Hamilton, Blodgett Creek from Hamilton,

Sunset fades to twilight along the Bitterroot River above Victor.

Mill Creek from Woodside, Big Creek from north of Victor, and Bass Creek from north of Stevensville.

 PADDLING

Canoeists, kayakers, and rafters choose from the Bitterroot's full length for day trips or a week-long expedition with no major rapids, all suitable as a canoe outing for non-expert paddlers. Most is Class 1 riffles, typically floatable all summer and fall. Avoid high flows in late spring. The Bitterroot can appeal to boaters who enjoy visitor services in towns, including a lot of good food with frequent landings and shuttles on the valley bike trail.

No large dams but five diversion structures present obstacles, with two dangerous blockages: Lost Horse Dam between Darby and Hamilton, and Sleeping Child Dam requiring portage 5 miles south of Hamilton. Upper river logjams can be troublesome, and irrigation withdrawals take a toll on fish and boatable levels, especially in dry years and between Woodside and Stevensville.

The lower reach, Florence to Lolo, remains much as Lewis and Clark saw it. The Bitterroot is famous for its golden cottonwoods in early October, when flows can bump up as irrigators halt diversions.

Sixteen public landings appear in *Paddling Montana* and provide for trips of 3 to 11 miles with camping at scattered public sites and below high-water lines. If ownership is in doubt, avoid houses and forego campfires—good practices regardless.

For a long trip—runoff permitting—start below Conner at Hannon Memorial access for 72 miles to Buckhouse Bridge, 5 miles up from the mouth, reached near the US 93 bridge south of Missoula. Or continue down the Clark Fork as many as 43 more miles with dam-free Class 2, altogether a significant 129-mile trip with a mandatory Clark Fork exit at Saint John's landing above Alberton Gorge's whitewater.

Blackfoot River

Length: 131 miles
Average flow: 1,600 cfs
Watershed: 2,286 square miles
Location: Northeast of Missoula
Hiking: Headwaters of the North Fork, short paths at landings

Boating: Kayak, raft, day trips and overnights
Whitewater: Class 1-3
Gauge: Bonner
Highlights: Moderate whitewater, recreational stream near Missoula

Popular among boaters and anglers, the Blackfoot was degraded by past mining but has improved with path-breaking reclamation efforts. In the 1970s the Nature Conservancy bought easements for protection and access and established the Blackfoot River Recreational Corridor for public use of selected private parcels cooperatively managed by Montana Fish, Wildlife and Parks and landowners along 29 mid-river miles between Russell Gates access and Johnsrud Park—a once-promising model that unfortunately did not see much duplication elsewhere.

But highlighting a trend that has seen many hundreds of successes across the nation, a dam was removed 1 mile above the Clark Fork confluence in 2005. Larger, 30-foot-tall Milltown Dam, just below the confluence, had trapped toxic mine tailings for a hundred years but was eliminated in 2010. Restoration of the site—now a state park—marks one of the largest river recovery projects in the Rockies.

The Blackfoot River nears its mouth at the Angevine Access upstream from Bonner. Dam removals have restored the lower river to a free-flowing stream.

In 1998 Montanans passed a statewide initiative banning further cyanide gold processing, stopping a mine proposal in the upper Blackfoot basin. Other mining threats remain, but Blackfoot Challenge and the Clark Fork Coalition work for protection and restoration.

Joining the Blackfoot near Ovando, the 35-mile-long North Fork flows from the Scapegoat Wilderness and the southern end of the Crown of the Continent ecosystem, where proponents seek region-wide wildland safeguards.

 ## FISH

Anglers cast for brown, rainbow, and cutthroat trout throughout the Blackfoot. The North Fork supports wild cutthroat and bull trout.

 ## ACCESS

From Missoula drive MT 200 east and upstream along the Blackfoot's lower 13 miles, turn left on Johnsrud Park/Blackfoot River Road, continue 17 miles to an upper junction with MT 200, and proceed east on it to headwaters.

 ## HIKING

A dirt road/trail leads upstream 3 miles from Whitaker Bridge; from MT 200 eastbound turn left on Johnsrud Park Road, go 7 miles to Whitaker Bridge, park on river right, and walk upstream on river left.

Short angler paths are found at Blackfoot landings scattered from the Ovando area (54 miles up from the mouth) downstream.

Trails follow the upper 19 miles of the North Fork and tributaries in Lolo and Flathead National Forests. Take MT 200 east to Ovando and turn northeast to the North Fork trailhead.

 ## PADDLING

This is one of Montana's most popular floating rivers, with strong flows and whitewater May and June, settling to lower runnable levels of Class 2+ rapids by mid-July and continuing all summer. *Paddling Montana* lists seventeen landings at 2- to 13-mile intervals. Call Montana Fish, Wildlife and Parks for a map and permit to camp between Russell Gates and Johnsrud landings.

From upstream of Lincoln down to the North Fork confluence near Ovando, expect tight turns and logjams in the small, seldom-paddled stream.

From Russell Gates access (off MT 200 west of Ovando) to Ninemile Prairie (off Johnsrud Park/Blackfoot River Road), 16 miles are mostly Class 2 with some Class 3 at higher flows.

From Ninemile Prairie to Whitaker Bridge, along Johnsrud Park Road, 6 miles of quiet water suit less-experienced paddlers.

Just below Whitaker, Thibodeau is the big rapid, Class 2-3, with boulders and a left-side route, followed by Class 2—or 3 at higher flows—for 7 miles to Johnsrud Park off MT 200.

From Johnsrud to Bonner (2 miles above the mouth), 11 miles of Class 2 see heavy use by paddlers and tubers on summer weekends.

For a 54-mile expedition—Class 2-3 early in summer and mostly Class 2 after levels drop—paddle from River Junction access (below the North Fork and south of Ovando) to Bonner.

Clark Fork River

Length: 133 at Missoula, 220 at Saint Regis, 346 at Pend Oreille Lake
Average flow: 21,586 cfs; 3,893 at Missoula, 7,162 at Saint Regis
Watershed: 21,747 square miles
Location: Southeast and northwest of Missoula
Hiking: Short walks
Boating: Raft, kayak, canoe, day trips and overnights

Whitewater: Class 1-2, Class 3-4 in Alberton Gorge
Gauge: Missoula, Saint Regis (above Flathead River), Cabinet Gorge (Idaho line)
Highlights: Missoula's river, whitewater at Alberton Gorge, day trips and long canoeing opportunity

This is nearly the longest and largest river within the Rocky Mountains of the United States—second only to the Snake, which runs for many of its miles across the Snake River Plain and outside the Rocky Mountains, whereas the Clark Fork is all Rockies. It begins with an intensively mined upper basin at Butte and winds through the I-90 corridor as America's longest Superfund toxic waste site for 130 miles. Conditions in the river have improved in recent decades, with trout returning.

Flows increase with the Blackfoot and Bitterroot Rivers at Missoula, then the Clark Fork thunders through big whitewater in Alberton Gorge above Superior, winds among

Below Rock Creek and upstream from Missoula the Clark Fork becomes a mature river with summerlong flows for paddling.

forested mountains of the Northern Rockies, doubles in volume with the Flathead River, stalls behind three dams, and enters Idaho as Lake Pend Oreille. Waters emerge below the dam-raised lake as the Pend Oreille River, which crosses northern Idaho and western Washington to join the Columbia just north of the Canada border.

Don't confuse this with the smaller "Clark's Fork" of central Wyoming and Montana, bound for the Yellowstone River and Atlantic Ocean (see Wyoming chapter).

One of the most remarkable glacial histories occurred here as continental glaciers advanced 15,000 years ago and ice 2,000 feet deep dammed the flow where the Clark Fork today empties into Lake Pend Oreille. The ice dam impounded Glacial Lake Missoula 200 miles upstream to Deer Lodge, covering 3,000 square miles—one-third the size of Lake Erie—with waterlines still visible on mountainsides. Water pressure broke weakening ice, releasing a half-mile-high deluge into the Columbia and scouring canyons down to Pacific tides. Once would have been astonishing, but this happened perhaps forty times on half-century cycles. Lower Clark Fork canyons from Saint Regis to Idaho reflect the erosive force of those ice age floods.

Today's river is severely impacted by mining and more, but restoration efforts of the Clark Fork Coalition and other groups are gaining traction. The removal of Milltown Dam above Missoula marked a major advance with removal of arsenic-tainted sediment and restoration of flows in 2010.

 FISH

Though Pacific-bound, the Clark Fork never saw salmon because waterfalls downstream on the Pend Oreille blocked migration. Now the river above Missoula is noted for rainbow and brown trout, and the middle river is one of Montana's good coldwater fisheries, transitioning to warmwater fish below the Flathead.

 ACCESS

I-90 follows the Clark Fork from Butte westward to Saint Regis, where the river doglegs east with MT 135 alongside, receives the Flathead River, then reverts westward with MT 200 beyond the banks. From headwaters to Missoula boaters use nineteen landings, with another twenty-nine below; see *Paddling Montana*.

 HIKING

Short walks can be taken at some access areas, and bike trails in Missoula run from the I-90 Bonner exit at Milltown down to McCormick Park, reached via the I-90 Orange Street exit and Cregg Lane.

At the I-90 milepost 72 parking area (eastbound only), a steep path drops to an enchanting rapid, rock wall, and beach above Alberton Gorge.

Below Saint Regis by 13 miles, at Ferry Landing, a "River Path" leads upstream on river right.

 PADDLING

Many upper miles are boatable in early summer, with Class 1-2 riffles and quiet water but also with diversions, low dams, and mining's legacy. Willows crowd serpentine shorelines through the agricultural valley.

Below Rock Creek—20 miles upstream from Missoula—boating levels persist all summer. Schwartz Creek (below Rock Creek) to Turah access (above the Blackfoot) is a popular 9 miles, Class 1-2.

A 4-mile "town stretch" from Sha-Ron access to McCormick Park attracts summer-time tubers and includes Brennan's Wave, a constructed hydraulic at Caras Park, popular with kayakers and surfers.

McCormick Park in Missoula to Kona Bridge is 9 miles—half of it winding through one of the West's largest cottonwood river deltas above the Bitterroot River's entry from the south. However, I do not recommend this reach to casual boaters. Anyone launching in Missoula must be aware that in the main channel 5.5 miles below McCormick, a hazardous irrigation dam requires mandatory portage of 100 yards with a difficult landing in swift water on the left; stop far upstream of the dangerous structure, which can be heard but is not easily seen.

Avoiding the portage, a popular 14 miles of Class 1-2 runs into the Clark Fork from Buckhouse Bridge on the beautiful lower Bitterroot. Start on the Bitterroot River at US 93 just south of Missoula and float to Kona Bridge. To reach the takeout, from

Downstream from Missoula the Clark Fork braids in cottonwood-lined channels where the Bitterroot River enters, creating one of the largest riparian deltas of rich lowland habitat in the Rockies.

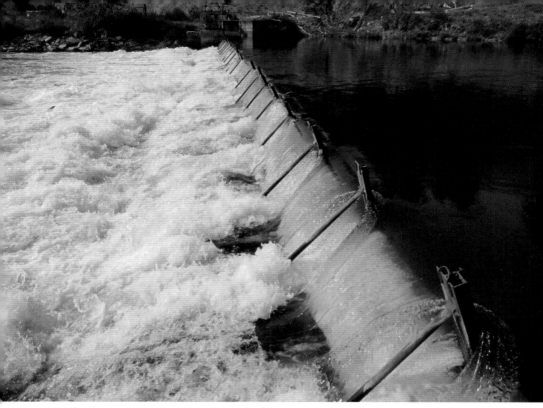

Paddlers downstream from Missoula must portage this hazardous irrigation dam blocking the channel above the mouth of the Bitterroot River. Floating here is not recommended for casual boaters.

south of Missoula on US 93 northbound, go left on Blue Mountain Road, west on Big Flat Road, and right on Kona Ranch Road to the bridge, river left.

Class 2 paddling continues 34 miles from the Bitterroot to Saint John's access: take I-90 exit 70. Visit in advance and don't miss it: Class 3+ Alberton Gorge awaits below!

Alberton ranks among the biggest whitewater flushes in the West, with summer runoff pushing 2,000 to 10,000 cfs and summerlong boatable flows in the 2,000 range. Spring-time runoff tops 30,000 cfs and remains high through June; levels above 10,000 present serious high-volume hazards. Hells Canyon of the Snake is the Rockies' only similar high-volume run (though far bigger), and Alberton is distinctive as an accessible day trip. At medium and low levels, Class 3-4 pool-drop rapids include big waves, holes, and rocks beneath canyon walls. I-90 tracks on higher slopes but is not intrusive. Put in near Cyr, off I-90 exit 70 westbound only, and run 10 miles to Tarkio landing or 16 to Forest Grove; commercial trips available.

Below Alberton Gorge minor rapids occur occasionally for 86 dam-free miles from Forest Grove to Thompson Falls, with sandy beaches in mid to late summer. For the Forest Grove put-in, take I-90 exit 61 to the river-right landing. Below, the river passes through Superior and Saint Regis.

Though mostly with gentle flows below the whitewater of Alberton Gorge, the lower Clark Fork rushes through a big-volume Class 2 rapid below Saint Regis and the Ferry Landing ramp.

The I-90 corridor westward to Saint Regis has houses and ranchland, but the highway is rarely seen along quiet forested shorelines. From Saint Regis, with access on river left north of town, to Ferry Landing on river right, the Clark Fork for 13 miles bends mostly away from MT 135, followed by 12 miles to the Paradise town ramp with the road alongside but rocky mountains rising high. Given the ruggedness of the Class 1-2 canyon there, it's a wonder that the rapids are not Class 4 or 5. Throughout, the Clark Fork from Alberton down offers a magnificent and accessible big-river experience. But non-experts beware: 4 miles below Ferry Landing, at Class 2+ Cascade Rapids, stay left of holes sudsing on river right. Below Plains 4 miles, another Class 2+ rapid can be sneaked far left or right at low flows—best to scout. Roadside shuttles are easy, but traffic's oppressive for biking.

At the town of Thompson Falls, flatwater backs up behind a chain of three dams extending through Lake Pend Oreille. Take out just east of town at the upper reach of the first reservoir.

Flathead River

Length: 158 miles counting Flathead Lake plus 115 of the North Fork, total 273
Average flow: 11,638 cfs
Watershed: 8,933 square miles
Location: North of Missoula, north and south of Polson
Hiking: Limited

Boating: Canoe, raft, day trips and overnights
Whitewater: Class 2-4
Gauge: Perma
Highlights: Extension of Flathead forks, Buffalo Rapids, long gentle reach

Though overshadowed by its stellar forks, the main-stem Flathead is also an exceptional river.

From the confluence of the North and Middle Forks to Flathead Lake, the upper main stem runs 51 miles, first riffling then languid through riparian lowlands featuring oxbows and wetlands above Flathead Lake—excellent habitat for waterfowl (and mosquitoes!). Most of the main-stem corridor above Flathead Lake is privately owned, with hay fields above wooded floodplains.

Below the 35-mile-long lake and its 205-foot-tall dam, the lower main stem flows through the Confederated Salish and Kootenai Tribes' reservation for 72 undeveloped miles. The first 7 include Buffalo Rapids; the remaining 65 have gentler flows with occasional roads nearby.

Below Buffalo Rapids the main-stem Flathead eases for 65 miles of broad waters, larger than the Clark Fork here where the two arteries meet, Flathead on the left and Clark Fork on the right.

The tribes require day-use and camping permits for the river below Fathead Lake—good for three days and available at the Polson Walmart. Get one! Violations cost $150.

The Flathead is larger than the Clark Fork where they meet, surprisingly comparable in size to the Yellowstone and larger than the Missouri where those two much longer rivers merge in North Dakota.

Six dam sites, unpopular with the tribes, were considered and rejected on the lower Flathead in past decades.

FISH

Native cutthroat and rare bull trout still migrate from Flathead Lake to spawning locations above, sometimes finning their way 150 miles upstream. Anglers attuned to migration schedules can find good fishing, often lackluster otherwise. Anadromous fish never journeyed here owing to downstream waterfalls on the Pend Oreille.

One of the greater environmental tragedies of the Flathead involves efforts to "improve" sport angling by planting nonnative lake trout in Flathead Lake during the 1960s. The voracious exotics targeted the Flathead's kokanee salmon. Introduced to the lake in 1914, the kokanee had become so plentiful that they filled tributaries upstream during migration season, with a mass of red fish feeding one of the continent's greatest concentrations of bald eagles along the North Fork, an enduring population of grizzly bears, and a host of other wildlife. After decimating the kokanee, the lake trout went to work on native cutthroat, which also migrated from the lake to spawn. Efforts to reestablish some measure of balance in the system have been thwarted by the popularity of lake trout among some anglers.

The lower Flathead supports lake whitefish but nonnatives dominate, including smallmouth bass, plus predatory northern pike originally introduced on the distant Little Blackfoot River (tributary to the Clark Fork, not Blackfoot) to attract anglers.

ACCESS

The upper main stem is reached at US 2 south of Columbia Falls. For the lower river, use MT 211 and 212 on the Salish and Kootenai Reservation.

HIKING

This is not a hiking river, as the upper main stem winds through private wetlands and the lower river through Indian reservation.

PADDLING

The upper main stem runs 51 miles from the North Fork–Middle Fork confluence to Flathead Lake, first with steady current and then slowly in swampy terrain below MT 35. I found the lower end of this expedition buggy with soggy shores, but interesting for the full Flathead experience—better in a canoe than raft, though sleeping on a raft here would be the way to go for those who are open to it, bugs permitting.

Shortening the trip to omit flatwater, Teakettle access appears above the US 2 bridge east of Columbia Falls, 13 miles below Blankenship Bridge (confluence of North and Middle Forks). In another 15 miles, Old Steel Bridge access is east of Kalispell. If going the whole way to the lake, take out in flatwater off MT 82 at Sportsman's Bridge near the inlet to the lake.

The main-stem Flathead flows out of Flathead Lake and through the big-volume torrent of Buffalo Rapids.

Below Flathead Lake and its dam, 2 miles of gentle flow are followed by 4 miles of high-volume Class 3-4 rapids, then another mile to Buffalo Bridge takeout. Drive southwest from Polson's lakeshore on Kerr Dam Road to the put-in below the dam. Summer flows average 11,000 cfs but vary with releases of 3,200 to 25,000. Call Kerr Dam for schedules. From 10,000 to 18,000 cfs is considered good whitewater, but that's *big*—Grand Canyon–style volume. This is one of the West's highest-volume, regularly runnable rapids, though short.

Four significant pitches start with a ledge—especially challenging at "low" flows of 3,000 to 6,000 cfs. Four linked drops culminate with Buffalo Rapids. Where cliffs climb high and the river narrows, an S-turn swings left then right. Scout by eddying out left, just above the drop. Climb the path up the rock face to inspect the left-side run. Boaters rarely ventured here a few decades ago; now 200 might pass on a busy day, including outfitters. Takeout for the 7-mile run is Buffalo Bridge; from Kerr Dam Road jog repeatedly westbound on Valley View Road, then turn north and west on Buffalo Bridge Road.

Virtually unnoticed, the Flathead below Buffalo Rapids continues 65 miles to the Clark Fork above Paradise. Mostly serene, clear water passes undeveloped riparian forest and prairie with broad views, birds, and wildlife. The lowest 25 miles have a railroad and MT 200 alongside.

With a permit from the tribes, boaters can run 20 miles from Buffalo Bridge to Sloan Bridge, 20 miles from Sloan to Dixon, and 14 miles from Dixon to Perma. From Perma the Flathead runs another 11 miles to the Clark Fork and onward 2 miles to the Paradise Bridge ramp, river right, making a Buffalo Bridge–Paradise trip of 67 miles possible. Long-trip aficionados can go another slow-moving 34 miles on the Clark Fork with most, but not all, Class 1 water (see Clark Fork) for a total length of 101 miles to the dammed-up Clark Fork at Thompson Falls.

Flathead River, North Fork

Length: 115 miles, 58 in the United States
Average flow: 2,963 cfs
Watershed: 1,566 square miles
Location: West side of Glacier National Park
Hiking: Tributaries in Glacier National Park

Boating: Raft, canoe, day trips and overnights
Whitewater: Class 1-2, some 3
Gauge: Glacier Rim
Highlights: Overnight canoe or raft trip, mountain scenery, clear water, wildlife

After its upper 57 Canadian miles, Montana's North Fork Flathead continues to the Middle Fork confluence. The east bank lies in Glacier National Park, with the west side mostly in Flathead National Forest.

Exceptionally clear blue-green water tinted from glacial runoff in the Livingston Range eastward covers a riverbed brilliantly shining with red, black, gray, and white metamorphic rocks, all backed by magnificent scenery. A west-side gravel road, not much seen from the river, runs the valley's length. In this habitat for grizzly bears, black bears, moose, mountain lions, otters, beavers, and bald eagles, I've seen tracks of eight different mammal species at a single campsite.

Coal mining in Canada at Cabin Creek, 8 miles north of the border, along with oil and gas exploration on the west side of the valley had long posed threats to this stream. After Earthjustice petitioned the United Nations to halt fossil fuel extraction in both countries, Congress passed the North Fork Watershed Protection Act in 2013, and in 2014 British Columbia compensated a bankrupt mining corporation that had sued the province over

Flowing from Canada, the North Fork Flathead borders Glacier National Park to the east and national forest land to the west. Early autumn is a good time to paddle this popular stream.

The North Fork Flathead is famously clear and blue-green in both its deep pools and fast water.

a mining ban. After forty years of protection efforts, the North Fork appears to be secure from mining and drilling.

From the international border to the mouth, Congress designated the North Fork as a National Wild and Scenic River. Most tributaries are pure and wild, including Trail, Whale, and Yakinikak Creeks—all proposed for Wild and Scenic status by Montanans for Healthy Rivers.

 FISH

Fishing can be good depending on migration of cutthroat. Bull trout survive here and must be released. The river's cold water and spare nutrients make for smaller and fewer fish than in Montana's classic trout streams, so the North Fork is rarely boated strictly as a fishing trip. Rainbow trout are found and caught in the lower North Fork, and genetic introgression by them is a serious threat to native westslope cutthroat.

 ACCESS

From the northeast corner of Columbia Falls, take MT 486/North Fork Road north with a right turn in 8 miles to the Blankenship Bridge ramp below the North Fork–Middle Fork confluence, or continue straight to Big Creek, Polebridge, and the Canadian border.

 HIKING

Trails in Glacier National Park link valley forests eastward to glacier-carved lakes and the Continental Divide. Minor paths can be found along the river, but no trails follow its length.

The sun sets on one of the North Fork Flathead's inviting cobble bars, with the Livingston Range of Glacier National Park rising in the background.

 PADDLING

The North Fork is one of the West's finest canoeing streams for experienced paddlers, with Class 2 and one or two minor Class 3 rapids that make for a premier semi-wild multiday float with easy road access—a rare combination.

Expect logjams against shores and possible blockages from the Canadian border to Polebridge—25 miles of swift water into July or later.

Polebridge to Big Creek is 18 miles of Class 1-2 with possible log issues but fewer of them, runnable all summer.

Big Creek to Glacier Rim for 12 miles has the largest rapids, Class 2+ at four drops and Class 3 at high flows in two pitches at Fool Hen Rapids, 3 miles above Glacier Rim landing; scout on river left.

Another 4 miles end at the Blankenship Bridge ramp on river left. Though few do it, paddlers can continue down the main stem for a 109-mile trip from Canada to Flathead Lake.

In my opinion, late-summer overnight trips on the North Fork are the finest extended canoe trip or easy raft trip in the Rockies. Good floating lingers into autumn, with yellow cottonwoods, chilly bug-free nights, and far fewer paddlers. Take all precautions for grizzly bears, which range both banks but favor the national park. I'd rather camp on the west side, where a permit is not required as of this writing but is being considered owing to increased use. See the Forest Service booklet *Three Forks of the Flathead Wild & Scenic River Float Guide*, and call Flathead National Forest for updates.

Flathead River, Middle Fork

Length: 109 miles plus 24 of Bowl and Basin Creeks, total 133
Average flow: 2,856 cfs
Watershed: 1,135 square miles
Location: Southeast of West Glacier
Hiking: Riverfront and tributaries, day hikes and backpacking

Boating: Raft, kayak, canoe, day trips and overnights
Whitewater: Class 2-4
Gauge: West Glacier
Highlights: Wilderness, roadless expedition, native trout, whitewater, canoeing

Running from the heart of a great American wilderness and then along the border of Glacier National Park, the Middle Fork Flathead is free of dams, diversions, and major shoreline development. Its upper half was called the "wildest river in Montana" by wildlife biologists Frank and John Craighead, and has long been revered as such. It's one of the Rockies' few dam-free waterways longer than 100 miles.

The upper Middle Fork flows 61 miles through the Bob Marshall and Great Bear Wilderness Areas at the core of the fourth-largest wild ecosystem in the West. Below the wilderness, the next 40 miles adjoin Glacier National Park and Flathead National Forest in a corridor shared with US 2 plus the Burlington Northern Santa Fe Railroad,

The Middle Fork Flathead presents several sets of Class 3-4 rapids among miles of easier water. Here the maze of the lower "Brothers" rapids below Spruce Park—named for John and Frank Craighead, who championed protection efforts—offers just enough room to ship oars and jet through.

but with virtually no development. Along the river's lower 8 miles the park occupies the north side, with private land and national forest southward. At Blankenship Bridge the Middle Fork meets the slightly larger North Fork, forming the main stem. The Middle Fork's journey through flowered meadows, conifers, and cottonwoods supports one of the West's strongest populations of grizzly bears, plus mountain goats and bald eagles.

This stream played a prominent role in the history of river conservation. It was here, while opposing plans for a dam at Spruce Park, that pioneering bear biologists John and Frank Craighead in the 1950s conceived the idea of a national system of protected rivers. This evolved into the National Wild and Scenic Rivers Act of 1968. Enrolled into this system along with the North and South Forks in 1976, the Middle Fork Flathead is the nation's fourth-longest designation from source to mouth. With national park, wilderness, and Wild and Scenic status, this river is one of the most highly protected anywhere. In 2019 Montanans for Healthy Rivers proposed Clack, Gateway, Schafer, and Strawberry Creeks as tributaries for Wild and Scenic status.

 ## FISH

The Middle Fork has plentiful native westslope cutthroat trout, while bull trout also thrive in cold tributaries and the river—one of the finest major native trout streams in the West. Nonnative rainbow trout were introduced to the lower Middle Fork in the past and have been advancing upstream and posing serious threats to native cutthroat. Montana Fish, Wildlife and Parks is considering installing barriers at some key tributaries for cutthroat survival.

 ## ACCESS

The lower Middle Fork is easily reached east of West Glacier by US 2, which runs up the valley to Bear Creek, where the road departs northeastward, ascending the Bear Creek corridor to the Continental Divide and leaving the upper Middle Fork accessible only by trail for 87 miles.

 ## HIKING

From Bear Creek a Forest Service trail ascends the Middle Fork 7 miles to Spruce Park and onward. Side paths reach the shores, but the main trail typically lies back from the riverfront in deep forest. The Continental Divide National Scenic Trail follows the Middle Fork's upriver extension of Strawberry Creek. The basin constitutes some of the lower forty-eight states' finest grizzly bear habitat; take precautions including bear canisters for food storage.

 ## PADDLING

The Middle Fork offers the unusual opportunity for remote float trips by packing or flying in to Schafer Meadows and floating out 27 miles to US 2 at Bear Creek, with a compelling option to continue another 46 road-accessible miles to the North Fork confluence and even farther down the main stem. Hire a bush pilot to fly into Schafer, or hike/horse-pack the 14-mile trail via Morrison Creek; from US 2 about 2 miles west of Marias Pass, drive south on gravel FR 569 for 6 miles, bear left after Challenge Creek, and continue 2 miles to the Morrison Creek trailhead.

From Bear Creek down, the Middle Fork Flathead has half a dozen road-accessible reaches of Class 2-4 rapids with lucidly clear water. Flathead National Forest river ranger Indigo Scott patrols here on the Class 2 Essex-to-Cascadilla reach.

For a shorter river trip—favored at lower flows—hike 6 miles to the mouth of Granite Creek, 11 miles downstream from Schaefer. Take US 2 west of Marias Pass, turn south on FR 569 for 6 miles, avoiding both 1651 westward and 569 eastward, and go straight on FR 9634 to the trailhead (take a Flathead National Forest map).

The Middle Fork drops 35 feet per mile, creating a lot of whitewater. Forest Service permits are not required as of 2020. Avoid high flows in early summer that can top 11,000 cfs. Typical boating levels are 1,000 or less, which may end by late July. Low flows then may be suited to inflatable kayaks—also easier to carry to the put-in.

The most challenging drops on the wild Middle Fork occur below the Spruce Park Guard Station (7 miles above Bear Creek)—Class 4, or 5 when high. Scout the last and largest pitch when you see tall rocks, river right.

On the road-accessible section below Bear Creek, the first 5 miles to Essex Bridge landing include two Class 3-4 drops. Look for mountain goats where the river passes a north-bank salt deposit.

From Essex to Paola Creek landing is 7 miles of scenic Class 2 with mountain views into Glacier National Park. From Paola to Cascadilla Creek is 12 miles of Class 2 with one Class 3 drop at high flows. The full 19 miles—Essex to Cascadilla—offer a rare overnight river trip through mountain country on clear and mild whitewater suitable for beginning rafters and experienced canoeists summerlong.

Another 7 miles of Class 2 below Cascadilla end at Moccasin Creek landing—not seen from the river and rarely used as a takeout because it requires dragging boats up Moccasin 200 yards. But that's easy with canoes or kayaks, and it makes possible a 26-mile trip at the Glacier Park boundary, all summer. For Class 2-3 boaters disembarking here, first scout and flag this obscure but must-do takeout (Class 4 below!).

Below Moccasin, 9 miles of Class 3-4 whitewater away from the road flow through John Stevens Canyon to West Glacier—the Middle Fork's most popular kayaking and commercial rafting reach.

Finally, 6 miles of Class 1-2 after June run from West Glacier to Blankenship Bridge— fine for most canoeists, with options to continue down the main stem.

See the Forest Service's *Three Forks of the Flathead Wild & Scenic River Float Guide.*

Flathead River, South Fork

Length: 98 miles plus 37 of Young's Creek, total 135 including Hungry Horse Reservoir	**Boating:** Small raft/inflatable kayak overnights, plus a canoe/kayak day trip
Average flow: 3,601 cfs	**Whitewater:** Class 2-3 with a major portage or takeout hike
Watershed: 1,675 square miles	**Gauge:** Twin Creek
Location: East of Kalispell	**Highlights:** Hike-in wilderness river expedition, native trout
Hiking: South Fork and tributary backpacking	

Although a 34-mile-long reservoir impounds the lower South Fork Flathead, 61 miles upstream flow through superb wilderness with some of the West's finest bull trout habitat. In memorable Flathead style, white, black, and red rocks cover the riverbed like an artistic mosaic.

Danaher and Young's Creeks join to form the upper South Fork, reached only by trail in the Bob Marshall Wilderness. Magnificent tributaries include the Spotted Bear River, flowing 32 miles to the South Fork 7 miles above the reservoir.

Boaters pack into the South Fork Flathead and float to the Mid Creek takeout with its 2-mile trail to the takeout road, avoiding this gorge that's too narrow for a raft but a scenic draw for hikers.

The entire Flathead system is a wonderland of multicolored metamorphic rocks, evident here along the South Fork above Meadow Creek Gorge.

The South Fork's free-flowing reach was designated Wild and Scenic in 1976. At that time local Montanans told me that the lower South Fork—flooded by Hungry Horse Dam in 1953—had been the finest part of the entire Flathead River system. Its damming unfortunately predated the river conservation movement in America, which began to gain traction with the Spruce Park dam fight on the Middle Fork Flathead just a few years later.

 FISH

The entire river and tributaries down to the reservoir remain a stronghold of west-slope cutthroat and bull trout. In the past, nonnative rainbow trout were introduced to the upper South Fork basin and populated twenty-one headwater lakes. The construction of Hungry Horse Dam provided a barrier to upriver migration of rainbows from their strongholds below, and the Montana Fish, Wildlife and Parks conducted a rainbow eradication program at the infected headwater lakes, effectively restoring the South Fork above Hungry Horse to a native cutthroat stream.

 ACCESS

From US 2 at Columbia Falls, drive east past the Hungry Horse Dam turnoff, go south on FR 38, and negotiate washboard gravel above the reservoir's east shore for 35 miles to Twin Creek and the South Fork's inlet to the reservoir. The road crosses to the west side and continues 17 miles up to the Meadow Creek trailhead.

HIKING

From the Meadow Creek trailhead, off-trail walking both upriver and down is spectacular; start on the trail and explore the bedrock watercourse and sublime gorge entrance downstream.

From road's end the South Fork Trail crosses the river on a high footbridge and leads upstream, with heavy horse traffic. Tempting side trails climb Big Salmon Creek, the White River, Gordon Creek, and the South Fork headwaters—Young's and Danaher Creeks. Take grizzly bear precautions. The 24-mile-long White River hides behind isolated peaks on both sides of its high-elevation valley reached with an epic long hike.

 PADDLING

Alaskan-like in remoteness, the upper South Fork requires not only a pack-in hike of substantial length, but also a pack-out at the end. This hard-earned float is typically a five-day expedition where rafters carry in gear or hire horse packers during the narrow seasonal window after the high water of early June subsides but before low flows start in mid-July. Rapids are relatively easy except for a lower reach, with take-out recommended above it.

From MT 83 near Seeley Lake, take Forest Service roads to the Pyramid Pass Trail, trek up it and descend Young's Creek to the South Fork, 17 miles altogether. Then float 37 miles to the Mid Creek takeout on river right (signed on a ledge—in any event do not miss!) above Meadow Creek Gorge.

Takeout requires an unusual 4-mile river-exit hike to the Meadow Creek trailhead and dirt road; horse packers can be arranged. A few intrepid boaters—ideally with inflatable kayaks on low flows—carry around narrows too thin for a boat to fit, then run Meadow Creek Gorge with its difficult and limited scout and chance of log blockage, and continue with another steep rapid followed by easy riffles to backwaters of Hungry Horse reservoir.

For a tantalizing, easy sampling of South Fork wonders, take a canoe or kayak run above the reservoir. Drive the South Fork road upstream from the reservoir to the Cedar Flats access, carry your boat down the quarter-mile trail, and float Class 1–2 transparent water 9 miles to a takeout below the Spotted Bear Ranger Station.

See the Forest Service's *Three Forks of the Flathead Wild & Scenic River Float Guide*.

Gallatin River

Length: 115 miles
Average flow: 1,046 cfs
Watershed: 13,851 square miles
Location: Southwest of Bozeman
Hiking: Headwaters in Yellowstone National Park

Boating: Raft, kayak, canoe, day trips
Whitewater: Class 2-4
Gauge: Gallatin Gateway
Highlights: Yellowstone National Park, whitewater, trout fishing

This river rises at Gallatin Lake in Yellowstone National Park followed by 10 miles of wild stream. Northward, beyond the park, the river drops into Gallatin Canyon—50 miles of riffles and rapids separating the Madison Range to the west from the Gallatin Range eastward. Below the canyon and southwest of Bozeman, 60 more miles of trout water wind through gravel bars, willows, and cottonwoods, and irrigation diversions deplete the river in summer before it reaches the triple confluence with the Jefferson and Madison, forming the Missouri River.

In this crucial wildlife corridor of the Greater Yellowstone Ecosystem, grizzly bears make their home at upper reaches and elk herds descend to lower elevations for winter.

 FISH

Though it still shelters some native westslope cutthroat, the Gallatin is prized as a "blue ribbon" rainbow trout stream, with 3,000 fish per mile in one section. Float fishing is not allowed in the canyon. On the lower river anglers target rainbow and brown trout.

Flowing from the northwestern corner of Yellowstone National Park, the Gallatin links that vital ecosystem with lower-elevation terrain to the north—especially important as a wildlife corridor in winter—and offers great whitewater and fish habitat.

With its turbulent canyon awaiting downstream, the Gallatin flows with fast water for canoeing at Taylor Creek during early summer's silty runoff.

 **ACCESS**

The upper river in Wyoming is reached via US 191, which follows the Gallatin downstream into Montana and through its canyon to the Bozeman area. The mouth lies just north of Three Forks.

 HIKING

Bighorn Pass reaches headwaters east of US 191 in the northwest corner of Yellowstone National Park. Downstream, paths approach the river from pullouts along the highway.

 PADDLING

Boating is not allowed in Yellowstone. Below, Gallatin Canyon ranks among Montana's most popular whitewater for rafting and kayaking through 40 miles of Class 2-4 rapids. Flows persist well into summer, with easy access off US 191.

From Taylor Creek—on the west side and 6 miles below the park—to the West Fork (16 miles downstream at the Big Sky turnoff), Class 2 boating draws kayakers and experienced canoeists after runoff declines in late June. Especially popular, 8 miles rush from Red Cliff access to Shady Rest landing below the West Fork and the Big Sky turnoff.

From Shady Rest to Squaw Creek, 17 miles feature canyon-constricted rapids. Class 2-3 steepens to 4 at Greek Creek, 10 miles below Shady Rest. From Squaw Creek to the canyon mouth another 8 miles run at Class 2-3, with takeout above a hazardous diversion dam that appears 1 mile above the canyon mouth.

The lower river—clogged with logjams, brush, and diversion dams—is not often boated.

Kootenai River

Length: 479 miles; 164 in the United States, 99 in Montana and 65 in Idaho
Average flow: 30,650 cfs at the mouth in British Columbia, 15,180 at the lower US-Canada border
Watershed: 19,384 square miles in Canada and the United States
Location: Libby and Troy

Hiking: Short trail at Kootenai Falls
Boating: Raft, canoe, kayak, day trips and overnights
Whitewater: Class 1-4, Class 5-6 at Kootenai Falls
Gauge: Leonia, Idaho
Highlights: Scenic cascade, canoe reach, imperiled fish, angling

This second-largest river in Montana is one of few big rivers of the interior West that's deeply forested throughout. It begins north of Canada's Kootenay National Park, and after exiting from the highest peaks of that spectacular preserve, flows south through the Rocky Mountain Trench at the western base of the Continental Divide—a mirror image of the upper Columbia, which is nearly connected and hydrologically linked by

A full-bodied river among the rainy northern mountains of Montana, the Kootenai is home to rare fish and some of the largest boatable water in the Rockies, flowing here past the mouth of the Yaak River.

groundwater, but rather flows northward in the same geologic formation before turning abruptly south from British Columbia to the Washington line.

For 50 miles in Montana and another 40 upstream in Canada, the Kootenai was impounded by Libby Dam in 1972—one of the last free-flowing river losses of such length and natural quality in the West. Below the dam the Kootenai runs across northern Montana and Idaho 164 miles before reentering Canada, where the "Kootenay" gains big volume from the Purcell Mountains and ends as the Columbia's third-largest tributary, behind the Snake and with barely less water than the Willamette.

In Montana, clear runoff below Libby Dam flows through a forested valley with a highway on the right side and railroad opposite, yet owing to the river's size and screening forest, it retains a sense of remoteness and free-flowing power.

Above Troy the river roars over Kootenai Falls—one of the most amazing hydrologic phenomena one is ever likely to see and, in my opinion, one of the most outstanding but little-known scenic attractions in the West. It's also the West's highest-volume waterfall not blocked by dams or dried up by diversions (Lower Yellowstone Falls and Washington's Snoqualmie Falls have less volume, Shoshone and Twin Falls on the Snake are entirely diverted much of the time, and Willamette Falls in Oregon is partially dammed). But don't expect Niagara—Kootenai Falls is not a sheer drop but an ornate composite of cascades and river-wide ledges through the course of a long, rocky S-bend. Rapids ease below and riffling flows enter Idaho, where the river meanders in the deep and geologically distinctive Purcell Trench toward Canada's Kootenay Reservoir.

Many ospreys nest here, and this is one of few Montana rivers where black bears are often seen, especially in spring. Bighorn sheep sometimes appear on cliffs across from the falls.

A registered National Natural Landmark, Kootenai Falls was threatened by hydropower plans in the 1970s. With opposition by tribes defending the site for spiritual values, and by river conservation groups, the proposal failed passage by the Federal Energy Regulatory Commission—a rare case of that agency not permitting a dam.

On another front, open-pit coal mining in the Fording River basin—tributary to the Elk and then the upper Kootenai reservoir in British Columbia—has discharged toxic amounts of selenium for decades and in 2020 was the suspected cause of a 93 percent population crash of westslope cutthroat trout downstream. The problem remains unresolved.

Kootenai shorelines in Montana are a mix of Kootenai National Forest and private land including the logging and mining towns of Libby and Troy.

 FISH

Until Libby Dam was built, the Kootenai ran unimpounded in Montana, and some anglers say it was the best native cutthroat fishery in the West. The dam altered flow regimes and temperatures, diminishing native fish populations including endangered white sturgeon. This largest freshwater fish in North America once grew to 16 feet and inhabited most large northwestern rivers. It survives in only a few, where some anglers still lobby for a sport season on the rare and ancient cartilaginous species. Libby Dam sharply reduced habitat, and releases geared to hydropower eliminated the flow regime essential for sturgeon reproduction. Since 2016 efforts have been waged to alter

The multi-pitch cascade of Kootenai Falls is one of the most astonishing but little-publicized hydrologic and scenic features of the Rockies, just off US 2 between Libby and Troy.

hydropower schedules and mimic natural conditions for sturgeon, native whitefish, and burbot—also at extinction risk owing to dam-induced temperature changes.

Though rainbow trout are synonymous with Montana for anglers, the Kootenai has the state's only native rainbows, a unique strain called Columbia River redband. With 2,500 (mostly rainbow) trout per mile, this is a popular sport fishery.

The Kootenai also supports native cutthroat, whitefish, bull trout in tributaries, and the red-and-green kokanee salmon, first introduced to Montana in 1914 at the Flathead and now appearing in many streams west of the Continental Divide.

 ACCESS

US 2 follows the Kootenai valley from Bonner's Ferry in Idaho upstream and eastward through Troy and Libby. MT 37 then angles north to Libby Dam and along the reservoir to British Columbia.

 HIKING

Spectacular paths tour the cliffs of Kootenai Falls at a low-key county park along US 2 between Libby and Troy. With off-trail scrambling at the falls' edge, this is among the most extraordinary short river walks in the West.

A major Kootenai tributary, the Yaak River begins in Canada and advances through dense green forests of northern Montana, tumbling over this waterfall with angular bedrock before joining the Kootenai.

 PADDLING

From Libby Dam to Libby is an excellent Class 1-2 big-volume day trip of 17 miles with strong flows all summer. I've overnighted this, but with difficulty finding a campsite. Beware of dam releases bumping levels up 4 feet. In autumn up to 160 bald eagles gather here. Put in at the Alexander Creek access, river-right below the dam. Take out at the Libby bridge.

Kootenai Falls' foaming extravaganza is generally considered unrunnable—a high-volume Class 5-6 drop unmatched for combined gradient, volume, and beauty.

Below the falls, 2 miles of Class 4 continue; expert kayakers put in below the falls.

From the Troy bridge access downstream, big-volume Class 2 riffles pass the Yaak River and can swell to sizable waves at high flows. Take out at Leonia, Idaho, for a 14-mile canoe trip, or go another 14 miles with nearly flat but scenic paddling to Bonner's Ferry; take out on river left off Cow Creek Road. When I did this 28-mile, three-day trip in early autumn, kokanee made quite a sight at the mouth of the Yaak, whose lower miles they ascended to spawn.

Madison River

Length: 148 miles plus 35 of the Gibbon River, total 183
Average flow: 1,719 cfs
Watershed: 12,002 square miles
Location: Northwest of Yellowstone National Park
Hiking: Day hikes and backpacking in headwaters and Bear Trap Canyon, short walks at Three Forks

Boating: Canoe, kayak, raft, drift boat, day trips
Whitewater: Class 1-5
Gauge: Ennis Lake
Highlights: Trout fishing, whitewater canyon

Beginning at the confluence of the Firehole and Gibbon Rivers in northwestern Yellowstone National Park, with astonishing geyser sources and habitat of Rocky Mountain megafauna, the Madison enters Montana and immediately pools behind Hebgen Dam.

Quake Lake lies 2 miles below, formed when a 7.5-magnitude earthquake triggered a whole mountainside to crumble, damming the river, depositing rock 400 feet up the opposite side, and killing twenty-eight campers. Remnants of the slide now create 4 miles of heavy rapids below the lake. The river then enters a wide valley and riffles through 57 miles renowned for trout fishing, with nutrient-rich waters and willow-lined shores.

The riffling Madison upstream from Ennis is one of the West's most revered trout-fishing streams.

Downstream from Ennis this section ends with silt-filled Ennis Reservoir and its dam that releases warm flows. Whitewater of Bear Trap Canyon follows for 9 miles, and in another 31 miles the cottonwood-lined Madison meets the Jefferson and Gallatin Rivers at Three Forks to form the Missouri River.

 ## FISH

Tens of thousands of anglers journey annually to this world-renowned trout-fishing river—one of the most storied angling destinations in the West, with 6,000 trout per mile and heavy use upstream from Ennis. Owing to conflicts between bank and float anglers, the Madison from Quake Lake to Lyons Bridge and from Ennis Bridge to Ennis Lake is closed to fishing from boats.

Whirling disease, in which cartilage and spinal deterioration cause trout to spin in circles and die, tragically struck here after starting in Europe. The plague spread from hatcheries to wild, naturalized, and hatchery trout across much of the West through stocking programs and with waterborne spores, birds that ate infected fish, and contaminated angling gear. Whirling disease can affect all trout species but mortality is less with browns, causing some rivers, including the Madison, to transition from rainbow to brown trout fisheries. Total trout populations here had fallen 90 percent in 1994 but have since recovered through brown trout dominance and perhaps genetically resistant rainbows.

The trail through Bear Trap Canyon clings to steep slopes and shorelines of the Madison River west of Bozeman.

 ACCESS

US 287/20 reaches the upper Madison in Yellowstone National Park and continues down to Ennis, then MT 84 and Madison Road lead to Three Forks.

 HIKING

In Yellowstone, US 287/20 winds through Madison Canyon with waterfront paths and views of monumental Mount Haynes southward. Downstream from the park boundary, interpretive exhibits reveal Quake Lake's geologic history at a visitor center off US 287.

North of Ennis and below Madison Dam, the BLM maintains a 15-mile out-and-back trail through Bear Trap Canyon with views to the river. From Bozeman drive west on MT 84 for 30 miles, then before crossing the Madison turn south on gravel and go 3 miles to the trailhead. Watch for rattlesnakes and poison ivy. Angler use is heavy mid-June through early July. Autumn is a great time to hike here.

At Three Forks, Missouri Headwaters State Park has short paths to the confluence of the Madison and Jefferson, and then the Gallatin, forming the Missouri.

Rocks and boulders from the landslide that formed Quake Lake just west of Yellowstone National Park have been eroded by the Madison River, but turbulent rapids remain, run here by two kayakers.

 **PADDLING**

Boating on the Madison is not allowed in Yellowstone National Park.

Downstream, 4 miles of Class 4-5 rapids below Quake Lake were formed by sharp boulders crushing into the river during the 1959 landslide—expert kayakers only.

Class 1-2 riffles follow for 36 miles from Raynolds Pass landing to Varney Bridge (9 miles upstream from Ennis), suited to rafts, canoes, and drift boats. But, unless you're fishing (and stopping to get out before casting), this willow-lined riffle is mostly uneventful for paddlers. Since the 1970s I've avoided canoeing the Madison because of heavy angler use. Midday paddling is an option. From Varney to Ennis Reservoir the shallow Madison braids with logjams.

Ennis Reservoir has filled with silt, and water warms to 85 degrees—lethal to trout. Below the dam, 1,500-foot-deep, roadless Bear Trap Canyon's Class 3-4 whitewater runs 9 miles, popular with kayakers and rafters. From Ennis drive north on US 287, turn east on Ennis Lake Road, and drop to the put-in below the dam. To take out, drive farther north on US 287 to Norris, turn east on MT 84, and descend to the landing. Flows of 1,500 to 2,200 cfs are good here; above 4,000 is extremely turbulent. See the BLM brochure *Bear Trap Canyon Wilderness Visitor's Guide.*

Below the canyon another 31 miles of Class 1-2 riffle to the mouth with access at Greycliff, Cobblestone, and Three Forks landings.

Marias River

Length: 171 miles plus 98 of Two Medicine River and Two Medicine Creek, total 269
Average flow: 870 cfs
Watershed: 8,495 square miles
Location: Northeast of Great Falls

Hiking: Headwaters, short riverfront paths
Boating: Multiday canoe trip
Whitewater: Class 1+
Gauge: Tiber Dam, Loma
Highlights: Cottonwood wildlife corridor, easy extended canoe trip

The lower Marias runs through one of the most beautiful river corridors of the Great Plains, striking with bluffs where the last Rocky Mountain topography flattens toward the prairie. The river's lower reach supports a host of wildlife along its wild journey to the Missouri River. In his journal Meriwether Lewis called the Marias "one of the most beautifully picturesque countries that I ever beheld."

Worlds away, this watershed begins at one of the more spectacular road-accessible locations in the Northern Rockies—Two Medicine Lake in southern Glacier National Park. Downstream, where Cut Bank Creek enters from a cluttered field of oil wells, the stream's name changes to Marias. Passing through rangeland, muddy waters reach Tiber Dam, and below it the run featured here lies hidden from all but those who go seeking it.

The lower Marias wanders across a wide sandstone canyon floor and through groves of girthy plains cottonwoods, home to coyotes, waterfowl, eagles, and more beavers than I've ever seen on a river.

Among the most beautiful rivers leaving the Rockies and entering the Great Plains, the Marias is like an intimate, picturesque version of the Missouri River to the south.

Key problems are not so evident, but like elsewhere, the regulation of floods by upriver dams has diminished qualities that depend on periodic high water. After an experimental flood release at Tiber Dam in 2006, USGS scientists confirmed that even minor floods have a beneficial effect, revitalizing the Marias's back channels, adding woody debris, depositing silt for cottonwood regermination, and enhancing wildlife and fish habitat.

 ## FISH

A little-known trout fishery thrives with cold clear water for 15 miles below the dam. As water warms downstream, walleye, sauger, and catfish take over. With the dam's effects and voracious exotics including pike, the Marias is not known for native fish, though some warmwater species survive near the Missouri.

 ## ACCESS

To reach the lower river, go north from Fort Benton on MT 223 for 40 miles and turn west to Tiber Dam.

 ## HIKING

For spectacular mountains at the headwaters, take US 2 to East Glacier Park, turn north on MT 49, and park at Two Medicine Lake for backcountry trailheads. For the lower river, wander the riparian forests from canoe-in campsites below Tiber Dam. Rattlesnakes favor fallen cottonwood limbs and trunks—careful reaching for firewood!

 ## PADDLING

For 75 miles the lower Marias makes for ideal canoeing—an intimate version of the famed White Cliffs section of the exponentially larger, windier, and muddier Missouri downstream. Some shorelines are public with the BLM and some private, but I've not seen even a single cowboy there.

Put in below Tiber Dam, where 500 cfs are normally released in summer, more in spring. In 16 miles MT 223 crosses, followed by 59 roadless miles to the Missouri at Loma; take out at the US 87 bridge for a 75-mile trip. Brace for mosquitoes in early summer. Going later is better if 500 cfs or preferably 700 to 1,500 continue.

For an add-on with big-water contrast, continue 23 miles on the Missouri to Coal Banks Landing, or the full 127 miles on the Missouri to US 191 for a total of 202 miles—in my opinion the best long expedition on the Great Plains.

Missouri River

Length: 2,341 miles plus 199 of the Jefferson, Beaverhead, and Red Rock Rivers, total 2,540; 750 miles at the Montana–North Dakota border
Average flow: 90,099 cfs at the mouth, 7,697 at Fort Benton, 10,074 at the North Dakota border above the Yellowstone
Watershed: 494,970 square miles

Location: South and east of Great Falls
Hiking: Riverfront paths
Boating: Long canoe trips
Whitewater: Class 1 but high volume
Gauge: Fort Benton
Highlights: Historic canoe trip, prairie cottonwood corridor

The longest dam-free section of the Missouri is a Montana classic, free-flowing for 213 miles east of Great Falls. This is significant mileage, though only one-tenth of the heavily dammed river's full length.

With headwaters, the Missouri is America's longest river. Counting upriver extensions of the Jefferson, Beaverhead, and Red Rock Rivers, the total comes to 2,540 miles—192 longer than the much larger Mississippi from its source at Lake Itasca to the Gulf of

One of the epic river journeys of the Rocky Mountain foothills and Great Plains, the Missouri flows freely for 213 miles between reservoirs in northern Montana. These are the famed White Cliffs below Coal Banks Landing.

Mexico, and far longer than the Ohio, which carries almost 100,000 cfs more water than the Mississippi where the two meet in Illinois.

Already a mature river born of tributaries at a place logically named Three Forks, the Missouri's first 15 miles offer renowned trout fishing to the low barricade of Toston Dam, followed by Canyon Ferry, Hauser, Upper Holter, and Holter Dams—altogether 70 miles of reservoirs north of Helena. Then 91 miles of mostly gentle big water run to Great Falls, popular among anglers.

Four run-of-river dams block the flow in and near Great Falls, the city being the namesake of now-forgotten cataracts that together plunged 400 feet. Two and a half times the height of Niagara, this gradient was converted to dams beginning in 1890. Only Crooked Falls remains a waterfall, though diminished by hydropower diversions.

One of the prototype studies that led to the National Wild and Scenic Rivers system was completed in the 1960s for the free-flowing section downstream of Great Falls, but protection was thwarted for decades by infighting among agencies and disinterest among Montana's politicians, who later in 1976 designated a 149-mile reach starting at Fort Benton. Within this section, the corridor from Coal Banks Landing to Charles M. Russell National Wildlife Refuge near US 191 was also named the Missouri Breaks National Monument in 2001, administered by the BLM.

Coal Banks Landing lies 45 miles below Fort Benton, and downstream from it the "White Cliffs" of limestone rise 200 feet—widely regarded as highlights of the Missouri. Through the Wild and Scenic reach, groves of plains cottonwoods shade some riverfronts, though their health and extent are greatly reduced by cattle grazing and altered flows, including diminished floods owing to dams upstream. Good riparian habitat remains at the mouths of Arrow Creek, the Judith River, and Cow Creek, thanks to those tributaries' deltas. The undeveloped Missouri corridor is habitat for pronghorns, beavers, mule deer, elk, golden eagles, white pelicans, and waterfowl. Native bighorn sheep were hunted to extinction but others were introduced; watch for them below Judith Landing.

Arguably our most historically significant western river, the Missouri was the route of Lewis and Clark and others in their wake. Aficionados now track the explorers' path and identify campsites and journal entries along the way; see *On the River with Lewis and Clark* by veteran river guide and writer Verne Huser.

 ## FISH

The upper river has trophy trout water, including the tailrace of Holter Dam near Wolf Creek.

The 149-mile Wild and Scenic reach hosts forty-nine species of fish, native and introduced, including one of only six remaining populations of paddlefish, which grow to 140 pounds but only in deep, turbid, undammed reaches of the Missouri, Yellowstone, Mississippi, and large tributaries. About fifty pallid sturgeon survive here. Other warmwater fishes include catfish, sauger, and northern pike.

 ## ACCESS

Headwaters join at Three Forks; from I-90 exit 278 follow signs for 4 miles to Missouri Headwaters State Park. Downstream shorelines are reached east of I-15 between Helena and Great Falls. The Missouri River Recreation Road parallels the water for 35 miles within the 91-mile free-flowing section upstream of Great Falls. For recreation sites take I-15 exit 226 at Wolf Creek and drive north.

From Great Falls drive northeast on US 87 to Fort Benton and the beginning of the long dam-free reach. For its downstream end, take US 191 northeast of Lewistown.

HIKING

To see the source, go to Missouri Headwaters State Park (fee), with short walks to the Madison-Jefferson confluence and three-quarters of a mile farther to the Madison-Gallatin confluence.

In the city of Great Falls, Crooked Falls is the only waterfall remaining undammed. For this obscure landmark that should be better known than it is, drive US 89 to the southeast side of the city, turn north on US 87, pass Malmstrom Air Force Base, turn east on 10th Avenue then left on Rainbow Dam Road, park at Rainbow Dam Overlook, and walk east on the gravel trail past Rainbow Dam to Crooked Falls.

Within the wild Fort Benton–US 191 reach, riverfront paths and off-trail walking include the famed White Cliffs below Coal Banks Landing. Just above Eagle Creek campsite, explore the slot canyon called Neat Coulee.

PADDLING

Mostly easy paddling is found through 60 miles or more of dam-free current between Holter Dam and Ulm Bridge, upstream of Great Falls, with roads and development alongside, but *Paddling Montana* cautions that rapids lie 1.5 miles below Hardy Bridge—23 miles below Holter Dam. Other access areas are possible.

Below Morony Dam—east and downstream of Great Falls—the Missouri's longest dam-free section begins with 3 miles of whitewater and continues as Class 1 for 184 miles to backwaters of Fort Peck Dam, 10 miles east of US 191. To miss the rapids but maximize the trip, canoeists can put in 16 miles below Morony at Carter Ferry (15 miles above Fort Benton) for a 168-mile float to US 191. Most long-distance paddlers settle for the 149-mile Wild and Scenic reach, Fort Benton to US 191, all Class 1.

Class 1, however, is a different animal here. Upstream wind is often a factor and potentially a safety issue with chop and deceptive eddy lines in the massive river.

The reach from Fort Benton to US 191 is boated by 3,000 or more people annually, typically out for five to ten days. Easily shuttled, a day trip runs 22 miles, Fort Benton to Loma. For another 23 miles to Coal Banks Landing the river winds through prairie hills. Below Coal Banks an isolated Missouri tours its white cliffs in a 46-mile section to Judith Landing.

The Missouri "breaks" of rugged badlands follow for 40 miles to Cow Island, with access 8 miles farther at Power Plant Ferry Road. Another 14 miles go to the main access at US 191, where most floaters take out. A final 17 free-flowing miles end at the more remote Rock Creek access with backwaters of Fort Peck Reservoir.

I carry water here rather than purifying the opaque river; lacking rapids and portages, extra weight is not so troublesome. Firewood is scarce, so bring a camp stove. Mosquitoes can be maddening in places, especially early in summer, and beware of rattlesnakes. Plan for interludes of thunderstorms—I'm not embarrassed to say that I've saved myself more than once with a good old-fashioned umbrella as I waited out short but dramatically drenching events (tempting as it is, avoid huddling under the cottonwoods in open, lightning-bolt terrain). I paddle especially during mornings, before winds pick up. All those qualifiers aside, the big river is fabulous and popular for beginner and intermediate paddlers, including youth and family groups.

See the BLM Lewistown District's set of four maps covering Fort Benton to US 191, *Upper Missouri National Wild & Scenic River*. Call the BLM in Fort Benton for maps and conditions.

Big surprise: A relatively unknown free-flowing section of the Missouri lies below both the Wild and Scenic reach and the 135-mile-long Fort Peck Reservoir and runs 185 miles to a ramp directly across from the confluence with the Yellowstone River near backwaters of Garrison Dam in North Dakota. Wide waters cross Montana's plains with breaks incised by ravines, and with waterfowl, raptors, and whooping cranes in spring and fall. Upstream, Fort Peck Dam alters water temperatures and releases clear flows—effects that fade after 60 miles, where native prairie fish reappear. Though US 2 parallels several miles northward, this free-flowing reach offers the quiet isolation of the plains. Unlike the Wild and Scenic section below Fort Benton, you'll likely see no people except maybe at four bridges. The north shore is Fort Peck Indian Reservation, but the tribal warden assured me there are no permit requirements or restrictions on canoeing or camping.

Rock Creek (Clark Fork Basin)

Length: 53 miles plus 40 of the Middle Fork, total 93
Average flow: 531 cfs
Watershed: 882 square miles
Location: Southeast of Missoula
Hiking: Angler paths, biking on a gravel road

Boating: Kayak, canoe, day trips
Whitewater: Class 1-2
Gauge: Clinton
Highlights: Trout fishing, scenic Class 1-2 mountain stream, biking

Rock Creek is the only river flowing north from the rugged complex of southwestern Montana mountain ranges and having no major highways, developments, or diversions. Along with the Middle and South Forks of the Flathead, this is one of three basins rated with "high aquatic integrity" by the Interior Columbia Basin Ecosystem Management Project of 2003.

With runoff from the Anaconda–Pintlar Wilderness, the Middle and East Forks flow north to form the main stem, where a gravel road follows alongside beneath cliffs and

A favorite of anglers, pine-clad Rock Creek flows north to the Clark Fork River upstream from Missoula, and its semi-wild basin links the Greater Yellowstone Ecosystem with the Crown of the Continent's pristine country to the north.

conifer-clad mountains. The creek meets the Clark Fork 20 miles upstream from Missoula (two smaller Rock Creeks flow to the Clark Fork west of Missoula).

This watershed is pivotal to three of the finest wild terrestrial ecosystems in the West: Crown of the Continent to the north, Selway/Salmon/central Idaho to the southwest, and Greater Yellowstone southeastward. The semi-wild Rock Creek basin is the best habitat bridge between these. Grizzly bears have recolonized headwaters, and Rock Creek is a highlight among other candidates for National Wild and Scenic River designation.

 ## FISH

One of few streams of "top biological integrity" listed by the state Department of Environmental Quality, the creek supports native bull trout and westslope cutthroat. Fishing, however, is mainly for nonnative brown and rainbow trout. These populate the lower river and unfortunately are spreading upstream. Whirling disease had killed rainbows here, causing a transition to brown trout.

During prime season and especially early summer, anglers crowd Rock Creek. Modest flows make the stream good for wading, and to reduce conflict, fishing from boats is restricted July through November.

 ## ACCESS

From I-90 exit 126 go south on Rock Creek Road, paved then turning to gravel.

 ## HIKING

The gravel road is fine for riverfront bicycling. Short paths reach the shores.

 ## PADDLING

Rock Creek is swift but whitewater is mostly limited to Dalles Rapids, Class 2+ below Harry's Flat Campground, 14 miles up from the mouth. However, logs may be encountered elsewhere, especially in lower reaches. Good boating flows unfortunately coincide with a notorious salmonfly hatch bringing out anglers in early June, and wading fishermen are difficult to avoid when levels drop in July. Boatable levels continue through August. In spite of this being a drop-dead-beautiful stream, I do not paddle here owing to the numbers of anglers.

Smith River

Length: 122 miles plus 41 of the North Fork, total 163
Average flow: 361 cfs
Watershed: 1,999 square miles
Location: South of Great Falls
Hiking: Riverfront paths at campsites

Boating: Canoe, raft, kayak, overnights
Whitewater: Class 1-2
Gauge: Fort Logan (upper), Eden (lower)
Highlights: Easy multiday wilderness trip, limestone canyon, fishing

Smith River headwaters rise in the Castle Mountains and meander through irrigated ranchland to the entrance of a limestone canyon separating the Big Belt and Little Belt Mountains, west and east respectively, as outliers to the main Rocky Mountain uplift and surrounded by prairie. Deer, elk, and otters live here.

The canyon section is proposed for Wild and Scenic designation by Montanans for Healthy Rivers, but threatening in 2020, an Australian corporation proposed a copper mine for 7,500 acres along Sheep Creek—the best rainbow trout spawning tributary and source of cold water at the Smith's canyon entrance. Plans are predicated on the belief that a plastic liner can contain toxins without leaking for decades and longer.

One of Montana's outstanding rivers for a multiday float trip, the Smith combines mild whitewater with wildness and canyon scenery.

FISH

Anglers flock here for rainbow and especially brown trout. Native cutthroat have retreated to tributaries including Tenderfoot Creek.

 ACCESS

From Livingston take US 89 north to White Sulfur Springs, jog east then north on MT 360, turn right on Smith River Road to the state park, then north to Camp Baker and the upper (southern) end of the canyon.

 HIKING

Riverfront paths beckon at campsites such as the lower canyon's Rattlesnake Bend, with its off-trail scramble to high overlooks.

 PADDLING

Mostly riffles, the Smith's usual trip winds 65 miles. The Smith canyon is one of Montana's most popular fishing and floating streams and the only one with permits required

The Smith River makes its sweeping arc beneath limestone cliffs at Rattlesnake Bend.

in advance, selected through a Montana Fish, Wildlife and Parks lottery. One in ten names are drawn, with a total of 900; apply in January with substantial fees. At the put-in, reserve campsites and get a map from the ranger.

Swift Class 1 steepens with two rocky Class 2s, though sharp bends and logs can trouble inexperienced paddlers on this two- to four-day outing. The largest rapids come after Rattlesnake Bend, 12 miles above Eden Bridge takeout.

Go early May through early July before flows drop. Look for at least an intimate 200 cfs for small rafts and some scraping and wading; some canoeists and kayakers squeak through on 150. Early dates may be cold and rainy. After irrigation ends in September, flows might resume.

For the put-in, see above. To take out, drive northward on the west side for two hours via gravel Upper Milligan Road to Eden Bridge. Avoid when wet. For an easier but longer route, which I took in foul weather, follow US 89 on the east side, cross the Little Belt Mountains (snow is possible in May) to Great Falls, take I-15 south to exit 270 at Ulm, and finally head south on Millegan Road to Eden Bridge. For shuttle listings, contact Montana Fish, Wildlife and Parks.

Below Eden Bridge the lower 20 miles can be boated through rolling hills and ranches, though few do it. Watch for fences.

Stillwater River (Yellowstone Basin)

Length: 71 miles
Average flow: 971 cfs
Watershed: 1,075 square miles
Location: Southwest of Columbus
Hiking: Headwater day hikes, backpacking

Boating: Kayak, canoe, small raft, day trips
Whitewater: Class 2-5
Gauge: Absarokee
Highlights: Wilderness headwaters, whitewater, swift mountain stream

The Stillwater begins northwest of Cooke City and drops through the heart of the Absaroka–Beartooth Wilderness (another Stillwater north of Kalispell flows languidly into the Flathead). Downstream from the Stillwater platinum mine, the river leaves Custer Gallatin National Forest and riffles through ranchland.

On a similar path, the West Fork runs 17 miles from the Beartooth Wilderness, then 12 miles with roads and ranch diversions to the main stem near Nye.

Tributary to the lower Stillwater and eastward, Rosebud Creek also drains the Beartooth Wilderness. Hydropower dams block West Rosebud, but East Rosebud flows 20 miles from wilderness lakes to the national forest boundary and was designated a National Wild and Scenic River in 2018. Other streams north of Yellowstone National Park, including the Boulder River and Rock Creek, share the region's stunning headwater scenery and wildness.

 FISH

Upper reaches support brook trout, while lower cottonwood corridors have rainbow and brown trout fishing at a few public access sites (see the Custer National Forest map).

Opening a window to mountain strongholds southward, trails up the Stillwater River show the resounding wildness of the Beartooth and Absaroka mountain ranges.

From the end of the road the Stillwater Canyon Trail leads upstream to wilderness. Downstream, the river plunges into severe and then milder whitewater as it nears the Great Plains.

 ACCESS

From I-90 at Columbus, turn south on MT 78 to Absarokee, go right on Stillwater River Road to Nye, jog left then right onto Nye Road, and go to the end.

 HIKING

Backpack the Stillwater Trail to high country toward Yellowstone. The West Fork and East Rosebud likewise have great hiking; take grizzly bear precautions.

 PADDLING

Paddling Montana reports Class 5 kayaking starting at the end of the road near Woodbine Campground. After 3 miles of Class 4-5, 10 miles of mostly Class 2 run to the Moraine access. From there to Cliff Swallow landing is 9 miles of Class 3 after early summer crests, Class 4 when higher. Beware of low-bridge hazards, Woodbine to Cliff Swallow.

Below Cliff Swallow landing—10 miles upstream from Absarokee—the remaining 24 miles are mostly swift Class 2, but stay right below the Absaroka fishing access. A large wave appears 1 mile above Whitebird and a big hole 1 mile below Swinging Bridge access, 5 miles above the mouth; stay right.

Upper reaches drop too low in mid-July; below Absarokee is usually boatable summerlong.

Yellowstone River

(See also the Wyoming chapter.)
Length: 692 miles, including 130 in Wyoming, plus 13 of the South Fork; total 705
Average flow: 12,523 cfs, 1,342 at the Wyoming-Montana line, 6,947 at Billings
Watershed: 69,413 square miles
Location: North of Yellowstone National Park and eastward across Montana

Hiking: Day hikes and backpacking at headwaters, angler paths at landings
Boating: Canoe, raft, drift boat, day trips and overnights, long trips
Whitewater: Class 2, one Class 3 reach
Gauge: Yellowstone Lake, Gardner River, Livingston, Billings, Forsyth
Highlights: Rockies and Great Plains interface, long canoeing river

The Yellowstone spans an outsized geography of both Rocky Mountains and Great Plains, and the river's beginnings in its namesake national park are a river highlight of the West.

After 130 miles the Yellowstone leaves the park, enters Montana, and flows through aptly named Paradise Valley between the Absaroka Range immediately east and the Gallatin Range to the west.

Legendary, monolithic, and cherished by many, the Yellowstone is a landmark river of the West, riffling here through upper Paradise Valley.

The Yellowstone turns eastward from its mountain fastness and downstream from Livingston crosses a Rockies-to-plains transition zone where cold water continues with good trout habitat.

At Livingston the river breaks out of the mountains and continues between receding sub-ranges. Then below Big Timber hundreds of miles of the Yellowstone cross the plains, joining the Missouri River just past the state line in North Dakota.

Hearty flows continue summerlong. At its mouth the Yellowstone averages 12,523 cfs where it meets the longer Missouri, which carries only 11,000.

Among nine major rivers flowing from the Rockies, only the Yellowstone and Salmon remain unblocked by storage reservoirs. Though the Yellowstone is often cited as the longest dam-free river in the United States outside Alaska, that's not quite true: It has no storage reservoirs, but six low-head diversion structures include one channel-wide dam of rock rubble that requires portage by canoeists and is scheduled for upgrading to a larger, formidable concrete dam.

But not to quibble, the Yellowstone has extraordinary natural qualities: pristine headwaters in the national park, a largely intact riparian corridor with cottonwood forests for 600 miles, an excellent assemblage of native fishes, and the longest high-quality canoe trip in America. With its size and range of habitat—high elevation to low—the Yellowstone is the central freshwater artery of Montana and of the Rockies' northeastern quadrant.

The Yellowstone's storied path incorporates exquisite wildness of headwaters, excellent trout fishing, and stunning scenery. Riparian habitat supports beavers, coyotes, wolves, and both mule and white-tailed deer. The Yellowstone excels more than any other river I know with a who's who of large birds: whistling swans, sandhill cranes, ospreys, various prairie raptors, white pelicans with glossy black wing bars, and more bald eagles than I've seen in summer on any other river outside Alaska.

Conservation

Downstream from Yellowstone National Park, 31 miles of the river through Paradise Valley were endangered in 1972 with flooding by Allenspur Dam, which would also have degraded hundreds of miles of habitat below by altering flows. Citizen and state opposition halted the project. This worthy reach still lacks protection under the Wild and Scenic Rivers Act, as of this writing.

Threats of diversions for fossil fuel development also led to a state reservation of water that precludes large withdrawals; the Yellowstone is America's only example of setting aside substantial flows in a large river for fish, wildlife, and hydrologic functions that maintain a healthy riverbed. However, a complementary program for protecting riparian habitat through easements, acquisition, or other arrangements along the river has not resulted in anything approaching a corridor of public open space. Land development could diminish qualities of the entire river, as it already has in Montana's upper reaches.

Though spared the dam, Paradise Valley has undergone a boom, with trophy homes rising from floodplains and terraces. Worse, with the riverfront investments came extensive riprapping of the banks intended to armor the new homes, in the process diminishing riparian values and habitat.

Meanwhile, on the lower river catastrophic oil spills have reoccurred from broken pipelines in 2011, 2015, and other times. Unit trains of oil tankers pose similar threats. Personal observation in floating the entire middle and lower river revealed places where crumbling bank erosion was alarmingly close to railroad tracks.

Though the Yellowstone has been spared storage reservoirs and industrial-scale withdrawals by the fossil fuel industries, irrigation systems developed during Montana's early days shunt flows into canals, and a multitude of pumps divert water. These are mostly minor intrusions, but on the lower river Intake Dam blocks migration of endangered pallid sturgeon. Only 125 of these ancient fish, growing to 5 feet, remain in the upper Missouri/Yellowstone basin, and the local population has not reproduced in the wild since dam construction a century ago. Hatchlings need to drift in the current for two weeks before they can swim on their own, and adequate free-flowing water across the fish's range has become rare. Some adult sturgeon survive in shorter reaches, but the species has been on life support through a captive breeding program—a stopgap response at best.

In spite of a national trend to remove unnecessary dams, the Army Corps of Engineers at this writing plans to replace the current rock-and-rapid structure at Intake with a solid-wall concrete dam estimated at $60 million (more costly now), though the planned fish passage facilities are not known to work for sturgeon, which are highly susceptible to even minor blockages of migration routes. American Rivers and other groups support dam removal with provisions for pumping irrigation water into canals for uninterrupted service to farmers. Elimination of this minor dam would open 167 miles to spawning sturgeon and other fish and would free the Yellowstone of its only full-width dam.

 FISH

The river between Yellowstone National Park and Livingston is known as one of the most famous streams in America for large rainbow trout. Coldwater angling continues downriver to Big Timber, where the river warms, though some trout survive to Billings. Fishing is best from late July—after cloudy flows from snowmelt subside—through fall.

The entire Yellowstone supports an exceptional assemblage of forty-five species of native fishes including ancient rare paddlefish, endangered pallid sturgeon, shovelnose sturgeon weighing 140 pounds, and burbot. Warmwater species also include native sauger, which need long migration routes, plus introduced walleye, northern pike, and channel catfish. The Bighorn River—a lower basin tributary mainly flowing through the Great Plains and so not featured here—is a top angling stream for introduced brown trout in the tailrace of Bighorn Dam.

 ## ACCESS

Downstream from Yellowstone National Park the river is reached by US 89 from Gardiner northward to Livingston. Middle and lower sections are accessed by roads off I-94, then by MT 16 through lower reaches to Sidney, and local roads to the mouth.

 ## HIKING

Below the national park, private land limits hiking through Paradise Valley and for most of the river's length. At Livingston the Levy Trail is a town-walk of 1 mile; take US 89 north, cross I-90, turn right on Ninth Street, and go to the end.

Otherwise, hiking along Montana's Yellowstone is limited to short walks at public ramps or on gravel bars and riparian flats reached by boat. Scattered federal and state land can be found on BLM maps.

 ## PADDLING

Just below the national park, Gardiner to Corwin Springs is 8 miles of Class 2-3 whitewater. From Gardiner on US 89 on the west side of the river, go east on Park Street to the end. However, this is a steep carry to the river, without parking there. Easier, drive from Gardiner north 3 miles on US 89 to McConnell access. Another 5 miles north on 89, find Corwin Springs landing near the next bridge over the Yellowstone.

Below Corwin comes the 9-mile Yankee Jim Canyon with a trio of pushy Class 3 rapids—the largest big-wave whitewater below the national park. Reach the Carbella takeout via gravel road west of US 89; from Gardiner drive 17 miles north and turn west.

Many paddlers favor the one- to three-day trip from Carbella to Livingston with its iconic Rocky Mountain views of Emigrant Peak, pyramidal to the east. But canoeing is excellent the whole way to the Missouri River—a 527-mile expedition, nearly dam-free, unconditionally the place to go for the West's longest canoe trip. I did this in September as a splendid twenty-day journey. Foul weather required three layover days, which left me with a lot of daily mileage, but doable in nearly steady current.

Below Carbella the Yellowstone is Class 1-2 suited for canoeists experienced in big water with strong currents and wave trains. Typical entrance to a rapid narrows with a definitive green-water tongue funneling into breaking waves, avoided by drawing left or right after starting down the drop.

Enigmatic, the middle and lower Yellowstone is semi-wild with features of a great wilderness expedition but also opportunities for exit at frequent ramps, resupply at small towns, and cell phone use through the interstate highway corridor for those who value the security that phones offer. However, the ranchland burgs and sprawling Billings are

Downstream from Columbus the Yellowstone riffles farther from its mountain origins and embarks across the Great Plains, complete with colorful sunsets across a spacious landscape.

not as convenient as they appear on maps—typically a mile from the river and not directly accessible or walkable with a heavy water jug. Drinking water supplies are not generally convenient or evident. I carried twelve gallons for my twenty-day solo trip; one refill would have been enough but I conveniently topped off twice: at Pompeys Pillar National Historic Park, 35 miles below Billings, and at the Forsyth town campground. I preferred not to drink river water, especially below Billings, but carried a filter for backup.

Though ranches, irrigation works, scattered houses, an interstate highway, and railroads with noise even all night at a few camps are all part of the mix, the river offers enticing views throughout, swift water, and mature cottonwood forests. As a large, healthy, free-flowing stream, the Yellowstone still creates dynamic new channels, carves banks, builds logjams, and nourishes wildlife habitat the way all arterial rivers once did when their natural processes remained intact.

Roads parallel both banks, though they are mostly unobtrusive if not hidden from the water and its floodplains, which are typically guarded beneath bluffs. *Paddling Montana* lists sixty-one public access areas—a ramp or path to the water every 5 to 10 miles or so.

Unlike the Missouri River—a Great Plains cousin—the Yellowstone has development but also natural amenities lacking on the more popular river to the north: clear water, hundreds of Class 2 rapids, mountain views, a nearly continuous cottonwood forest, and the virtual absence of other boaters, in contrast to the Missouri below Fort Benton with thousands of floaters per year.

Consider the Yellowstone in three unequal sections:

1. Carbella to Livingston: Starting at the Carbella ramp, Class 2 rapids run 46 miles through Paradise Valley, passing ranches and the abrupt rise of the Absaroka Mountains—views now unfortunately marred by trophy homes. Yet the river is still beautiful. This reach has some of America's best-known brown and rainbow trout fishing.

2. Livingston to Billings: 132 miles of Class 1 with many Class 2 wave trains, mountain views, islands, rocky bluffs, cottonwoods, and ranches. Having turned east at Livingston, the Yellowstone transitions from the Rockies to the Great Plains, though peaks linger in the distance and the river brushes against small mountains.

3. Billings to the Missouri River: 351 miles. At Billings the river passes refineries, urban traffic, the odor and foam of sewage, and air heavily scented by the oil and gas industries, though downstream all that fades quickly and the Yellowstone resumes as an artery linking the Rockies with the plains. Cattle, hay fields, road crossings, a railroad, and I-94 share this corridor, but the vacation homes and drift-boat anglers common above Big Timber are gone.

Long sections of the lower river have a surprisingly wild feel with wide gentle flows, Canada geese honking in multitudes, white pelicans in elegant flight, and not a person appearing for miles or even days. Cottonwood forests are magnificent though badly infested by Russian olive trees in lower miles.

For the final 85 miles from Glendive to the mouth, I-94 and the railroad have turned away, leaving the Yellowstone serenely wilder beneath bluffs of the Great Plains. It seems that only the buffalo are absent.

At Billings the Yellowstone encounters the stark encroachment of the fossil fuel industry with oil and gas facilities at the riverbank.

Leaving the gas industry behind as fast as it had appeared, the Yellowstone crosses the plains of eastern Montana, where flows hesitate at six diversion structures. All but one are minor, including Rancher Dam here below the mouth of the Bighorn River.

The Yellowstone's six low diversion dams all appear from Billings to Intake Dam on the lower river. All deserve floaters' attention. First, Huntley diversion dam blocks the right side of an island 14 miles below Billings; stay left of the island for uninterrupted easy passage. Waco Dam appears in another 36 miles; again, stay left of the island for open water. Rancher Dam comes in another 36 miles (below the Bighorn River); I dragged over the rocky low rubble at extreme left. Myers Dam comes 15 miles farther; stay far left for a Class 2 drop at low flows, likely turbulent when higher.

Larger, Forsyth Dam rises in another 41 miles; go extreme right for a 3-foot plunge next to the southern bank, doable in low flows, likely with increased turbulence when higher; stop far upstream along the brushy bank to scout and carry if in doubt. In another 167 miles (16 miles below Glendive), Intake Dam extends river-wide—a formidable rock pile planned for upgrading to a concrete-wall structure. The existing dam, as of 2020, includes a unique cable car strung overhead that drops boulders onto the rock dam when needed. Carry right to avoid the steep drop and left-side canal.

All of the Yellowstone's dams require keen alertness, pose potential dangers, and may require portages if proper approaches are not taken.

For extended Yellowstone trips, acquire twelve BLM maps, *Yellowstone River Floaters' Guide*, from Springdale (below Livingston) to the mouth. For upper reaches and a map missing from the BLM supply, I managed with photocopies from the DeLorme *Montana Atlas*.

The fully mature Yellowstone carries more water than the Missouri where the two behemoths meet just across the Montana state line in North Dakota, not far below this gravel bar campsite near Sydney.

To avoid wildlife stress, I recommend Yellowstone travel not in early summer but later, after young birds have fledged and wildlife becomes less vulnerable. Late summer and early autumn bring beautifully clear green water. Lower levels make rapids distinct, gravel bars exposed, and campsites available, although the current is slower and weather risky in September.

The full Yellowstone is an epic journey, incomparable in scale, taking paddlers away for hundreds of miles on a truly great American river expedition.

The lower Yellowstone is a vital wildlife corridor, supporting both mule deer—grazing the river edge here—and white-tailed deer.

Rivers of Wyoming

River recreation in the Rocky Mountain region of this predominantly semiarid state is concentrated in the northwestern quadrant, where the extraordinary waters of the Yellowstone, Snake, and Green Rivers take form and largely define the renowned Greater Yellowstone Ecosystem. River running and streamside hiking here are among the finest in the West. Comprised of ten contiguous mountain ranges that overflow into Montana and Idaho, this wild and water-laced landscape with 108,800 miles of streams statewide is enormously important for its wildlife habitat and also for the gifts that these rivers offer to people and whole basins extending far downstream.

Snowmelt from the stunning Tetons—the quintessential glaciated peaks of the Rockies—and from neighboring ranges feed water to a host of excellent streams radiating outward and ultimately ending in far-flung estuaries of not only the Pacific and Gulf of Mexico but also the Gulf of California. This is the most notable crown of headwaters in the West. Runoff from Wyoming's rivers and streams ultimately touches twenty states before drifting out to sea—the highest such number in America. Remarkably, all those states are reached by waters from just three northwestern Wyoming counties: Teton, Park, and Sublette.

While the Greater Yellowstone region's mountain complex gives rise to the most significant cluster of waterways in Wyoming, the drier Medicine Bow Range in the southeast drains to the North Platte, and an eastern outlier of the Rockies—the Bighorn

From wild headwaters the North Fork Shoshone gathers downward momentum with US 20 alongside as the eastern gateway to Yellowstone.

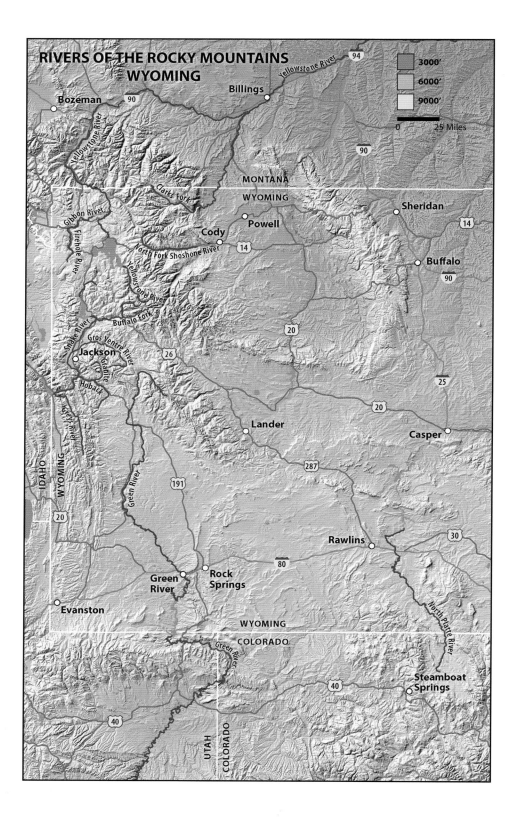

RIVERS OF THE ROCKY MOUNTAINS
WYOMING

3000'
6000'
9000'

0   25 Miles

Bozeman   90   Yellowstone River   94

Billings   Yellowstone River

90

Clarks Fork

MONTANA

WYOMING

Sheridan   14

Gibbon River

Firehole River   Cody   Powell   14   Buffalo

North Fork Shoshone River   90

Yellowstone River

Buffalo Fork

Snake River   Gros Ventre River   20

Jackson   26   Granite

Hoback   25

Greys River   20   Lander   Casper

IDAHO   287

WYOMING   191   Green River   20   Rawlins   30

80

Green River   Rock
River   Springs

Evanston   North Platte River

WYOMING

COLORADO   Green River

UTAH   40   Steamboat
Springs

40

COLORADO

Mountains—sheds water to the lower Bighorn River, though at that point it's dammed and entering the Great Plains.

Fishing in the Greater Yellowstone region is legendary. Here reside some of the healthiest native trout populations in the West, including Snake River finespotted cutthroat—genetically the same as Yellowstone cutthroat, though each has its regional name.

The rare Bonneville cutthroat—endemic to the landlocked Bear River basin of Utah, Wyoming, and Idaho, plus other tributaries to the ancestral Bonneville Lake of ice age vintage—maintains a limited stronghold in

WYOMING RIVERS
Buffalo Fork (Snake River Basin)
Clark's Fork (Yellowstone Basin)
Firehole and Gibbon Rivers
Granite Creek
Green River
Grey's River
Gros Ventre River
Hoback River
Platte River, North
Shoshone River, North Fork
Snake River
Yellowstone River

southwest Wyoming's Smith's Fork of the Bear River. Also extremely restricted, Colorado River cutthroat survive in La Barge and Fontenelle Creeks flowing to the Green River from the east face of the Wyoming Range, and also in the Little Snake River basin (no relation to the Snake River of Teton and Idaho fame), which flows south to the Yampa at Wyoming's south-central border.

Other declining native fishes include the bluehead sucker, flannelmouth sucker, roundtail chub, and leatherside chub—perhaps less showy but no less deserving of their share of life. These warmwater natives are abundant in only a few select streams on the west side of the Continental Divide.

While fine reaches of rivers remain in Wyoming's northwest corner, the state's waterways overall have been widely degraded. Oil and gas drilling and other fossil fuel development have taken political priority, to put it lightly, and fossil fuel extraction has impaired water quality and quantity in many streams. Overgrazing on arid lands has resulted in degraded riparian corridors. Invasive species such as tamarisk on floodplains and brown trout in coldwater streams crowd out and compete with natives. Even though Wyoming has the lowest population density in the West—five people per square mile—development pressures in recreation hot spots such as Jackson Hole, along with the sporadically booming and busting phases of fossil fuel towns, all threaten streams and riparian habitat.

Most of Wyoming's rivers pour into reservoirs or are debilitated, at least to some extent, by diversions, and so Wyoming waters—like others throughout the interior West—lack continuity with downstream aquatic ecosystems. However, significant reaches remain free-flowing and at least somewhat natural.

Until 2009 only one waterway was included in the National Wild and Scenic Rivers system: the upper Clark's Fork of the Yellowstone. An unlikely but significant bill was then passed designating portions of the upper Snake River and fifteen tributaries as the "Snake River Headwaters." Even then, not all worthy streams were included owing to opposition by county commissioners outside the core Teton County area, and ultimately by the Wyoming congressional delegation that reluctantly moved the bill through Congress, chiefly in respect for their Wyoming colleague, Senator Craig Thomas of the Yellowstone area, who authored and sponsored the insightful legislation but passed away while it was pending.

A sizable group of Wyoming streams continue to offer important habitat and recreational qualities, and some, including the upper Yellowstone, the Clark's Fork, and the Snake with its upper tributaries, are exceptional from a national perspective.

Buffalo Fork (Snake River Basin)

Length: 26 miles plus 27 of the South Buffalo Fork, total 53	**Hiking:** Day hikes and backpacking
Average flow: 546 cfs	**Boating:** Canoe, day trips
Watershed: 327 square miles	**Whitewater:** Class 1-2
Location: Northeast of Jackson, east of Moran	**Gauge:** Moran
	Highlights: Easy paddling, wilderness headwaters, wildlife

The North Buffalo Fork and South Buffalo Fork (not North Fork or South Fork Buffalo) run 25 and 27 miles respectively through woodlands and wetlands of the Teton Wilderness. The main stem continues 26 miles through riparian thickets where moose browse. Roads lie on either side of the lower river, though they don't encroach. Some frontage is owned by guest ranches, but main-stem shorelines mainly lie in Bridger-Teton National Forest and in Grand Teton National Park, where the Buffalo Fork meets the Snake River.

Largely protected, this river includes important wildlands at the core of the Greater Yellowstone Ecosystem and supports bald eagles, wild trout, and grizzly bears.

 FISH

This is one of the Rockies' larger streams where nearly all fish are native, with Snake River cutthroat doing well.

The Buffalo Fork curves through willows and moose habitat as it approaches Grand Teton National Park and the Snake River.

The North Buffalo Fork nears its confluence with the South Buffalo Fork in the Teton Wilderness.

 ## ACCESS

From Grand Teton National Park at Moran Junction, take US 287 east 3 miles, turn north on Buffalo Valley Road, and go to the end.

 ## HIKING

The Buffalo Forks trail system starts by paralleling the upper main stem, though without many views to the water, and continues up both the North and South Buffalo to link with a vast forested trail network, not much used by hikers, who tend to prefer the high country of the Tetons, but heavily used by horse packers and elk hunters in autumn.

 ## PADDLING

Not often paddled, the main-stem Buffalo is a Class 1 float with riffles and great views of the Tetons through willows and riparian habitat of moose and cutthroat. Prep for bugs in summer. Boating is not allowed on this stream in Grand Teton National Park; take out above it.

From US 287 drive 10 miles east on Buffalo Fork Road, and put in below the campground at Turpin Meadows Bridge. For takeout of the 13-mile glide, from Moran Junction take US 287 east 3 miles to the bridge and a small river-left pullout with a path to the water. Park 200 yards back west at the 287/Buffalo Fork Road intersection if necessary.

Clark's Fork (Yellowstone Basin)

Length: 152 miles; 65 in Wyoming, 87 in Montana
Average flow: 1,047 cfs
Watershed: 2,795 square miles
Location: Northwest of Cody
Hiking: Day hikes and backpacking

Boating: Canoe, kayak, day trips
Whitewater: Class 2+, Class 4-6
Gauge: Belfry, Montana (lower river)
Highlights: Wildest canyon in the West

I regard the upper Clark's Fork of the Yellowstone as the wildest river in the United States outside Alaska. This owes to an extraordinary 2,000-foot-deep canyon with vertical walls, virtually unrunnable whitewater, and no road or trail along or to the river in its canyon reach.

Don't be confused: The similarly spelled Clark Fork is entirely different, flowing west to the Columbia River. The Clark's Fork (often spelled "Clarks" Fork, though there was only one William Clark!) is one-twentieth the volume of its western cousin but significant as it flows from Montana into Wyoming and back into Montana to meet the Yellowstone.

The stream begins near Cooke City, Montana, in mountains checkered by past mining. It quickly flows southeast into Wyoming and for 20 miles gathers tributaries draining south from the formidable Beartooth Plateau.

The Clark's Fork of the Yellowstone starts its dramatic descent in forests at southern edges of the Beartooth Plateau along the Wyoming-Montana border. Here Pilot Peak rises on the horizon.

For another 20 miles the river plunges through its forbidding canyon, dropping 1,200 feet through 6 miles and thundering over multiple waterfalls within "The Box"—a gorge unlike any other for its granite walls, whitewater intensity, wildness, and untapped flows.

Below the canyon the river enters a trail-accessible, U-shaped, glacier-carved valley that spills out into dry terrain where the Rocky Mountains flatten to the Great Plains. Another 100 miles of lower river with roads, a railroad, seventeen diversion dams, and ranches cross Wyoming and Montana to augment the Yellowstone on the Great Plains near Billings.

The upper watershed is prime for grizzly bears and also wolves, which know that large herds of elk, pronghorn, mule deer, and white-tailed deer descend the Sunlight Creek drainage in late autumn to forage at lower elevations. A thousand mixed ungulates have been seen grazing together in this Wyoming Serengeti.

In 1990 Congress designated a 21-mile reach of the Clark's Fork as Wyoming's first National Wild and Scenic River, but not before a half mile at the lower end was omitted for an irrigation dam— never built.

Pounding through "The Box," the Clark's Fork is arguably the wildest river in the United States outside Alaska, churning in a canyon that's virtually inaccessible and neither boatable nor hikeable in any normal sense of the words.

In 1995 a gold-mining plan threatened headwaters, and after engagement by American Rivers, the Greater Yellowstone Coalition, and other groups, federal agencies acquired the mining rights for protection. More recently, gas fracking surged in the lower basin with potential to degrade the Clark's Fork and Yellowstone Rivers.

 FISH

Both the upper Clark's Fork and Sunlight Creek support Yellowstone cutthroat. Above and below its canyon, the Clark's Fork also has rainbow trout, brown trout, and native mountain whitefish. Below the canyon, the Wyoming Game and Fish Department stocks hatchery trout.

Downstream in Montana, a cottonwood corridor where one might expect excellent habitat is diminished by diversions reducing the flow and by cloudy irrigation return flows, while access is restricted by a lack of public land. Some anglers manage to find an unusual mix of brown, rainbow, and cutthroat trout plus native mountain whitefish and introduced grayling. Warmwater fish populate the Great Plains reach downstream.

A bridge of the Chief Joseph Highway offers this view straight down to the depths of Sunlight Creek in its own box canyon that's similar but smaller than that of the Clark's Fork.

 ACCESS

From the west and Cooke City, drive east on US 212 along the upper river, then bear right on WY 296. From the southeast and Cody, go northwest on WY 120 and west on Chief Joseph Highway/WY 296 west.

 HIKING

From US 212 east of Cooke City, turn right on WY 296, drive 5 miles, and just past Hunter Peak Campground park on the left at the Clark's Fork trailhead. This path climbs to the northern canyon rim and after 12 miles emerges at four-wheel FR 119, which continues eastward down to the canyon mouth. For sensational views, I needed to bushwhack a bit off-trail to rock outcrops at the canyon's north rim.

Another trail follows the south rim of Dead Indian Creek Canyon to the canyon of the Clark's Fork below The Box, 6 miles out and back. Find the trailhead just off Chief Joseph Highway 1 mile east of Sunlight Creek Bridge—itself worth a stroll from the south-side parking lot for breathtaking views of Sunlight Canyon, a smaller but to-scale version of The Box.

Though rarely paddled, the upper Clark's Fork offers a chance for an athletic adventure in low-water boating and spectacular mountain views during late summer, starting with this canoe portage at a small waterfall above Fox Creek.

 PADDLING

Not for everyone, the tiny, intimate upper Clark's Fork has a scenic Class 2 run of 4 miles in high mountain terrain with extraordinary views of Pilot Peak—one of the more memorable scenes of Rocky Mountain peaks from a runnable river. Wait for high flows to subside in midsummer or so, and count on a few logs to surmount and shallows to wade, but I've enjoyed adventure paddling here in late August even with a dozen drags given a nominal flow of 50 cfs. To put in, take US 212 east from Cooke City 5 miles, and across the highway from Fox Creek Campground carry to the base of a 6-foot waterfall, or simply put in nearer the road and drag around the falls. Take out at a roadside pullout 3.5 miles east from the put-in or 1 mile west of the 212/296 intersection. Park visibly or flag this nondescript takeout. Class 5 below!

From the WY 296 intersection onward the Clark's Fork is a Class 4–6 descent. Two Class 5 upper sections are followed by the famous Box with seventeen strenuous portages, many requiring rock climbing and teamwork in belaying—one of the most demanding whitewater descents in the West.

The lower Clark's Fork across Montana to the Yellowstone River can be paddled but is riddled with diversion dams, and shorelines are mostly private.

Firehole and Gibbon Rivers

Length: Firehole, 32 miles; Gibbon, 35 miles
Average flow: Firehole, 307 cfs; Gibbon, 127 cfs
Watershed: Firehole, 262 square miles; Gibbon, 125 square miles
Location: West-central side of Yellowstone National Park

Hiking: Geothermal boardwalks, day hikes, tributary backpacking
Boating: Not permitted
Whitewater: Rapids and waterfalls
Gauge: Firehole near West Yellowstone, Gibbon at Madison Junction
Highlights: Geysers and geothermal features, wildlife

As twin sources to the upper Madison River in Yellowstone National Park, the Firehole and Gibbon have exceptional geologic and wildlife values (see the Montana chapter for the Madison).

The Firehole flows 10 miles from Madison Lake through wildlands, riffles within a stone's throw of the iconic Old Faithful Geyser, and continues 22 miles with Yellowstone's Grand Loop Road nearby. North of the Firehole, the Gibbon River is longer

Known principally for Old Faithful, but also for myriad other geysers and geothermal attractions, the Firehole River farther downstream plummets over Firehole Falls, seen with a short stroll off a side road near the western entrance to Yellowstone.

but with a much skinnier watershed and flows south and west from similar wetland and geothermal headwaters.

The two basins offer the greatest hydrothermal display in the world, including half of all global hydrothermal features. Bison and elk graze along the Firehole and tributaries. Heated water spurs growth of algae, bacteria, and invertebrates and keeps sections of these rivers ice-free and uniquely productive for fish at high elevations year-round.

Unfortunately, the invasion of New Zealand mud snails has radically altered ecological balances. First discovered in the park in 1994, the snails reached devastating densities in thermally influenced waters, outcompeted native invertebrates, and consumed algae needed as food for other species. The Firehole and Gibbon are graphic examples of how rivers within fully protected jurisdictions—and that appear pristine to casual observers—are vulnerable to degradation from exotic species spread without our knowledge,

The Firehole River of western Yellowstone National Park collects steaming discharges from the largest geothermal complex on earth, seen here at Black Sand Basin.

Fairy Creek curves across bison-grazed meadows before joining the Firehole River and then the Madison in Yellowstone National Park.

The Firehole and Gibbon Rivers join to form the Madison, here in western Yellowstone National Park near the Wyoming-Montana border. A fly fisherman works his craft even as autumn snowstorms fill the sky. Mount Haynes fills the background.

control, or restorative remedy. If you wade in these rivers, thoroughly clean your shoes or waders afterwards—I was surprised to not see this advice posted by the Park Service where many people were wading downstream from the thermal features.

 ## FISH

Native fish ventured no higher than Firehole Falls, just above the Gibbon confluence, but brown trout were stocked as early as 1890. Rainbows were likewise introduced to the upper Firehole. Though stocking in the park was halted in 1955, both species persist. Mountain whitefish are native to the Madison below Firehole Falls.

 ## ACCESS

For 22 miles the Firehole is paralleled by Yellowstone's Grand Loop Road, which likewise follows most of the Gibbon.

 ## HIKING

Short paved and boardwalk trails are strolled by thousands daily through the Firehole basin and also the Norris Geyser Basin of the upper Gibbon. Get out of the car and see Gibbon Rapids at an unmarked pull-off 2 miles west of Norris; also, a brilliantly orange and utterly bizarre travertine cone can be seen at water's edge from below a pull-off just downstream. Gibbon Falls is a busy but worthwhile stop on the highway.

The Gibbon River rushes through rapids and erodes bedrock volcanic formations west of Norris.

Trails reach the upper Firehole via the Shoshone Lake Trail south of Old Faithful. Tributary Nez Perce Creek—north of the Lower Geyser Basin—flows west from the park's Central Plateau, reached via a 10-mile trail one way, though from the Grand Loop Road it's a mile to the first river view. Take grizzly bear precautions.

At the lower Firehole, short paths reveal canyon waterfalls near the park's west entrance off the 2-mile-long Firehole Falls Road—a minor scenic byway that offers some of the park's most awesome cascade-waterfall views.

PADDLING

No boating is allowed on rivers in Yellowstone National Park.

Granite Creek

Length: 23 miles
Average flow: 127 cfs
Watershed: 85 square miles
Location: Southeast of Jackson
Hiking: Day hikes and backpacking
Boating: Canoe, kayak, day trips

Whitewater: Class 2
Gauge: None, but comparable to one-fifth Grey's River
Highlights: Waterfall, hot spring, intimate canoe trip

Granite Creek is the major tributary to the Hoback River as it flows from Bridger–Teton National Forest toward the Snake River south of Jackson.

 FISH

The creek has small native Snake River cutthroat.

 ACCESS

From Jackson take US 89 south 13 miles to Hoback Junction, turn east on US 191, go 10 miles, turn left on Granite Creek Road, and continue on gravel 10 miles through meadows to a hot spring developed in 1933 with a deck.

Granite Creek riffles through Bridger-Teton National Forest as it nears the Hoback River.

HIKING

The Granite Creek Trail follows the upper 12 miles of this stream in the Gros Ventre Wilderness, reached from a trailhead at road's end.

The gravel road along the lower creek is unplowed in winter and groomed for snow-mobiles, but with that significant disclaimer, the route is used for cross-country skiing to the hot springs and for launching winter expeditions into the headwaters' fabulous backcountry skiing terrain through the Gros Ventre Range.

 PADDLING

Not much paddled, the lower 10 miles of Granite Creek are an excellent early summer Class 2 treat—a rare opportunity for canoeing on a small, lively Rocky Mountain stream at high elevation with mountain views. Beware of logs and tight bends. Paddlers can continue down the Hoback to the Snake River.

Below its waterfall, Granite Creek presents a rare opportunity to canoe or kayak on relatively easy whitewater at high elevations in the Rockies of Wyoming.

Green River

Length: 769 miles, 323 in Wyoming
Average flow: 5,303 cfs, 1,614 at the Wyoming-Utah line
Watershed: 44,143 square miles, 13,785 in Wyoming
Location: North and south of Pinedale
Hiking: Headwaters day hikes and backpacking

Boating: Canoe, kayak, raft, day trips and overnights
Whitewater: Class 1-3
Gauge: Daniel (near Pinedale), La Barge, Fontenelle Dam
Highlights: High country, fishing, canoeing

The Green's upper 10 miles drain the Wind River Range of 13,000-foot peaks, followed by the 5-mile-long Green River Lakes with their classic backdrop of Squaretop Mountain.

The river then sweeps north and west in a riffling arc that hinges together the north–south aligned Wind River Mountains with the east–west Gros Ventre Range; the valley of the upper Green is the principal connection between wild country of the Winds and the Greater Yellowstone Ecosystem westward. The river bends south past Kendall Warm Springs—only home of the endangered Kendall Warm Springs dace, precariously close to the road and to people seeking a warm-springs bath. The upper basin is also known as a bastion for globally imperiled endemic plants.

In early spring the upper Green River near Moose Creek awaits the rush of snowmelt from the skyward rise of the Wind River Range to the east.

The upper Green River emerges beneath the shadow of Squaretop Mountain—a landmark of the stunning Wind River Mountains' granite and glaciated uplift.

With 180 essentially dam-free miles (four low diversion dams but no storage reservoirs), the upper Green is the longest nearly free-flowing section of sizable stream in Wyoming (on the Great Plains, the Powder is longer but much smaller).

Above the US 191 bridge northwest of Pinedale, the Green was recommended for National Wild and Scenic River protection by the original planners of that program in the 1960s, but Wyoming's delegation declined owing to a local irrigation scheme at Kendall that never passed economic muster—even for the Bureau of Reclamation. Gas extraction now poses a serious threat to the upper basin; 10,000 new wells have been proposed, with the specter of pollution, water losses, and latticeworks of roads fragmenting a fragile landscape. How this plays out in the climate-change era of fossil fuels remains to be seen.

Far downstream at its mouth in Utah the Green is much longer than the Colorado River where the two meet (769 versus 439 miles) but carries less water—5,303 cfs compared to the Colorado's 7,600 at the confluence.

 ## FISH

Known nationally, the upper Green offers excellent fishing for introduced rainbow and brown trout.

Flowing into the Green from the west and just above Fontenelle Reservoir, La Barge Creek runs 45 miles from the Wyoming Range as one of the Green's largest tributaries and best habitat for rare Colorado River cutthroat.

 ## ACCESS

On US 191 west of Pinedale by 6 miles, turn north on WY 352, which becomes gravel toward Green River Lakes. Lower sections of the river are reached off US 189 from west of Pinedale and southward to Fontenelle Dam, then via WY 372.

 ## HIKING

A riverfront trail reaches headwater lakes, the monumental rise of Squaretop Mountain, and stellar backcountry that continues to the Wind River Range's glaciated heights.

 ## PADDLING

From the outlet of Green River Lakes, Class 1-2 riffles flow with a few short drops of easy Class 3 that can be carried. Crossing sagebrush uplands, the stream gathers tributaries from the Wind River Mountains to the east and the Gros Ventre Range to the west, and in 52 miles—with a few intermediate takeouts—reaches US 191 northwest of Pinedale, with access on river left above the bridge.

Ranches follow with scattered BLM parcels for the next 93 miles below 191, including several landings, four diversion dams, and a fence or maybe more (see *Paddle and Portage*), leading to backwaters of the river's first storage reservoir behind Fontenelle Dam, 127 feet high. Take out at Names Hill Landing off US 189, milepost 79, south of La Barge 5 miles. The full 145 miles from Green River Lakes to Fontenelle is the longest river trip in Wyoming's Rocky Mountains, though interrupted by several diversion dams.

In its final Wyoming reach the Green meanders 65 miles through sagebrush steppe from Fontenelle Dam to backwaters of Flaming Gorge Dam near the town of Green River, but the stream is blocked by a diversion dam, and tamarisk has infested the floodplain.

Be prepared for maddening quantities of mosquitoes all along the Green in summer, which, to be honest, have deterred me from paddling here except for the scenic headwaters above Kendall. See the Colorado chapter for the Green River's significant mileage below Flaming Gorge.

Grey's River

Length: 65 miles
Average flow: 646 cfs
Watershed: 455 square miles
Location: South of Jackson and Alpine
Hiking: Paralleling gravel road

Boating: Kayak, canoe, day trips, overnight possible
Whitewater: Class 2-4
Gauge: Alpine
Highlights: Road-accessible mountain river, whitewater

The Grey's River is an undeveloped but sizeable mountain stream, second-largest tributary to the upper Snake, Wyoming's second-longest river with no dams (except for its lowest mile, impounded by the Snake River's Palisades Dam), and a stronghold of Snake River cutthroat trout. It flows north in a high valley with the Wyoming Range edging the east side and the Salt River Range shadowing the west, ending in Palisades Reservoir of the Snake. Designation as a National Wild and Scenic River in 2009 was precluded by Lincoln County Commissioners' opposition.

Headwaters mark the southernmost extension of the Greater Yellowstone Ecosystem with its network of contiguous wild land and rivers. To the south, the watershed

The Grey's River is exceptional for kayaking, canoeing, and fishing at the southern end of the Greater Yellowstone region.

Below Lynx Creek the Grey's River rapids steepen, and below Squaw Creek this Class 4 rock garden challenges paddlers.

adjoins that of La Barge Creek—tributary to the Green and one of few streams with native Colorado River cutthroat. Headwaters also border those of the Smith's Fork Bear River—refuge for rare Bonneville cutthroat of the Salt Lake basin. In this pivotal position, the Grey's watershed is the best natural-area connection linking the Yellowstone complex southward.

This is one of the Rockies' outstanding semi-wild rivers, with road access to a paradise of clear water, riffles, rapids, wildlife habitat, and wetlands. A major downside to visiting here is fairly heavy traffic on the dusty road.

 FISH

Brown trout thrive along with rainbows and brook trout. In spite of the nonnative stocking, which started in the early 1900s and continued until this century, wild cutthroat do relatively well, as do mountain whitefish and mottled sculpins.

 ACCESS

From Jackson go south on US 89 to Alpine, turn left on Grey's River Road/FR 10138, and drive upstream on often-washboarded gravel, which continues 60 miles to Tri-Basin Divide.

HIKING

Riverfront paths can be found at many dispersed campsites.

PADDLING

Not paddled much, this river offers outstanding Class 2-4 whitewater for 30 miles from Cabin Creek Bridge to the mouth, with shuttles on the riverfront road. Flows are adequate for at least low-water boating through most summers.

My favorite reach is about midway down the river's length: Paddle from the Grey's River bridge leading to the Meadows Guard Station (3 miles above Deadman's Ranch) to the Grey's bridge at White Creek, 9 miles by road. Nearly constant Class 2 rapids feature views to peaks of the Salt Range as the stream winds through willows and penetrates spruce forests.

Below the bridge at White Creek an excellent Class 2 run continues with mountain views. Combined with the reach above, this is perhaps Wyoming's best two-day paddle through semi-wild terrain, though virtually no one runs it as an overnight trip.

The 10 miles below Lynx Creek accelerate with Class 3-4 to the mouth of Squaw Creek and amp up to Class 4+ in the 5 miles above Bridge picnic area, 1 mile above Palisades Reservoir.

Gros Ventre River

Length: 75 miles	**Boating:** Kayak, canoe, day trips
Average flow: 733 cfs	**Whitewater:** Class 2-4
Watershed: 624 square miles	**Gauge:** Kelly
Location: Northeast of Jackson	**Highlights:** Whitewater, geology, wildlife
Hiking: Day hikes, headwaters backpacking, river strolls	

Flowing through a mostly wild basin and drawing on waters of the Gros Ventre (Grow-VONT) Range to the south, this is the largest tributary to the Snake above the Henry's Fork. Strategically located, headwaters form the key connection between the Greater Yellowstone Ecosystem and the 100-mile-long Wind River Range eastward.

Sourced deep within the folds of the Gros Ventre Mountains, the undammed river flows east, north, and then principally west to the Snake River just downstream from Grand Teton National Park. The upper 18 miles through wild meadows are reached only by trail. The next section continues in an open valley with a gravel road. Most of the corridor lies in Bridger-Teton National Forest except for several guest ranches and

Brightened by summer's narrowleaf cottonwoods, the Gros Ventre River recedes to rocky levels below a landslide whose legacy from a century ago persists in boulders and cobbles.

inholdings. Downstream from the community of Kelly, the lower Gros Ventre divides Grand Teton National Park from Jackson Hole National Elk Refuge to the south.

The middle river pools in two natural lakes formed by landslides—unusual because most mountain lakes are glacial in origin. Lower Slide Lake formed in 1925 when a massive landslide formed a debris dam that failed two years later, releasing a tidal wave engulfing the village of Kelly. A rocky Class 3-4 rapid remains at the lake's outlet as legacy of the slide and cataclysmic flood.

Moose and wolves thrive here, and the nation's largest herd of elk passes through the basin each autumn on its way to the National Elk Refuge. Bighorn sheep can often be seen scrambling on red cliffs north of Lower Slide Lake.

Near the mouth, at the southern border of Grand Teton National Park, summer diversions completely dry up the lower Gros Ventre, seen from US 89. Upstream 6 miles, the abandoned Newbold Dam was removed in 2013, opening most of the river to migrating native fish.

 FISH

The Gros Ventre and most tributaries are habitat of Snake River cutthroat, growing to 14 inches. This is one of the larger streams in the Rockies that's relatively unaffected by introduced trout. Native mountain whitefish, sculpins, and daces also thrive.

The Crystal Creek Trail climbs from the Gros Ventre River and into high country connecting to the Granite Creek and Hoback basins to the south. Steve Schmitz fords early summer snowmelt at the beginning of a trans–Gros Ventre Range backpacking expedition.

 **ACCESS**

From Jackson take US 89/191 north 8 miles to Gros Ventre Junction, turn right on Gros Ventre Road, beyond the village of Kelly turn east, pass Lower and Upper Slide Lakes, and continue on gravel and then a roughening two-track to road's end.

 HIKING

Streamside strolling is good through the narrowleaf cottonwood forest at Gros Ventre Campground, 4 miles up from US 89.

Gros Ventre Road is excellent for mountain biking with nominal traffic, occasional views of the Tetons and the river, and no killer climbs even deep in the heart of the Rockies.

Trailheads at Crystal Creek and the upper basin lead to spacious ridges and rolling summits of the Gros Ventre Wilderness. Light use makes this basin distinctive from Teton highlands westward; backpack here in subtler but still enthralling terrain to avoid the crowds.

 PADDLING

For the upper run of Class 1–2 through meadows and mini-canyons, drive the Gros Ventre Road from Kelly upstream 24 miles to the elk feeding grounds, then another 3 miles to a roadside put-in. Serpentine flatwater through wetlands picks up with Class 2 riffles, ending after 8 miles at the Warden Bridge, 1 mile above Upper Slide Lake.

Next, after paddling through Upper Slide Lake, Class 2–3 plus a Class 4 drop run 7 miles to the mouth of Crystal Creek. Class 2 then follows for 4 miles to Lower Slide Lake and a river-right takeout at Horsetail Creek.

The Gros Ventre's most notable whitewater starts immediately below Lower Slide Lake's outlet amid rubble from the 1925 landslide. High water through June is a tumult of Class 4 holes, waves, and boulders. Lower flows make a technical run for kayakers, but the landslide's legacy of sharp fractured rock is hazardous in the event of a swim or delayed roll. Take out in 3 miles at the park boundary.

Downstream, boating on swift Class 2 riffles among cottonwoods is not permitted in the national park.

Hoback River

Length: 53 miles
Average flow: 501 cfs
Watershed: 567 square miles
Location: Southeast of Jackson
Hiking: Tributary day hikes and backpacking
Boating: Canoe, kayak, raft, day trips

Whitewater: Class 2-2+
Gauge: None, but comparable to Grey's River
Highlights: Class 2+ canoeing, cutthroat trout

The Hoback is a major dam-free Snake River tributary providing habitat linkage between the Wyoming Range to the south and the Gros Ventre Range to the northeast, all within the Greater Yellowstone Ecosystem.

After 12 miles of northbound headwaters, the stream passes the US 191 wide spot of Bondurant and then rushes westward 25 miles, accompanied but not crowded by 191 to the Snake River. Congress designated the lower Hoback and tributary Granite Creek as National Wild and Scenic Rivers in 2009. While most of the basin lies in Bridger–Teton National Forest, and the middle 20 miles are only lightly developed, the lower 6 miles—closer to the tourist hot spot of Jackson—face intense development pressure.

One of the Rockies' sweetest Class 2+ canoeing runs, the Hoback links headwaters between the Gros Ventre and Wyoming Ranges with the Snake River downstream from Jackson Hole. Straight ahead is the Hoback's confluence with Granite Creek.

Meanwhile in the upper basin, fossil fuel companies have proposed drilling on 64,000 acres—an ominous threat to water quality, habitat, and wildness, making this a battleground for the Jackson Hole Conservation Alliance. Unlike in the upper Green River watershed eastward, most gas drilling plans here have been rejected, and key drilling rights have been acquired for protection.

FISH

The main stem and tributaries are good wild cutthroat habitat.

ACCESS

From Jackson take US 89 south 16 miles to Hoback Junction and turn left on US 191 to Bondurant.

HIKING

No trails parallel the Hoback. Wilderness backpacking is good in the upper Granite Creek basin.

PADDLING

Starting at Bondurant the Hoback offers excellent Class 2+ paddling for 25 miles—a rare length of summerlong flows through a mountain landscape and forested canyon with relatively easy rapids. Put in alongside US 191 west of Bondurant or, for more water in summer, 8 miles lower at Granite Creek. Lively Class 2 rapids approach Class 3 through June. Take out at the Hoback bridge and US 191/89 intersection.

In early summer Granite Creek can be combined with the lower Hoback. Boaters can also continue down the Snake 8 miles with big water but no major rapids to the Elbow access, where the Snake turns west before entering its Class 3-4 Alpine Canyon.

Platte River, North

Length: 565 miles, 47 at the Colorado-Wyoming line
Average flow: 4,675 cfs at the mouth in Nebraska, 430 at the Colorado-Wyoming line, 1,682 at Encampment
Watershed: 30,900 square miles
Location: Southwest of Laramie

Hiking: Day hikes and backpacking
Boating: Raft, kayak, day trips and overnights
Whitewater: Class 2-3+
Gauge: Northgate, Colorado
Highlights: Cottonwood forest, whitewater, overnight rafting

The North Platte starts in Colorado and soon enters Wyoming, runs 200 miles north to Casper, then 365 miles east to the South Platte confluence in Nebraska. Dam-free upper reaches include one of the West's finest cottonwood forests.

Sinuous and sluggish across the North Park basin in Colorado, headwaters gather twin tributaries, Illinois and Michigan Creeks, from Arapaho National Wildlife Refuge. Near CO 125, just south of Wyoming, the North Platte drops into a rugged canyon running 20 miles north, mostly within the Platte River Wilderness.

Below the canyon the river continues 45 miles through foothills, with small rapids and several diversion dams. Beyond the Encampment River confluence the North Platte

Beginning in Colorado, the North Platte winds from meandering wetland sources and enters its intriguing canyon leading northward to cottonwood forests before settling into its lower-river fate of reservoirs and oil-industry encroachments across Wyoming.

riffles another 75 miles to Seminole Reservoir—first among a chain of dams through a developed corridor eastward.

 ## FISH

Native fish are mostly gone. The river is now a popular brown and rainbow trout fishery.

 ## ACCESS

From I-80 at Laramie, take WY 44/230 southwest to CO 127, then bear right on CO 125, which reenters Wyoming as WY 230, to Encampment. In Colorado, take CO 14 west from Fort Collins, cross the Front Range to Walden, and go north on CO 125.

 ## HIKING

The Platte River Trail of Northgate Canyon runs from Six Mile Campground down and back 5 miles, or at low flows ford to the east side and continue to Pickaroon Campground.

 ## PADDLING

The attraction here is Northgate Canyon just north of the Colorado-Wyoming line, busy on summer weekends. Class 3 whitewater increases to 4 when high and pushes 11 miles through the Platte River Wilderness, boatable until August.

From Colorado drive north on CO 125 through Walden and Cowdrey, go left at the CO 127 intersection, cross the North Platte, and at the Routt ramp sign turn right. To take out, from the Routt ramp drive north on CO 125, enter Wyoming where 125 becomes WY 230, go 4 miles to milepost 123, turn right (east) on CR 492, and continue 2 miles to Six Mile Campground and a steep path to the water. Forest Service regulations ban canoes here.

Continue boating below Six Mile another 7 miles with Class 2+ to Medicine Bow National Forest's Pickaroon Campground; from the CR 492/WY 230 intersection drive 4 miles north on 230, then turn right (east) on rough dirt to the takeout. The North Platte from Routt ramp to Pickaroon makes an 18-mile overnight trip through July, runnable in kayaks later.

Below Pickaroon 18 more miles of Class 2 traverse foothills and drier country to Bennett Peak Campground; from Riverside take WY 230 east 4 miles, turn left on CR 660, go 12 miles on gravel, and follow Bennett Peak Road/BLM Road 3404 for 7 miles to the campground/takeout. Get a Medicine Bow map, and prep for mosquitoes, especially on lower reaches.

At Riverside the Encampment River joins after flowing through its own remote 20-mile-long canyon of Class 4-5 whitewater, drawing expert kayakers in late July.

For paddlers enjoying cottonwood mileage, *Paddle and Portage* lists additional North Platte boating: 25 miles from Bennett Peak, with four diversion structures, ends at Johnson Landing in Saratoga across from the town park via Walnut Street. Another 45 miles stretch from Saratoga to I-80; take I-80 exit 228 and turn south on River Access Road. Finally, 25 miles run from I-80 to the North Platte's first reservoir; to take out use I-80 exit 219 and follow Seminole Reservoir Road north 10 miles to a landing. In all, *Paddle and Portage* describes 135 miles of nearly dam-free river running from Northgate Canyon to Seminole Reservoir.

Shoshone River, North Fork

Length: 65 miles
Average flow: 884 cfs
Watershed: 788 square miles
Location: West of Cody
Hiking: Short walks at campgrounds, backpacking to headwaters and up Elk Fork

Boating: Road-accessible raft, kayak, and canoe day trips and overnights
Whitewater: Class 2-3+
Gauge: Wapiti
Highlights: Whitewater, cliff-bound canyon, easy access

The Shoshone's North and South Forks drain the east side of the Greater Yellowstone region. The North Fork begins at the divide between the Shoshone and Sunlight Creek/Clark's Fork basin and flows through the North Absaroka Wilderness before reaching US 20. The road then parallels the river for 32 miles through Shoshone National Forest to Buffalo Bill Reservoir. Nine Forest Service campgrounds along the highway serve as overflow for Yellowstone crowds and fill in summer.

The North Fork is one of the Rockies' premier road-accessible rivers for extraordinary scenery that combines the best views of both high mountains and dry canyons, good whitewater, and campsites. Even at a roadside camp, a grizzly showed up while we were there.

Cliffs of the North Fork Shoshone's Palisades rise above the shores upstream from Newton Creek.

FISH

The North Fork is fished heavily for introduced brook, rainbow, and hybridized trout, with some native cutthroats.

ACCESS

From Cody drive west and up the North Fork on US 20—the main route to Yellowstone's east entrance.

HIKING

Campgrounds and five other Forest Service recreation sites along the North Fork have short paths to the water. East of the Yellowstone boundary 3 miles and just east of Pahaska Campground, the North Fork Shoshone Trail heads upstream 15 roadless miles to headwaters; however, the main trail starts with a long climb away from the river, and horses pound this route heavily.

A beautiful trail, which I prefer, ascends the Elk Fork, which joins the North Fork from the south. Expect heavy horse use here too, and this is grizzly bear central.

Sunset reflects on rapids of the North Fork Shoshone in its mid-section near Newton Creek.

After an approach of 10 miles via gravel road above Buffalo Bill Reservoir, the upper South Fork has a trail reaching 30 miles into headwaters and prime grizzly country of Washakie Wilderness; I'll pass on hiking alone there.

 PADDLING

The North Fork runs 33 stunningly scenic miles from the Yellowstone park boundary to Buffalo Bill Reservoir in Class 2-3 whitewater through craggy canyons with US 20 and Forest Service recreation sites for access. Flows are good to mid-July for rafts and all summer for kayaks and advanced whitewater canoeists. The road is busy but has an adequate shoulder for biking shuttles.

From Threemile Campground—2 miles east of the park boundary—to the upper of two successive bridges above Rex Hale Campground or Newton Creek, 12 miles of whitewater include Class 3 rapids.

Runnable for kayaks and canoes even in late summer, my favorite reach is from the second bridge above Rex Hale Campground to Horse Creek picnic area (above the Holy City rock exhibit)—10 miles of Class 2 when low with spectacular canyon and mountain scenery, good for an overnight trip even with the road. Flag the Horse Creek takeout—a gravel bar where the road access is hidden—or be ready for whitewater below.

Three Class 3 rapids follow immediately below Horse Creek, with takeout possible at the Holy City exhibit. Class 2-3 then continues 13 miles. Below the national forest boundary the river enters a wide valley with ranches, homesites, and diversions, but flows remain swift in a shallow entrenched gorge to Buffalo Bill Reservoir.

Snake River

(See also Snake River in Idaho.)
Length: 1,080 miles total, 152 in Wyoming
Average flow: 56,900 cfs at the mouth in Washington, 5,175 at the Wyoming-Idaho line
Watershed: 108,000 square miles, 3,917 in Wyoming
Location: North and south of Jackson

Hiking: Day hikes along the river, tributary backpacking
Boating: Raft, canoe, kayak, drift boat, day trips, overnights possible
Whitewater: Class 1-4
Gauge: Moran, Flat Creek, Alpine
Highlights: Wild headwaters, wildlife, whitewater, scenery, fishing, geology

Wyoming's Snake River has wilderness headwaters, the finest large-river riparian habitat in the interior West, an exceptional native cutthroat trout fishery, the most renowned scenic mountain float trip in America, and a magnificent forested canyon with one of the nation's most popular whitewater descents.

After its upper 40 miles through wilderness, the Snake River's first road access appears near the southern entrance to Yellowstone National Park, where this enchanting gorge sweeps southward.

The upper 40 miles are roadless from the Teton Wilderness of Bridger-Teton National Forest and southern Yellowstone National Park—one of the great headwater streams of the West and choice habitat of grizzly bears, wolves, moose, and elk. The river then traverses Rockefeller Memorial Parkway to Jackson Reservoir and Grand Teton National Park. Below the 18-mile-long flatwater—formerly a natural lake having one-third the dammed-up acreage—this sizable stream averaging 2,000 cfs winds the length of Grand Teton National Park. It curves in front of the 13,770-foot Grand Teton and sub-peaks in full view. Riparian frontage supports moose, elk, bison, beavers, trumpeter swans, and white pelicans.

Downstream from the park boundary for 24 miles, levees, built to prevent flooding of ranchland, were upgraded by the Army Corps of Engineers and now shield high-end residential development.

At the southern end of Jackson Hole, the Snake drops 19 miles through a narrowing valley that separates the Snake River Range to the west from the Wyoming Range to the east.

Finally the river rushes 9 miles through Alpine Canyon—one of the most popular whitewater runs in the West, ending 2 miles above Palisades Reservoir. The canyon sometimes sees 130,000 user days a year in a single reach—possibly the most in the nation (Colorado's Arkansas has more boaters but includes multiple paddling reaches). Total floating on all sections of the upper Snake in Wyoming is about 250,000.

Conservation

Despite wild headwaters and all its superlatives, the Snake has not escaped degradation. Built by the federal Bureau of Reclamation for Idaho irrigators, Jackson Lake Dam flooded riverfront wetlands and drastically altered flows downstream by lowering levels in winter and eliminating most floods. Low winter releases impair fish, and without floods, Engelmann spruce invade bottomlands once dominated by cottonwoods, which are essential for many wildlife species.

Downstream from the park, levees confine the flow, prevent the river from maintaining its floodplains, channelize the current, and perversely cause aggradation or accumulation of gravel in the riverbed, which ultimately renders the levees less effective by raising the level of the river between them. Worsening this, the west side of the river—with increasing development—is seismically sinking relative to the east side, which means that geologic forces are inexorably pushing the river west. Top-end housing pressures and encroachments throughout the region are intense with the tourism and second-home draw of Jackson Hole and its postcard mountain views.

 ## FISH

The river and many tributaries remain excellent habitat of Snake River finespotted cutthroat trout (genetically the same as Yellowstone cutthroat). Waters are heavily fished for these and introduced rainbows.

 ## ACCESS

At the southern end of Yellowstone National Park, views of the Lewis River—the northernmost upper Snake tributary—can be seen from the Lewis Falls Trail and from small and unmarked but spectacular pullouts along US 89 north from the park boundary

A skiff of fresh snow blankets the Ansel Adams overlook in Grand Teton National Park, where growing spruces are gradually commandeering the view to the river.

by 7 miles. The uppermost road access to the Snake River is 2 miles south of the park boundary where US 89 crosses at Flagg Ranch.

Farther south on US 89 below Jackson Lake Dam and upstream from the Moran entrance station, Oxbow Bend's pullouts and paths are good for spotting moose, trumpeter swans, and other waterfowl. Continuing south 6 miles, Deadman's Bar landing lies halfway between Moran and park headquarters at Moose; from US 89 turn west at the sign. Half a mile farther south on 89, the Snake River Overlook of the Teton Range was immortalized by photographer Ansel Adams in 1942, though growing spruce trees now obscure much of the view to the river.

North of Moose by 4 miles a gravel turnoff from US 89 drops west to Schwabacher Landing. At Moose the park road bridges the river, with a ramp on river right.

West of Jackson, WY 22 crosses at Wilson Bridge with access to a levee-top trail on the east side and boat ramp on the west side. South of Jackson 8 miles, US 26/89 crosses the river at South Park with another ramp. The highway continues 5 miles to a landing at Hoback Junction.

US 26/89 farther south reaches two ramps at the entrance of Alpine Canyon, followed by pullouts with river views.

 HIKING

For an epic backpack trip to Snake River headwaters, drive north on US 89 from Jackson, north of Moran turn east on Pacific Creek Road, and go to the end; hike up Pacific Creek, go left up Mink Creek, then down to Fox Park and the diminutive upper Snake.

A longer, 40-mile option follows Snake frontage from Flagg Ranch, south of the Yellowstone Park entrance. All this is prime grizzly habitat, so take precautions.

A remarkable sheer-wall basalt gorge can be seen from near Yellowstone's south entrance; pull off on the east side of US 89 half a mile south of the gate and walk along rimrock downstream.

Short paths explore the riverfront at the Oxbow below Jackson Lake Dam, Deadman's Bar, Schwabacher Landing, and Moose (see above).

Hundreds of miles of superb hiking on tributary trails beckon in southern Yellowstone National Park, Grand Teton National Park, and Bridger-Teton National Forest.

South of Jackson, the best view of Alpine Canyon is the short path to Lunch Counter Rapids; drive US 89 southwest from West Table ramp 5 miles (2 miles past Wolf Creek) to a pullout and steep path to the Lunch Counter ledge.

 PADDLING

At the Moose visitor center get a permit (fee) to boat within Grand Teton National Park; no limits on numbers. Some 70,000 people annually float on several reaches in the park, so expect company. Boating is permitted in the park on the Snake River but not on tributaries.

Wildlife viewing is a great attraction here, but respect animals' needs. If you affect wildlife behavior, you're too close. Tempting as it is, I avoid early- and late-day boating; that's when waterfowl and riparian wildlife feed the most. I avoid wildlife-rich areas such as backwaters and wetlands in spring and early summer.

To start at the uppermost road-accessible place, the Snake from just south of the Yellowstone entrance to the Flagg Ranch bridge is Class 2 for 3 miles after high water subsides in July—a thrilling descent through the narrow basalt canyon.

From Flagg Ranch and into Jackson Lake Reservoir, a 10-mile canoe trip with Class 1-2 riffles through midsummer runs 6 miles in a wild valley, then crosses 4 miles of reservoir to Lizard Creek Campground—6 miles by road south of Flagg Ranch. Beware of afternoon wind on this exposed flatwater crossing; hug shorelines if waves threaten.

From Jackson Lake Dam to Pacific Creek is 5 miles of Class 1 paddling. This and sections below are America's finest example of a full-bodied river flowing through high Rocky Mountain terrain with views to glacier-carved peaks.

Pacific Creek to Deadman's Bar is 10 miles of Class 1-2 on wide waters flowing strong all summer. For the takeout—occasionally missed with some consequence on this large river with road-free shorelines—watch carefully using the *Snake River Guide: Grand Teton National Park* by Verne Huser and Buzz Belknap, or at least a map from the visitor center.

Deadman's to Moose is another 10 miles with dynamically changing logjams. Novice boaters otherwise drawn to the Snake's swift but rapid-free flows must beware. Definitely ask about hazards and log-free passages when acquiring your permit at the Moose visitor center. Even major channels become blocked. Be prepared to quickly stop and safely reach shore or solid footing if boat dragging or lifting over logs is required. At all costs avoid being washed into fallen trees and—worst-case scenario with an upset—aggressively swim and climb on top of logs without getting washed under them. See *Snake River Guide*, above. For interpretive details about the Snake River, see *A Naturalist's Guide to the Snake River* by Margaret Creel.

As it flows through Alpine Canyon south of Jackson Hole, the Snake River's whitewater is one of the most floated reaches in the West, seen here at daybreak before the summer rush of rafts appear at Lunch Counter Rapids.

From Moose ramp to Wilson bridge and ramp, 14 miles of swift Class 1-2 water include 5 more miles through Grand Teton National Park. Below it levees crowd shorelines, but mountain views continue. Downstream from Wilson, another 14 miles wind to South Park bridge and ramp. Then South Park down to East Table Creek is 19 miles (16 by road), Class 2 on stronger flows, with mountainsides rising sharply from the river and with intermediate access.

From East Table ramp or 1 mile westward at West Table landing, the powerful Class 3 rapids of Alpine Canyon rise to Class 4 when high in June. Principally a raft and kayak destination, expert canoeists also paddle here after snowmelt subsides in July or so—still a big-volume river. For East Table, drive 21 miles south from Jackson on US 89. Take out 9 miles downriver at Sheep Gulch ramp.

Virtually all boating on Wyoming's Snake is done as day trips, though it's possible to navigate the full 72 miles from Jackson Dam to East Table. Just don't camp in the national park (which means a long first day or starting midway through the park mileage), and private land should also be avoided. Some scattered BLM parcels and islands appear between the park and Hoback Junction. Forest Service frontage can be found below there but, with roadside camping a problem, from May 1 through Labor Day national forest camping is officially restricted to campgrounds.

Yellowstone River

(See also the Montana chapter.)
Length: 130 miles in Wyoming plus 13 of the South Fork, total 143 in Wyoming
Average flow: 1,342 cfs at the Wyoming-Montana line
Watershed: 2,232 square miles in Wyoming

Location: Yellowstone National Park
Hiking: Day hikes and backpacking
Boating: Not permitted in Yellowstone National Park
Gauge: Yellowstone Lake
Highlights: Wild headwaters, waterfalls, wildlife

Within our first national park, designated in 1872, the upper Yellowstone in Wyoming was the first long reach of river protected under federal law and is still the third-longest river within national parks; only the Colorado in Grand Canyon National Park and the Chitina in Wrangell–St. Elias National Park are longer. The stream begins in one of the wildest enclaves of the lower forty-eight states, loops through bison-grazed wetlands of Hayden Valley, plunges over what I regard as the West's most impressive waterfall, and carves a canyon unlike any other. The tributary Lamar River supports the park's second-strongest concentration of megafauna, including wolves and grizzly bears.

Named for the sulfuric hue of volcanic bedrock downstream from its captivating waterfalls, the Yellowstone carves one of the great canyons of the West.

Though most of its mileage lies in Montana, the Yellowstone River has illustrious beginnings in Wyoming, climaxed here with the plunge of Lower Yellowstone Falls.

FISH

Yellowstone cutthroat are the native trout found throughout the upper Yellowstone basin. Exotic lake trout have thrived in Yellowstone Lake. Fishing Bridge, on the East Entrance Road near its intersection with the Grand Loop Road, is a good place to see fish. Angling is popular in the Hayden Valley area and in most locations with easy road access. A fishing permit is required from the National Park Service, though no Wyoming licence is needed. Anglers should always beware of grizzly bears and possible hazards.

ACCESS

The river is reached by the Grand Loop Road in Yellowstone National Park between Fishing Bridge and Tower Junction.

HIKING

Start with a Yellowstone National Park map. Headwaters lie south of Yellowstone Lake. From the Fishing Bridge recreation area at US 20, the Thorofare Trail heads south along the lake's 22-mile eastern shore, ascends the upper river 11 miles to the Thorofare

The Hayden Valley of the Yellowstone ranks as one of the West's premier enclaves to see bison, elk, and other wildlife.

The Yellowstone River churns through extraordinary geologic formations as it nears the Tower-Roosevelt area of the national park.

Creek confluence, then continues another 18 miles southward in the Teton Wilderness of Bridger-Teton National Forest. This low-gradient mileage is grizzly bear heaven, and horse packing is usually the mode of choice for many long miles through lodgepole pines.

More accessible, the Howard Eaton Trail runs north from Yellowstone Lake and past wetlands along the roadless east side of the river and along the eastern edge of Hayden Valley. From the Fishing Bridge trailhead the hike leads north 11 miles to Upper Falls—a 108-foot drop more directly seen via paved walkways south of Canyon Village.

A mile north of Upper Falls, Lower Falls is even more spectacular with its 308-foot drop reached by a paved and crowded but must-do trail stair-stepping down 500 feet to the brink—one of the most thrilling views of a waterfall in America. This is also the tallest large-volume falls nationwide—nearly twice the height (but nowhere near the volume) of Niagara Falls. Go early or late in the day to avoid the rush, fed heavily by tour busses, or visit in shoulder seasons.

South of Canyon Village, on the southeast rim, a park road leads to Artist Point and its short walk to the perfectly framed Lower Falls. Park there for Uncle Tom's Trail descending 328 stair-steps to the base of the Yellowstone's Grand Canyon—truly grand with yellow sulfurous rock, steep walls, and massive flow.

For a rigorous river tramp, the Seven Mile Hole Trail's 11-mile round-trip drops 1,400 feet to the water. East of Canyon Village, on the northwest rim, the trailhead lies along the road to Inspiration Point.

Moving downstream, drive to the park's Northeast Entrance Road at Tower Junction, turn east, and cross the Yellowstone. Half a mile farther at a picnic area on the south side of the road, a trail high above the east bank of the Yellowstone runs upriver 2 miles with fabulous views to rapids plunging past mineralized hot-spring shorelines in the incised canyon.

The fading light of a summer evening silhouettes a lone bison grazing above the Yellowstone River.

Also east of Tower Junction and on the east side of the Yellowstone bridge, an unmarked but fine trail leads downstream 1 mile to the Lamar River's mouth.

Another trail starts 3.7 miles west of Tower Junction at Hellroaring Trailhead. Hike north 1 mile to a Yellowstone footbridge that's a thrill in its own right.

For a 13-mile backpack trip, cross the footbridge, stay left at the Coyote Creek Trail junction, and continue to the ford of Hellroaring Creek (when too high, which is usually until July, return to the car or walk 2 miles up the creek to a bridge, then back down the other side). Beyond Hellroaring the trail rigorously climbs to higher country north of the river but descends again for 5 more miles of frontage. At the Blacktail Deer Creek Trail junction go left, cross the Yellowstone on another footbridge, and climb the Blacktail Trail 1,000 feet to its western trailhead along the Grand Loop Road 6.7 miles east of Mammoth, with a highway shuttle needed back east to the Hellroaring Trailhead.

 PADDLING

Boating is not allowed on the Yellowstone River in the national park. Below, this river offers the longest canoe journey in the West; see the Montana chapter.

APPENDIX: WHITEWATER AND LONG RIVER TRIPS

The table below lists boating runs by whitewater class, which is determined by the hardest rapid. For many rivers, more than one reach can be paddled.

The "long trip" mileage covers runnable lengths of 30 miles and more, without large dams, major portages, or Class 5 whitewater, and with camping possibilities. Two mileage entries mean there are separate long reaches on that river. Many of these are seldom run as extended overnight outings.

Where it's necessary or possible to continue down the larger receiving river to a lower takeout, numbers may include the greater mileage (Yampa into the Green, Salmon into the Snake, etc.). See narratives in state-by-state chapters. A few trips include downstream extensions from the Rocky Mountains into the Great Plains or Colorado Plateau. In the last column, "w/" means with continuous mileage of the river that follows.

RIVER	CLASS 1	CLASS 2	CLASS 3	CLASS 4	CLASS 5	LONG TRIP (MILEAGE)
Colorado						
Animas	X	X	X	X	X	
Arkansas		X		X	X	55
Boulder Creek			X	X	X	
Cache la Poudre		X	X	X	X	
Clear Creek		X	X	X		
Colorado	X	X	X	X	X	66, 130 or 241
Crystal		X	X	X	X	
Dolores		X	X	X		173, 206 w/Colorado
Eagle		X	X			40, limited camping
Elk		X	X			
Green	X	X	X	X		377 including UT
Gunnison		X	X		X	59
Platte, South			X			
Rio Grande		X	X			
Roaring Fork		X	X	X		31, 42 w/Colorado
San Juan			X			
San Miguel		X	X			36 with low dams, limited camping
Taylor		X	X	X		
White		X				70 including UT
Yampa		X	X		X	134 with low dams; 50 or 71 w/Green

RIVER	CLASS 1	CLASS 2	CLASS 3	CLASS 4	CLASS 5	LONG TRIP (MILEAGE)
Idaho						
Big Wood						
Boise		X				
Boise, North Fork			X	X		
Boise, Middle Fork		X	X			30
Boise, South Fork			X	X		
Bruneau				X		60
Jarbidge				X	X	30
Clearwater, Middle Fork and Main Stem	X	X				98, 107 w/Selway
Clearwater, North Fork			X	X		
Henry's Fork	X	X	X			
Lochsa			X	X		
Payette		X	X			
Payette, North Fork	X	X	X		X	
Payette, South Fork		X	X	X		
Salmon		X	X	X		363, 425 w/Snake
Salmon, East Fork		X				
Salmon, Middle Fork				X		100
Selway		X	X	X		47
Snake, "South Fork"		X				78
Snake, Southern Idaho	X	X			X	
Snake, Hells Canyon			X	X		105
St. Joe	X	X	X	X		69
Montana						
Bitterroot		X				72, 120 w/Clark Fork
Blackfoot		X	X			52
Clark Fork		X		X		34, 86
Flathead		X	X	X		65, 72 w/Clark Fork
Flathead, North Fork		X	X			59, 109 w/upper main stem
Flathead, Middle Fork		X	X	X		73
Flathead, South Fork		X	X			37
Gallatin		X		X		
Kootenai		X	X	X	X	34
Madison		X		X		
Marias	X	X				75, 202 w/Missouri
Missouri	X	X				91, 168, 185
Rock Creek (Clark Fork Basin)		X				
Smith	X	X				80
Stillwater (Yellowstone Basin)		X	X	X	X	
Yellowstone		X	X			527

RIVER	CLASS 1	CLASS 2	CLASS 3	CLASS 4	CLASS 5	LONG TRIP (MILEAGE)
Wyoming						
Buffalo Fork (Snake River Basin)	X					
Clark's Fork (Yellowstone Basin)		X			X	
Granite Creek		X				
Green		X				52, 93 with low dams
Grey's		X	X	X		30
Gros Ventre		X		X		
Hoback		X	X			33 w/Snake
Platte, North		X	X	X		36, 134 with low dams
Shoshone, North Fork		X	X			33
Snake		X	X	X		72

SOURCES

For information regarding some of the rivers—especially the most difficult whitewater—I relied on other published guidebooks. For paddlers doing challenging whitewater, or those who want detailed guidance about how to approach and run rapids, consult the books below, but with all the usual precautions. Many thanks to these fine authors and the knowledge they've imparted.

COLORADO

Paddling Colorado, Dunbar Hardy, 2009
The Floater's Guide to Colorado (with special attention to geology), Doug Wheat, 1983

IDAHO

Paddling Idaho, Greg Stahl, 2016
Guide to Idaho Paddling (with Class 1 and 2 water), Katherine Daly and Ron Watters, 1999
Idaho: The Whitewater State, Grant Amaral, 1992
Idaho Whitewater, Greg Moore and Don McClaran, 1989

MONTANA

Paddling Montana, Kit Fischer, 2015 and 2021

WYOMING

Paddle and Portage: The Floater's Guide to Wyoming Rivers, Dan Lewis, 1991

For river narratives I drew heavily from many sources in previous books of mine (see www.timpalmer.org) and from sources and consultations for my work with the Western Rivers Conservancy; see their website and the *Great Rivers of the West* report.

It's time to go home after a good day on the river.

RIVER INDEX

ABOUT THE AUTHOR

I'm Tim Palmer. I grew up in the Appalachian foothills of Pennsylvania and now live on the south coast of Oregon, but I've spent a lot of time on the rivers of the Rockies and lived along a number of them for years. My thirty books about rivers, the American landscape, adventure travel, and the environment have all been built around a lifetime of canoeing, rafting, hiking, backcountry skiing, exploring, photographing, learning about our waters and landscapes, and working for their protection.

It has been an honor to receive the Ansel Adams Award for "superlative photography" from the Sierra Club in 2019 and the National Conservation Achievement Award for

Author and photographer Tim Palmer. PHOTO BY DAVE HERASIMTSCHUK

With a trail through its length, Nez Perce Creek flows from headwaters deep in Yellowstone National Park and through lodgepole groves, meadows, and wetlands to its confluence with the Firehole in Wyoming.

communications given by the National Wildlife Federation in 2011. Also the Distinguished Alumni Award from the College of Arts and Architecture at Pennsylvania State University, where I got my start in landscape architecture. For my writing, photography, and activism in river conservation, American Rivers granted me its first Lifetime Achievement Award back in 1988—now a lifetime ago! *Paddler* magazine named me one of the "ten greatest river conservationists of our time," and in 2000 it included me as one of its "100 great paddlers of the last century." In 2020 the River Management Society honored me with its Frank Church Wild and Scenic Rivers Award.

After college I worked for ten years as an environmental planner. I'm a Visiting Scholar with the Department of Geography at Portland State University and have been an Associate of the Riparia Center in the Department of Geography at Pennsylvania State University. I often speak and give slide shows at conferences nationwide. Let me show you my work at www.timpalmer.org.

TIM AND PHOTOGRAPHY

For many years I used a Canon A-1, but most of the photos here were taken with a Canon 5D digital camera with 17-200 L series zoom lenses and a 50 mm L series lens.

Major tributary to the Firehole, the Gibbon River sprays over its largest waterfall—a busy site for travelers in Yellowstone National Park in Wyoming.

For adventures when a small kit is needed, I pack a Fujifilm digital X-E2. When boating, I carry a waterproof Canon PowerShot in my pocket.

With the goal of showing landscapes as accurately and realistically as possible, I limit myself to minor post-photo adjustments for contrast and color under Apple's most basic photo program. I use no artificial light or filters, and do nothing to alter the content of the photos. The overriding principle of my work is to show the world as it is, and to share with others the beauty and adventures that I've been privileged to see and experience in nature.

OTHER BOOKS BY TIM PALMER

America's Great Forest Trails (2021)
America's Great Mountain Trails (2019)
America's Great River Journeys (2018)
Twilight of the Hemlocks and Beeches (2018)
Wild and Scenic Rivers: An American Legacy (2017)
America's Great National Forests, Wildernesses, and Grasslands (2016)
Rivers of Oregon (2016)
Field Guide to Oregon Rivers (2014)
California Glaciers (2012)

Field Guide to California Rivers (2012)
Rivers of California (2010)
Luminous Mountains: The Sierra Nevada of California (2008)
Trees and Forests of America (2008)
Rivers of America (2006)
California Wild (2004)
Oregon: Preserving the Spirit and Beauty of Our Land (2003)
Pacific High: Adventures in the Coast Ranges from Baja to Alaska (2002)
The Heart of America: Our Landscape, Our Future (1999)
The Columbia (1997)
America by Rivers (1996)
Lifelines: The Case for River Conservation (1994)
Yosemite: The Promise of Wildness (1994)
The Wild and Scenic Rivers of America (1993)
California's Threatened Environment (1993)
The Snake River: Window to the West (1991)
The Sierra Nevada: A Mountain Journey (1988)
Endangered Rivers and the Conservation Movement (1986)
Youghiogheny: Appalachian River (1984)
Stanislaus: The Struggle for a River (1982)
Rivers of Pennsylvania (1980)